Water Walk America

Angel Hinman

WestBow
PRESS

A DIVISION OF THOMAS NELSON

WestBow Press books may be ordered through booksellers or by contacting:

WestBow Press
A Division of Thomas Nelson
1663 Liberty Drive
Bloomington, IN 47403
www.westbowpress.com
1-(866) 928-1240

ISBN: 978-1-4497-7162-1 (sc)
ISBN: 978-1-4497-7163-8 (e)
ISBN: 978-1-4497-7161-4 (hc)

Library of Congress Control Number: 2012919224

Printed in the United States of America

WestBow Press rev. date: 11/21/2012

Contents

This work is lovingly dedicated to Isaac and all the other water walkers around the world. Every step you have taken to collect water urged us to press on when we thought we couldn't make it another mile.

"For whoever gives you a cup of water to drink in my name, because you belong to Christ, assuredly, I say to you, he will by no means lose his reward." Mark 9:41 NKJV

Author's Note

All over the world there are people hurting and in pain. Some are without clean water, some are without food. Some people have everything under the sun but are incapable of realizing true joy, and still others are dwelling in the wilderness of despair. My husband and I understood the global clean water crisis and we had to *do* something. My greatest hope for you is that you might not be able to go on watching an injustice. Instead, I pray you find what makes your heart break and try and help that situation in whatever capacity you can. Don't expect to find all the answers on solving global problems in the pages of this book. I simply request that you let our misadventures spur you to *do* something.

As we were doing something, we came across a nation's worth of individuals that blessed us with their acceptance, giving, caring and love. As my husband walked across America and I supported him we learned patriotism as we fell in love with our land, our fellow Americans and all the beauty that this great country of ours' holds. In a time of immense conflict between political parties, economic instability and a soaring lack of unity, we are proud to report that though we may fight hard, we as a nation love even harder. I invite you to fall in love with America, as Brook and I did in 2011.

When I decided to write this book, Brook and I prayed for a vision as to how to implement our story to continue making an impact long after we stopped walking. In that prayer time, we felt called to donate 100 percent of author royalties to charity: water. I will not make a single penny off of the book you are about to read; each dime that could go to buying a new car for me or paying my rent is going to a far more worthy cause, bringing clean water to those without access to it.

Finally, I wish I could report to the world that I am a perfectly behaved young lady, but I suspect you will find as you read on that this is not the case. I am a young woman who yearns to be better for my God, my community, my family, my friends, and now for my readers. However, I have made grave mistakes in my years here on Earth. I make a preemptive plea now that as you read this story, you will look beyond my flaws to the lessons I learned in overcoming my own weaknesses. I studied the Psalms as we traveled across America and in Psalm 145:8 the Psalmist urges us to remember that "The Lord is gracious and merciful, slow to anger and abounding in steadfast love." I have prayed ceaselessly that you might get a glimpse of the beautiful faithfulness that my Jesus has in store for all of us who believe in Him; through the steadfast love I experienced on this journey.

My greatest desire in writing this book is to see my God glorified. I hope you enjoy my family's story, have a newfound patriotism, and are inspired to *do* something as you read this book, but most of all I hope that you will enjoy watching how the work of God is perfect, precise and full of miracles.

To God be the Glory,

Angel

Preparation: The Beginning of the End

"But as God has distributed to each one, as the Lord has called each one, so let him walk."

1 Corinthians 7:17 NKJV

I'd like to introduce you to my husband. He's a darling man. Brook is five feet, four and three eighths inches tall, with sparkling green eyes and a wild red beard. Built brawny, he has become accustomed to his friends calling him either a Buff Hobbit (or a Bobbit) or a Fierce Leprechaun. He is young, only 23 years old when this story takes place. His name is Brook but he is my Billy. My Billy is a strange sort of man, who feels life so deeply that his mind must resemble an abyss. He never stops thinking and lives everyday hoping to experience anything, everything, all things. He is a modern day disciple that loves God and immerses himself in the teachings of Jesus. He is restless, rebellious, wild, and at times the very definition of crazy.

My husband comes up with some outlandish ideas. He's tried to convince me to live in a myriad of strange places: a box truck, an RV, a yurt, a camper and once he even suggested we experience what citizens of third world countries go through by living in a cardboard refrigerator box. All of this is discussed in complete seriousness on his part and either complete aggravation or sarcasm on mine.

Whatever the reason for his desire of odd living conditions, it must be said that I rarely fall prey to his insanity. Typically when these ideas propel their way into Brook's mind he gets obsessed for a while, until either something zanier is able to fill the space that the previous idea has occupied, or until I

1

beg and plead for him to hush up and leave me alone because I refuse to live in a tiny yurt in the 21st century. However, there have been times that I was overcome by who knows what and relented.

One of these times was during the second trimester of my pregnancy. We spent those sweet months living in a two hundred square foot cabin with no running water, toilet, shower or sink. We had an outhouse, and the cabin was within walking distance to his parent's home where there were all the amenities of modern life, but I still didn't have a *toilet!* Our bed was up on a platform that he had built and our sofa was underneath. We had our TV to watch, though we rarely did. We kept our clothes, toiletries and other necessities on shelves and cooked in a microwave, a toaster oven or on the grill outside. I had a bucket I kept at the foot of our bed that I'd use for bathroom emergencies throughout the middle of the night when there was no way that I was climbing down the ladder from the bed and stumbling through the dark to get to the outhouse. It was very rustic for most people's standards, to put it mildly, but we were surprisingly comfortable and (secretly) I enjoyed the novelty of minimalism.

Brook's minimalist tendencies have rubbed off on me throughout our relationship, though the extreme conditions he relishes in I can't exactly understand or (usually) endure without some lapse of brain function. His experimental ideas aren't limited to living arrangements. They extend to just about every other corner of life. For example, we do not buy new clothes. We buy clothes from thrift stores, which is fine and dandy with me because we can get more for our money and I love the thrill of searching for a bargain. One day, Brook needed dress pants for an event. I took him to a thrift store where he was able to try on decent pants by popular designers and manufacturers. Do you know what pants he chose? Purple disco pants from circa 1970. He actually wears them. In fact, he wore them to my best friend's wedding.

We were given a Honda Element around the time we got married; man did I love that car. I drove it primarily, but we found we needed a second vehicle, so we went car shopping. The first car we bought together was an early 90's model, teal blue Geo Metro. When we bought it, gas was heading towards four dollars a gallon and the 45 mpg that the little car achieved wasn't good enough for Brook. One day I was getting off the bus to go home when to my elation, a teal blue Geo Metro drove by that was actually crappier than the one that my husband and I owned. This one had cardboard duct taped all over it! My elation quickly turned to horror as I realized that the driver of the even crappier car was my Billy. He had duct taped cardboard all over the car to increase aero dynamics on the Geo and to get an extra five miles per gallon, achieving a total of 52 mpg, a feat he still brags about to this day. We resold the car a few months later, and he somehow managed to hawk the thing off for double what we paid for it, even with the cardboard still attached.

All the things that we Americans value; speed, comfort, convenience, instant gratification, these are things that are lost to my husband's way of life. He does everything slowly, meticulously evaluating every iota of information that deals with making a decision.

As I'm sure you've realized, comfort is relative in our household. Last winter we did not have central heat and our bedroom would get down to forty five degrees on the coldest nights (don't worry, we heated our son's nursery and the rest of the house with space heaters as was necessary). Even though it was cold enough to see your breath and I could barely move from the weight of all the blankets that were piled on me in bed, we managed to endure. While I struggled for warmth each night, guess what my husband decided was an absolute necessity? Brook insisted that he had to mount a heater with a pull string right above the commode. You'd go in and pull the string before you'd use the bathroom, and when you were ready the seat would be warm for you, because nobody likes a cold toilet seat you know. Clearly my husband is maintaining an existence that most of us have to scratch our heads and wonder about, and it is obvious that his logical processes don't always equate to common sense for the rest of us humans, but he continues on his quest to be whatever it is that he aspires to be.

This barrage of events exemplifies some of the quirks of my husband. Brook operates on a different level than the masses. I have become accustomed to the oddities of his nature. His inability to be normal is something I embraced long ago. I often think that there is nothing my husband could say that would surprise me or truly disturb me and my daily existence. Recently, he yet again proved me wrong. I was in for the surprise and disturbance of a lifetime.

"Angel, would you read this for me?" Brook writes a lot; song lyrics, poems, ideas, etc. When he handed me a piece of paper at the beginning of February 2011, I wasn't anticipating what I was about to read. I innocently grabbed the paper and figured I'd be looking over a poem.

"Join me as I spend 120 days walking across America promoting the need for clean water for nearly 1 billion people on this Earth. People who are dying because they don't even have the luxury of a toilet to drink out of. Yes, I said toilet. A lot of people spend their entire lives walking just to collect water that isn't even as good as the water in your toilet, water that isn't even as good as the water in your toilet after you've used the bathroom in it. I'm going to spend four months of my life walking so that hopefully thousands of people can stop walking and start living. Hopefully you're willing to support me in this and together we can actually *do something...*"

It wasn't a poem, but it certainly stirred a strong emotional response in me, the way only poetry can. The second I finished reading that crazy note of Brook's about his idea, I knew something was happening and I could no more change that fact than sprout a third ear. Brook revealed that for a long time he'd been praying about a walk across America. He had always dreamed of an epic adventure like this, but he wanted to do it for a good reason. As he had been praying for a reason to abandon all normalcy and tradition, he was given the clean water crisis. This simple note was the culmination of what he felt God had charged him with. Much to my surprise, I felt peace. Protests didn't erupt from my mouth and I had no desire to argue with Brook or God. Thus began the Water Walk America campaign.

We didn't tell anyone for a few weeks. We wanted some time to work out our original plan before we presented our idea to the world. At first we had it in mind that I would remain in Wilmington, NC, where we lived at the time and continue working while Brook journeyed on his own. He originally calculated that he could do the walk in approximately four months, and I knew I could take time off and be with him a good portion of that time. When we began telling our close friends and family about the idea, everyone would look at me and ask how I felt about the big change. Brook's friends immediately asked how I felt. I guess I forget how bizarre my lifestyle is compared to others and therefore laughed initially at all of the people who were concerned for me. I was in full support of Brook walking over 3,000 miles alone, in the summer heat, far away from me, possibly without access to communication devices to let me know he was alive. Perhaps I am just as strange as my husband, actually I find myself wondering if this is true pretty often. I was almost worry-free about my husband gallivanting across America alone.

Only one concern ambled around in the back of my mind; we were beginning to plan the walk and all the while our then 16 month old son KO was getting more insane by the second. KO is our wild child. I always wanted three or four children; that was before I experienced KO. He is fiercely strong. He rolled over in the hospital crib when he was first born even though he was a preemie with underdeveloped lungs. While he was being treated in his first days of life, he had this box that was kept over his body that helped keep the oxygen treatment enclosed around him. Brook and I left his side to rest on the third day of his life, and when we returned he didn't have the box on anymore. When we asked the nurse why, she laughingly told us that he had *lifted* it up on his own and therefore she figured he was ready to take a break from it. KO has giant brown eyes like me and curly blonde hair. He is as adventurous as his father and as silly as his mother, which at times can be a lethal combination. He is also absolutely fearless and gets into everything.

One morning I started cooking his breakfast while Brook was off at work. In the ten minutes it takes for me to prepare his breakfast, Kiernan O'Malley had unrolled an entire roll of toilet paper and dragged it around the house after eating a decent amount of it. Before that he had climbed up the laundry pile and used it as a boost to reach and take a bite out of Brook's deodorant. It was just then, while my son was running around with toilet paper stuck in his teeth and breath that smelled like pleasant armpit that I realized that I was going to be the sole survivor on a planet with only a destructive pygmy that eats everything in sight to keep me company once Brook was gone. This came as a bit of a shock to me, and I had to truly contemplate whether I'd be ok without my wingman for an entire summer. I offered KO his hash browns (though I considered giving him some shampoo and bar soap since he seems to like that kind of thing) and said a simple prayer, "God, please let us know what is right for our family."

After KO's toiletry eating binge, I did a lot of thinking, praying, soul searching and organizing. Some people clean when they are stressed. I like to journal. If that doesn't cut it, I organize. I spent the afternoon organizing the clothes KO had outgrown and all the clothes that we needed to put away for winter. As I folded, separated, and categorized our sweaters, I called out to God begging to know how He expected me to decide between either carting a 16 month old wild child through the backwoods of America while my husband walked, or somehow work a part time job and live the life of a single parent while my husband crossed the country without me. God caught my attention as I was organizing; He reminded me to look beyond myself. He also gave me a shove to take a break from the packing and read my Bible that day. I was studying Matthew and I had come to Matthew 19:14, in which Jesus lovingly calls "the little children" to himself. Six huge boxes later, I'd labeled everything and divided it according to season, size, and style. I had also come to the conclusion that KO and I weren't going to sit around while Brook got to have the experience of a lifetime! God wanted us to take this leap of faith as a family so I braced myself for the jump.

That night Brook and I talked about the walk. We had a decent balance in our bank account because we'd been saving to buy our first home. If we sold the majority of our furniture and excess stuff, we'd be able to easily afford the summer as long as people would feed us and house us as we went along. We had positions working for the city, and though we both felt we were leaving our employers and future career opportunities in the dust, we knew it was for something far more rewarding than we could imagine. Besides our jobs, we had obligations at our church that we felt responsible for, but our pastor and congregation supported us in an incredible way. Our family was poised to help any way that they could and were interested (if not excited) in how our weird little adventure would turn out. We embarked on the journey of planning this monumental endeavor with a small army of supporters cheering us on before we even started the walk.

"Did you know yoo-hoos come in 11 ounce cans? It says twelve 11 ounce cans right on the box. I pondered it for about two hours the other day." Brook suffers from a curious disorder which I refer to as Numberitis. Sufferers of Numberitis are extremely intrigued when companies like Yoo-hoo decide to sell 11-ounce cans instead of twelve ounce like everyone else on the entire planet. Numberitis sufferers are the people who, when pumping gas and their tank fills up at 10.64 gallons, *must* pump until they reach 10.75. They also keep track of numbers in a way normal people don't, i.e. Brook knows exactly how many kilowatts per hour we are supposed to use in our apartment on an average day, and if it is different than it is supposed to be he has to know why. Yes, he checks it every day. For an anniversary present one year, Brook took me to see the Biltmore Estate in Asheville, North Carolina for the first time. While there, we got ice cream and the total was $5.49. Brook looked like he was about to issue an attack on the little screen that showed the bill total (because it was one cent from an even number), when the poor high-school aged clerk asked him in genuine fear, "Is everything o.k., sir?"

Numberitis is beyond annoying, gets in the way of progress, and generally drives those around the sufferer insane. When Brook has a bad case of Numberitis I typically recite, "Love is patient. Love is kind..." from 1 Corinthians 13:4, over and over again in my mind. However, his disorder has its occasional perks. For example, Brook is able to calculate the exact cost per ounce of everything at the grocery store and we have saved hundreds of dollars because he is a human calculator (and, yes I know that grocery stores do that for you on the little labels that they stick to the shelves, however, according to Brook, they are often off by a few cents). Though you would think that Numberitis would come in handy as we were considering what charity to benefit from our efforts, the choice was fairly obvious to us. We didn't have to employ extensive calculations to choose what organization could turn the highest profit off of our walking investment.

The organization charity: water is fantastic for many reasons. The first reason that was so important to us is that they are able to privately raise money for all of their operating costs so that they can use one hundred percent of public donations to fund the projects that give people in developing nation's access to clean water. The second reason we were drawn to them was because they can show documented proof of their wells via GPS, photos, and satellite images. In a world with its fair share of crooks and swindlers, it is refreshing to find an organization who finds it important to demonstrate their work with visible evidence. I was extremely excited with the choice of charity: water as the beneficiary of my husband's and my hard work because I knew they could do the most good with the money donated on our behalf. charity: water was the obvious pick for us, and we continue to be proud of our decision to have our efforts benefit the work they do to this day.

Starting a campaign with charity: water was simple. All we had to do was create a user account, set a goal, upload a picture and type a brief note about our mission. It was one of the most elementary parts of our campaign and we both highly recommend it to anyone considering fundraising on their own. After choosing a water organization to raise money for and setting up our campaign, we knew the first thing that needed to be done was to plan an itinerary and route that would allow Brook the safest roadways with the closest access to cities possible. This was a lot harder than we'd thought it'd be. I never realized it but it can be illegal to walk alongside of most major roads. This is understandable for safety reasons but it certainly made it difficult to find a route that worked. Not only is it illegal to walk on a lot of government owned property (i.e. roadways), but it is obviously illegal to walk onto private property. In many areas, our options were either Brook getting ticketed for illegal walking alongside the highway or him running the risk of getting shot by some strung out farmer because he was trespassing. As I'd rather explain to my son that his father was ticketed doing the right thing than he was killed by a psycho hillbilly, I begged Brook to pray about a route that would be safe, fun, scenic and lead to as much fundraising (and as few deranged lunatics) as possible.

Finally, we were able to agree on a route that didn't force either of us to be alone in the desert of Nevada for extended periods of time in which aliens could abduct us. Brook would start with his toes dipped into the Pacific

Ocean in Oregon, and walk from there all the way across the great states back to New York and end with his toes dipped in the Atlantic. Our initial route was changed to end in our home state of sweet ol' North Carolina early in our trek. The walk was going to be about 3,300 miles(I'm rounding but if you want to know exactly how many miles, feet, inches and centimeters, ask the guy I married who suffers from Numberitis), take around 120 days(or so we thought) to complete, and we hoped it would end with a lot of changed lives. Once we got the route down we began getting a video filmed, edited and distributed that detailed our plan and got attention. With the video posted on our blog, our charity: water campaign site and facebook page, we had the basis of a modern day campaign. After we got through the kinks of our campaign tools, we sat back and reviewed everything that was coming, and made a list of what we needed to do.

Brook and Angel's To Do List:

◆Send letters/emails to everyone along our route asking for fellow walkers, hosts, and most of all, donations to charity: water.

◆Get vehicle with enough space for one wild boy and his mother to survive a summer on the road together.

◆Pray.

◆Move out of apartment.

◆Get a summer's worth of sunscreen (that Brook will refuse to wear and will therefore be forgotten and shoved to the bottom of his pack where it will explode and get all over his granola and clean underwear, causing him to be sunburnt, hungry and have dirty boxers).

◆Figure out how on earth KO will get a nap everyday amidst fundraising and traveling so much. Also, figure out how Angel will be able to fundraise while chasing KO down and keeping him from conquering everything in sight.

◆Pray a lot more.

◆Get corporate sponsors to give Brook free stuff and support charity: water.

◆Thank everyone in the country who supports us.

◆Pray even more.

The list was much longer but I figured you would get a good idea of what was going on in our minds from the abbreviated version. There was an incredible amount of things to do and an incredible amount of prayers needing to take flight to heaven.

To give you an idea of what was happening in our family during this planning time, let's discuss number 2 on the list. We had two cars when we started our trip planning and they were tiny. I don't mind roughing it, but I have my limits, and being trapped in an itty bitty space with the wildest buffalo boy (KO, not Brook) in the world for extended periods of time didn't sound like a dream come true. I told Brook to start looking into alternative vehicle options for us. Of course he took this as an opportunity to be as eccentric as possible.

"Honey, what do you think of this?" He turned his laptop around one day after asking this and the screen candidly displayed a stretch limo. I started laughing, thinking it was a joke, and then I realized he was serious. "Oh. You are serious?! I can barely parallel park a car, how do you think I'd navigate that submarine through traffic?! And honestly, I said I needed more space, not a spaceship!" I almost fainted when he showed me a great deal on a hearse. So he was stuck on a limo for a while. When I told my ten year old sister Caeley that I might be driving a limo around the country for the summer, she very casually asked, "Will your limo have a hot tub?" Brook heard her and replied that a hot tub could certainly be arranged. At which point Caeley erupted with "THAT IS SO COOL!" I live in an alternate reality. This planning thing was exhausting; I couldn't wait to drop Brook off in Oregon and say, "See you in a few days Billy!" then speed off in my stretch limo with KO.

One day Brook's parents offered up their giant SUV for our trip's purposes. Though the price of gas was skyrocketing (again) we figured it would be worth it for the space, as opposed to a stretch limo. We gratefully accepted their offer. Many of the logistical details fell into place quickly and easily. What came as a struggle from the beginning of the preparation, especially for me, was having the right mindset going into the walk. It wasn't easy to imagine what we were facing because I didn't know anyone who had ever done this kind of walk the way we were, with a baby in tow, and I was having a difficult time coping with the unknowns.

The walk finally made sense to me a few weeks after Brook had told me about his plan. We ran out of toilet paper one day in March as we were preparing for the trip. I was sitting on the john and calling for Brook to get me some toilet paper when I realized we were out. As in no squares of cottony goodness anywhere in our apartment out. I was not a happy camper. Brook brought me some napkins and the trash can and told me to do my business "third world style." When I was stranded and muttering under my breath about the indignity of it all, I realized that I was a spoiled brat to be so angry over something that millions of people have to deal with everyday. I flushed my toilet, and then washed my hands fiercely. And as I looked in the bathroom mirror, I understood. I was profoundly inspired at the work that Brook and I were gearing up for. Maybe, somewhere in Africa, there was a woman my age with a husband and a son who was stranded on her "commode," but wasn't so fortunate as to have napkins in the kitchen and clean water and soap to wash her hands. Perhaps she didn't even have a flushing toilet, but rather a small hole in the ground. Maybe she got a disease or sickness from her situation, whereas I only suffered mild discomfort. The sacrifices I was preparing myself to make were going to be worthwhile, and that day in March made it all clear.

Having clean water is a huge blessing that I took for granted until I met Isaac, Esther, Carol and Edith. These four individuals were Ugandans visiting the United States as part of the Mwangaza Children's Choir. We were so fortunate to interview them on April 6th, 2011. That was the first day I ever honestly considered how incredible it is to be able to walk to the sink to get a glass of safe drinking water. It is also the first day in my life that I considered kidnapping.

This group was part of a collective that was touring the States and performing traditional African song and dance routines to Christian praise music. The children had competed in their home country to land the opportunity to be in the choir; many of them overcame incredible obstacles to get to practice. When they would share their stories of triumph during performances, the audience would be weeping. We gathered together with the three children and Edith, who was one of their mentors, to discuss what it was like walking for water in Uganda.

Isaac was 11 years old, but he was "going to make 12 on July 25," the day after my own birthday. He weighed about 80 pounds soaking wet and was the height of the average American 3rd grader. He had large brown eyes and was playful and silly; his stories were chilling but they were told in the most matter of fact, simplistic way. You would have thought he was discussing a trip to the grocery store rather than relaying his dangerous adventures and the painful, back-breaking work of fetching water, which he started doing at the age of four.

One day, when Isaac was very young, younger than 11, he went with his cousins and little sister to the water source to get water for their chores, bathing and to drink. He was in charge of all of the other little children and he felt the weight of responsibility heavily, probably as much as he felt the heavy jerry can weighing down on his head on the return home. When the children arrived, unsupervised by an adult, to the water source, they were greeted by a man who offered Isaac some cigarettes and then tried to kiss him. Sexual predators prey on the women and children who walk to get their water every day all over the world. Isaac said he still had to get water because if he returned home without it he would certainly be severely punished. He also had to ensure that all of his cousins and himself escaped from the man unharmed.

Eleven year old Isaac balances our half full Jerry can on his head!

After Isaac told me about his dangerous experiences traveling to the water source, the above just being one of them, I was broken. This little boy had come close to dangers that I have never been exposed to. The only sexual predator I've ever experienced was some stranger at a Halloween festival that grabbed my butt, and here is this little boy telling me his story without a tear or look of angst, but rather laughter in his eyes and an obvious awareness of his ability to provide protection for his family, *at 11*. I was completely unprepared for the beatings, harassment, physical injuries, and exhaustion these kids were describing that they endured on their walks to get water.

After our interview with the four Ugandans, we took our jerry can that would eventually accompany us across America outside and filled it about halfway full with water at a spigot. Then we asked them to show us how they held it back home when they walked. It was so heavy! I tried lifting it and it was a strain to hold it in one hand and walk in a straight line. They placed it on their heads, just as they did at home, they explained. Then they walked swiftly across the parking lot as though it were mere air on their head. I felt guilty enough asking them to lift the heavy can, but when they marched around with it balanced on their heads I felt something far deeper than guilt stir inside. I looked at Brook and I could tell he was feeling it too. When we got in the car afterwards, I looked at him and he said:

"If that little boy has to walk for water, and little boys and girls like him all over the world are carrying around jugs that heavy, causing who knows what kind of damage to their bodies, I think I can handle putting one foot in front of the other for a few months. Especially if it means I can go to sleep at night knowing that maybe some kids somewhere won't have to walk for unsafe water again."

I know that there are horrible things happening at home here in America, I saw a lot of them over my summer adventure: tornadoes and natural disasters, drugs, prostitution, abuse, neglect, fighting, killing, poverty and cruelty; all of the evils of the world can be found in my own country. However, I don't think that I will ever meet an American child who has to walk 4-10 miles a day for dirty drinking water that has the potential to kill them or make them very sick. I certainly don't think that the clean water crisis is the only problem that needs fixing in this world, but the stories of Esther, Isaac, Edith and Carol certainly made me grateful for the showers, clean drinking water and sanitary toilets I had access to. I wanted to kidnap Isaac and keep him as my own that day, him and the little girls as well, because I was wounded knowing they would be returning to such dangerous and unfortunate circumstances before we had even completed our walk across the country. Their grinning faces and honest stories were the greatest catalyst to my willingness to partake in this adventure, and continued to inspire both Brook and I long after we'd left North Carolina for our journey.

I've introduced you to my husband and son, but I haven't properly described myself. In many ways I am the opposite of Brook. He is serious, I am not. I take joy in being silly and having fun. I think laughter is one of the greatest gifts we get to experience and work hard to bring mirth to my loved ones. For all Brook's knowledge and deep thoughts, and for all my goofiness, we both agree that I am by far more productive than he is. I do not appreciate idle behavior; I graduated from college with my bachelor's degree when I was twenty years old, with a new born baby on my hip, a thirty hour a week job and volunteer obligations. It is unnatural to see me with a frown on my face or a wrinkled brow. Where Brook is so organized that he can calculate how many ounces of rice are left in the cupboard, I am hopelessly scatterbrained to the point that I will forget we have rice in the cupboard and go buy a new bag for a recipe rather than check to see what we already have. I am admittedly far too ditzy and am absolutely terrible at keeping track of my car keys. I am the oldest of four girls and am bossy to a fault. Most of all, I love to help others and I diligently try to model the love and acceptance of Jesus everywhere I go and with every act that I perform. Though I fail often, I keep on trying.

Now that you have an idea of how opposite Brook's and my nature are, imagine shopping with these two types of people; a serious, brooding adventurer and his purposeful, bossy, sarcastic sidekick. It sounds like a disaster waiting to happen doesn't it?

Brook is extremely tactile. I forgot this when it came time to start gathering gear for his walk. As he would be walking approximately 3,300 miles, we figured the most important gear we would purchase would be high quality walking shoes, so we went shoe shopping. We visited a local outdoor equipment retailer that had a special section of equipment and shoes that was recommended for individuals who wanted to hike the Appalachian Trail. Brook stood in front of the display that had about seventy different types of shoes and got a petrified look on his face. I started piling up boxes of shoes and asking the store clerk for all sorts of models in Brook's size. Brook just muttered, "I forgot socks."

When I handed him the first pair to try on he looked at me, looked at the box, saw the price tag and said "Next pair please."

"Brook, I think one of the wisest investments we can make this summer is buying good shoes. You are *walking* across America; you need shoes that will help you," I calmly explained.

"Well, we can find good shoes that aren't that expensive."

"Ok, these are twenty dollars cheaper. Try these," and I shoved a box at him.

"Umm, I was hoping for a pair that was at least seventy five dollars cheaper," he whined.

"You want to spend fifty dollars or less on a pair of shoes that you will be standing in for hours on end, every day, on who knows what kind of terrain for miles and miles?" I asked incredulously.

"Well, yeah." He then proceeded to tell me that he didn't know what he was going to need, and what he was going to like because he had never done this before, so he'd rather put less money into a pair of shoes in case he ended up hating it and having to wear it anyway to recoup cost. So we agreed to both be open-minded and try our hardest to agree on a pair of shoes that was high-quality and not worth a small fortune.

He tried on about 14 pairs of shoes at that first store. We bought one pair. When we left, two hours after we'd arrived, the poor clerk who'd been helping us had at least ten more gray hairs and would need to get his blood pressure checked if he saw Brook walk in the store again. What was even worse was that as soon as we got home Brook started doing price checks on the pair of shoes we'd decided on and found three places that advertised a lower price for the same shoes. We ended up returning those blasted shoes and purchasing them elsewhere at a lower price later in the week.

I wish I could say that it was just the shoes that we went through this amount of trouble for but it wasn't. We shopped for days trying to find the right clothes for his walk. I wanted him to have a white or yellow shirt to be more noticeable, but he found a purple Under Armor shirt that he ended up wearing nearly every single day of his walk. The man adores purple. Then we argued over a backpack. He insisted the overnight hiker's pack we owned would work, while I told him he just needed to get a new day pack. I loaded three suitcases full of clothes for KO, Brook and me. He went right behind me and reduced it to two suitcases. He halved the amount of toys I was going to bring to play with KO, and I doubled the amount of blankets he had been in charge of packing.

The last week before we left for Oregon was one of the longest weeks of my life. Brook and I both got so muddled at who had put what in the car and who had taken what out that we ended up just slamming the door and hitting the road, both completely unaware of how wacky and unsuitable our assortment of equipment would turn out to be for our long journey.

I have an immense capacity for adventure and fearlessness. I married a guy who suggests buying a hearse for a road trip. You've got to be fearless to unite yourself with that guy. However, I struggle with fear of the unknown. I have complete faith that God exists, but I occasionally worry about my life so much that I forget He is everywhere, taking care of everything, and that my insignificant little existence is not worth so much worry. As the days drew nearer and nearer to our departure, I felt my worries creep in over and over again. Would God find safe homes for my son, husband and I to sleep in over the summer? Would He open hearts all over the country and allow people to consider their immense blessings, especially the blessing of having clean water, and then donate out of thanks for their own fortunate situation? Would God keep Brook safe from escaped convicts and hungry bears? Could God help Brook and I turn our sacrifice and efforts into something that would change lives and if yes, would He do it?

My greatest fear was that at the end of the summer, after months of effort and hard work, personal sacrifice and doing our best, the only people that would donate would be our family and immediate friends. When I voiced this fear to Brook, he said "That's ok with me, because if we hadn't decided to do this, they never would have given and where would we be then?"

Between Brook's response to my fear induced question, and reading "Trust in the Lord with all your heart and lean not on your own understanding," in Proverbs 3:5, I began to relinquish my silly worries to Him who carries all burdens. Where would I be if I didn't take this plunge with my husband and son? I would be working, lying out on the beach and maintaining an aimless existence. The fear of not being good enough for the world wasn't powerful enough to stop me, and I am grateful to God for His ability to encourage me to continue on this path.

I have a healthy respect for the dangers that exist in this world, but I refused to let the thoughts of fearful situations and scenarios enter into my mind and cripple me from action after that day. No fear is worth wasting my life. Because I was able to look past my worries, I joined my darling husband and brought my little bear cub of a son on the greatest adventure I could never have thought of. I was able to do God's good work and help the poor. I only hope that I can raise my son and any other children I have to be able to look past fear and look towards fulfillment. Being fearful only caused me to waste time, and there are few things worse than wasted time.

With my fears behind me, the world seemed so exciting. Finally the day arrived when it was time to set off for our trip. The car was packed, goodbyes were exchanged, and after three months of planning and preparation we set off on the journey of a lifetime. On May 23rd, 2011, we set off for the coast of Oregon where we planned for Brook to start his walk on June 1st. The world was one big unknown to me as we pulled onto the highway that day, which is probably one of the greatest blessings that we humans take for granted. If I had known what was in store for me I might not have left that day with Brook! Thankfully the future is a mystery, and as the miles flew by on our drive out to Oregon, the anticipation in Brook's and my spirit soared.

Oregon: Becoming Accustomed to Homelessness

"All this is evidence that God's judgment is right, and as a result you will be counted worthy of the kingdom of God, for which you are suffering." 2 Thessalonians 1:5 NIV

Getting to Oregon was an adventure all of its own. We could only spend 2-3 hours in the car before Kiernan O'Malley would lose it and need *out*. We stopped and played at parks, rest stops, city pools, and anywhere that he could stretch his legs and charge headfirst into a patch of grass. Our SUV was passing through Missouri just as the phenomenal tornadoes swept Joplin up in a torrent. We stopped for the night in St. Louis after weathering the hail, sleet and rain on the road. We were deeply saddened by the devastation we saw, but inspired as well by the heroic tales of the families joining together, saving their loved ones and attempting to rebuild so quickly after all had been lost.

I'll never forget watching as one man stood up on national television crying his eyes out, begging for any news on where his son might be. This image moved me both because the man was so humble and desperate that he could plead on national broadcasts for help, and because I was so close to Joplin and helpless to aid him in his misery. If after experiencing the devastation of a lost child, home and community, he could be so bold as to ask for help on national television and keep his wits about him, I certainly hoped Brook and I could be so bold if we ever got the chance to beg for help for our cause, our own 'children'. I truly had kidnapped Isaac in my heart and considered him a child that I was responsible to provide clean water for. If I didn't as one of his guardians, and we are all guardians of the poor and helpless if we consider Jesus as our Savior, then who would?

I still don't know if that man found his son but I certainly prayed for him and his prosperity. I hope the good Lord heard a whole lot of prayers on his behalf that day from people all over America. With the Joplin tragedy fresh in our thoughts, we continued out to Oregon with our own cyclones of unfortunate occurrences, exhaustion, self doubt and homesickness to battle on the horizon.

As we inched closer to Oregon the temperature dropped, and it didn't stop until it hit the comfy upper 50's or lower 60's during the day. When you are born and raised in the sweet, sticky humidity of the south, 50-60 degree days in June are unacceptable. We had gravely under packed for colder temperatures, which we would later discover in some very inopportune ways, but until then, we shivered from the rainy cold in our simple sweaters with the car heater on full blast.

After a week of driving and gearing ourselves up for our grand walk, we pulled into Portland, Oregon, where we planned to spend our last night before the walk in an upscale chain hotel with all the comforts that we could imagine. We paid for a room with a king size bed and a huge TV. When we entered the room we turned the heater on high and enjoyed the day in the hotel pool and hot tub. We went to a city park and played that afternoon. All the comfort almost fooled us into forgetting what the next day would bring. We went to sleep in glorious fashion on a luxurious mattress, in a warm room, after a day of family fun. The next morning we filled our bellies with free hot breakfast, something we found new and exciting that day but would grow to despise in the months ahead. Then we checked out of our hotel haven and headed west to the coast where the real adventure finally began.

The drive to the coast was a rainy one, with both Brook and I somewhere between shocked that the day had finally arrived and excited that we were getting started. I sat in the car completely amazed at where our life was going.

I asked Brook what was going through his head, as the car rolled by tree after tree and we drew ever closer to Cape Meares. Like a nervous kid on the first day of school his words spilled out in quiet rapidity, "I'm just glad the time is finally here. It's kind of like when we were waiting for KO; I am just excited the day has come to start walking. But it sucks that I am getting such a late start."

We got out to the coast around 10:30 a.m., and were aggravated to find that where we had chosen to begin there was no way to get your feet in the ocean unless you jumped off a cliff. Brook was so set on sticking his toes in the Pacific ocean and walking those same toes all the way back to the Atlantic that he consulted a map to see if there was anywhere within the vicinity of Cape Meares to do so, but to no avail. Though it was nearly traumatic, he sucked it up and made his very first concession of the grand walk that he had planned in his mind. He didn't get to dip his toes in one ocean, but he did climb up onto the lookout that was at the very edge of the United States of America. He prepared his pack with granola bars, water, and a small arsenal of toilet paper, and then it was time. At eleven a.m. on June 1st, I said a prayer that my husband's body would be strong, our path would be safe, and that our impact would be large. Clean water for those in need was our goal, and I prayed that we could meet it with God's help and provision. I put KO on my back in a carrier pack and we set off together on the first steps of the walk. I filmed the first few feet and held it together long enough to not bust out the tears until I turned off the camera, but man did I shake with joy and elation as I said good bye to Brook after those first steps and watched him head off on his part of our journey, the journey of walking 3,300 miles almost completely alone. The walk had begun.

The three of us at Cape Meares just before Brook took his first steps.

For Brook, the beginning of the walk was about as anti-climactic as it could have been. He didn't get to begin with his feet in the ocean while a loud symphony played some sort of battle march. He simply put one foot in front of the other and began walking. From that fateful day in June until we completed the walk, events occurred almost every day that we certainly hadn't planned on, so the anti-climactic beginning certainly should have clued us in had we been forward thinkers. As Brook walked slowly into the distance and I wrestled KO into the car, I wondered what the next few months would look like and how we would all turn out after this journey. I never wondered if we'd finish; I knew we had to. However, I wondered how sane and composed we'd be after the end of this trek.

Later in the day I drove by Brook to check on him and met him with a late lunch. He was a trooper and marched on after a ten minute scarf-down session, and I didn't check on him again for a few hours. I found a campsite in Tillamook National Forest and set up the tent, then went to find him again. The second time I caught up with him, he was hurting, hungry and tired. He had been going strong for 5 hours. I told him I'd pick him up after two more hours.

When I picked him up he had just finished 21.5 miles and walked for seven hours. His joints and leg muscles ached and there were already blisters formed on his toes. He had chaffed between his legs and under his arms. He ate about 1000 calories at dinner and drank some "medicine" (also known as cheap beer) and we hit the sack, hoping for a peaceful night's rest. Before bed, we noticed that clouds were rolling in again and since all it ever does in the Pacific Northwest is rain, we tied the rain fly down to the ground and to the front of the car for extra protection over our tent from the moisture.

At three a.m. we were awoken to KO's screams because he had peed through his diaper all over our bedding in the tent in the 35 degree tundra of Oregon's Tillamook National Forest. Once we got him dried, changed, calmed down and back to sleep, our new friend and road companion showed up. That night he showed up not softly; but rather as a ferocious beast that wanted to drench us in his company. Big, hard, loud pelts of rain crashed into our tent, especially where I had forgotten to zip up our rain fly properly. We woke up around 6 am freezing, soaked, grouchy and smelling of baby pee.

We made breakfast in a foggy headed stupor trying to avoid the water that fell from the trees every time the wind would blow. I was pulling out of our campsite to go drop Brook off where I had picked him up the night before when all of a sudden Brook shouted "ANGEL!"

I turned around to see the cause of his distress and found that the tent had moved about ten feet forward because it was still tied down to the front of the car. It says in Proverbs 14:11 that "the tent of the upright flourishes." "Clearly, we aren't in an upright position today," I thought to myself. Then it started to rain again.

I dropped Brook off and wished him luck; the poor guy had to start off his walking in torrential down pour, after a miserable night's sleep knowing that his tent had surely seen better days. I was driving back to camp looking forward to playing with KO and trying to recoup the day when I arrived and was startled to find a work van parked directly in front of my campsite. Not just any work van, but one containing about 15 inmates from a local Oregon prison. The foreman came over, he was a non inmate, and assured me that they'd be out of the way soon. He proceeded to tell me all about the great hikes that I could go on nearby. I suppose some people hike in rain storms with 30 pound kids on their backs but I am not one of them.

I had to use the bathroom when we first got back to camp but the inmates were working on a construction project in the bathroom so I waited until I saw(or thought that I saw) that they were done with their jobs. I walked to the bathroom with KO and opened the door. And there was an inmate using the john. Now it is awkward to walk in on someone in the ladies room using the bathroom, and it is even more awkward to walk in on someone of the opposite sex using the bathroom, but it is about a million times more awkward to walk in on someone who is the opposite sex and is a convicted felon wearing their bright orange vest that says "INMATE" using the facilities. Trust me, I'd know.

What was I supposed to do then? I was about to explode, all the other inmates were standing around trying not to laugh as they had just witnessed me open the bathroom door on this guy and I'm holding my wild buffalo son in my arms. I waited until the occupant of the toilet left the premises, walked in and used the bathroom and walked out with my head held high, because what else could I do?

Isn't it fascinating that no two people share the exact same life experiences, especially when it comes to moments like this one? How many other people will I meet in my life that have walked in on an inmate using the bathroom at a campground in the middle of a national forest in the freezing cold rain in June? My guess is none.

Brook texted me that day and asked me to come pick him up earlier than originally planned. He finished his second day after 18.5 miles barely able to move. Tillamook National Forest isn't a flat place. Oregon in general isn't a flat place. His calves and knees ached from the constant up and downs of the road. The second day of his walk he also encountered more hair pin turns and having to jump out of the way of cars than he had the first day. He barely muttered two words when I picked him up. He had a lot of medicine that night, and slept a little better, which rejuvenated him enough to make it to a little town called Forest Grove the next day.

Forest Grove, Oregon, happened to be the place where Brook's ancestors first settled and prospered in America. We found all this out accidentally. We were calling everyone once we arrived in a cell service area to give them an update and Wendy, Brook's mom, mentioned that we had a distant relative that lived there. We got his contact information and actually got a hold of him. His name is Hubert; he and his lovely wife Florence were some of the most hospitable folks I've come across. They were well into their eighties, history buffs and major collectors. I called them when we arrived and they saw us the next day. We walked into their home and immediately all the alarms in my brain went off, "Not baby proof! Not baby proof!"

There was an antique doll collection on display, and some of the most fragile looking seashells I have ever seen, casually nesting on coffee tables. Their pride and joy was the large hoard of rare rocks and minerals. I was intrigued by their collections, not because I have a massive interest in rocks, minerals or antique dolls, but because these two people had worked so diligently to gather these things and were so passionate about the stories each item had.

The stories continued as Hubert gave us a history lesson and a tour of the historic "Hinman House" where Brook's great great great grandfather had lived. The property had three Sequoia trees in the front yard and the largest Sequoia tree in all of Oregon was one of these. I thought to myself about the similarities between Brook, myself and KO and the lonely giants that were resting there in that front yard. These trees seemed to be awkwardly planted in a place far from their home. I realized that those trees were making me homesick. I already had a longing for the sticky heat of North Carolina summer.

The yard was stunning but the house was the main attraction, so as we entered the historic dwelling place of Brook's forefathers I tried to forget home and focus on the present adventure. Seeing your ancestral home is an odd event. It is two parts inspiring and exhilarating, and one part eerie. We got excited to walk where, decades past, individuals carrying DNA that would eventually be passed on to Brook and KO had walked. When the floor creaked, and when I looked out the window into the back yard, I realized that we were hearing and seeing an updated form of what Brook's ancestors heard and saw when they lived in the house many years before. It was eerie to me, knowing that I'd never meet the people who settled here. I'd never know what they felt, how they acted, but I still would have the walking, breathing result of their procreation by my side so long as I had KO and Brook with me. Their lives shaped who my spouse and son would become, and I would never get to thank them (or heckle them) about the physical and mental qualities that they passed on to our generation. I was in love with Hubert and Florence for sharing this moment with our family, and will forever be grateful that I have seen the home in which my husband's family history in America began.

Looking back, I realize now that God wanted our little family to be inspired as soon as we could be on our walk. He sent us through Forest Grove that we might get the opportunity to learn our family history, and carry that history all 3,300 miles back home where we enjoyed sharing it with our other family members, many of which had never been to the Hinman House. He also provided a generous hotel manager there in town that gave us our first discounted hotel room when he heard our story. Most of all we got to meet Hubert and Florence, whom have devoted their lives to historical documentation of their family and the collection of items with intricately woven stories. They were ever so kind to us when we were beginning our journey.

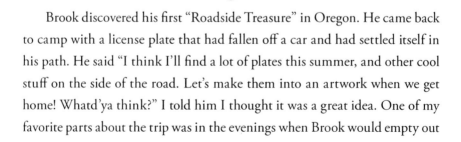

Brook discovered his first "Roadside Treasure" in Oregon. He came back to camp with a license plate that had fallen off a car and had settled itself in his path. He said "I think I'll find a lot of plates this summer, and other cool stuff on the side of the road. Let's make them into an artwork when we get home! Whatd'ya think?" I told him I thought it was a great idea. One of my favorite parts about the trip was in the evenings when Brook would empty out his daily stash of "treasures." We have car emblems, license plates, CD's, and an assortment of other old junk that we collected and have big plans for.

One of the first days he brought back a "Roadside Treasure" I asked him what his day was like. He said "Well, you know what my morning is like. We wake up, I make sure every crevice that could chafe is lubricated and my blisters are all doctored up. I pack my sack, and I tromp off. I keep tromping for about four hours before I take a rest. I sit and eat and read my Bible for about half an hour. Then I walk for another four or five hours. While I walk, I listen to music and sermons. Maybe someone will stop and offer me a ride that I can't take, or maybe I will take a second break and chat with people that are in my path, you know, share the clean water mission. But they don't change much, my days, I mean."

The United States of America is a strange place full of even stranger people. I would categorize myself as somewhat strange. If there was a scale to measure strange, with one end being normal or mildly quirky and the other end being extremely eccentric-handle with caution, I would be somewhere in the middle. The lady who checks out your books at the library who may wear slightly too much pink lipstick that tends to get on her teeth is on the normal end of the spectrum and the guy muttering to himself about the aliens who inserted a chip in his brain when he was abducted last week that rides your city bus would be on the other end. I was walking with KO one day, contemplating what makes us strange when I realized that I had a list of personal quirks a mile long.

I have an aversion to white foods; anything that is purely white freaks me out. I have to have mashed potatoes with pepper and butter so that they aren't that awful color. I can't stand how it feels when my bones can feel other people's bones. Holding Brook's hand has never been a romantic experience but rather a test of my ability to endure the gut wrenching feeling of his knuckles painfully close to mine. Chalk disturbs me. I have to eat a pickle every single day. Wondering what makes me strange is kind of strange. When you have so much time to think, as Brook and I both did over the summer you wonder about everything. I thoughtfully considered more things than I feel appropriate to list. However, it was a freeing notion that I had time to just wonder. Being out in the woods of this country, surrounded by trees, mountains or hills, and lots of rocks, but with no access to technology changes your way of thinking.

My brain didn't process things the same way when I was living an adventure as it did when living a life in which my goals were to pay the bills and get by or just "take it easy." When I was on the road, I considered why things were the way they were. I thought about why women take so much time to groom, me included, while I felt content with my appearance in the grime and filth of five days without a shower. Why do we have to drive or fly everywhere? Why isn't walking more popular? Why do we have to do everything so fast and 'easy'? Nothing gives you the opportunity to ponder like a stint of homelessness and joblessness, and though it may sound like lunacy, I highly recommend it.

As we were getting accustomed to what it means to live out of our car, it became grossly evident that we were in need of an entire mind shift to be able to get through this task. Ponderings aside, our first month on the road was incredibly difficult. Before we left North Carolina I promised myself and God that I would become a more devoted Bible reader since I'd have so much time to be in the Word on the road. Throughout this tale, you will get to hear the words that God sent to me through my Bible study, Words that got our little family through moments when we thought there was absolutely no way we could go on. It was in my study of the Word that I found strength to overcome the daily hurdles of living out of a car, and to put all those ponderings of mine in order.

I don't care how survival savvy or in shape you are, when you are out on the road, living out of your car there are some things you aren't prepared for. Things that are totally taken for granted at home have an elevated or even mystical appeal. Take for example a nail file. I forgot to bring a nail file with me, and the first week while we were in and around Portland I forgot to buy one, then we were in the middle of nowhere. When you are in the middle of nowhere, if you are lucky enough to find items like nail files, which are considered a luxury, then you are going to have to pay big bucks. Nail files, even the cheapo, disposable, only good once kind that no woman in her right mind would want are $4.50. That is about 8 times what they are worth, in my opinion, and so my nails suffered. I waited four weeks to file my nails before I was finally able to find a pack of emery boards for a dollar. I did a happy dance when I found those nail files.

Nail filing aside, there are real and practical examples of the things we just completely take for granted when we are living in our modern homes. Preparing a meal becomes something of a burden rather than a pleasure on the road. At home, you can stop at the grocers on your way back from work, pick up any of the thousands of different items available for purchase and then prepare a delicious, nutritious and savory meal in minutes on a stovetop or in an oven. We cooked everything on a single burner propane stove on our trip. That means when we ate spaghetti, which we did over and over again, we had to first cook the noodles then cook the sauce. The result was a never hot meal. And the wind could throw off the entire process! The flame for the burner was exposed so if even a little wind was blowing, we'd have to reposition the stove or hover over it defending our meager cooker from the elements. We lost our can opener every other day. It was like the car ate the can opener each and every time we would use it. One awful night, on a particularly windy evening, Brook and I ended up chewing on a block of uncooked Ramen noodles because we couldn't get the stove to light because of the wind and we couldn't find the can opener to open anything else. We knew the hard ramen would fill our bellies, so we crunched on it between groans and laughter at our situation.

We kept all of our non-perishable foods in a laundry basket in the back of the truck, which drove Brook crazy. He hated going back to that laundry basket because it was never in order. He organized the canned goods in it at least once every two days in order to try and streamline the ease of digging out what we used most. And don't even get me started on variety. We are so blessed to have variety in our grocery stores. When your major food groups are peanut butter, canned beans and ramen noodles, which are the easiest foods to carry on the road, you understand the true gloriousness of variety. There were many times in Oregon and throughout the trip that I'd walk into a convenience store and open mouth gape at the freezer pizzas, hoping I wasn't drooling. Knowing that I couldn't cook a freezer pizza for at least four months as an American brought me to an embarrassing level of discomfort.

Our diet consisted mainly of rice and beans, yogurt, jarred fruit, ramen noodles, canned soup, canned veggies, eggs, granola bars and the dreaded peanut butter fold-over. To make a peanut butter fold-over you need a piece of bread and some peanut butter. We used the crunchy kind, but creamy works as well. You take a knife and pile peanut butter on it, then smear the stuff on one half of the bread and then proceed to fold it over, in half. It is neither appetizing, nor tasty, but it gets the job done. Brook's back pack always had at least two of these delicacies, as well as three granola bars in it.

Back home we ate a lot of meat. We loved to cook and were regular shoppers at our neighborhood farmer's market. Fresh produce was a huge part of our diet. To go from eating everything fresh, yummy and meaty, to eating out of a can or a box was not an easy transition. I actually got excited about McDonald's dollar burgers at that point in the trip because I was so tired of rice and beans. By the end of the journey I never wanted to see a golden arch again, or a peanut butter fold-over for that matter. Until that June of 2011, the blessings of an electric stove, a working fridge and a stocked grocery store right up the road escaped my attention. I remember dreaming about these things like they were magical treasures; they were my holy grail throughout Oregon.

In Oregon, we were getting our fanny's kicked trying to learn this new lifestyle. We had so many blunders and fights over how to clean dishes without using all of the water we had in our Jerry can, how to position the car for optimal flat sleeping, and how to do just about everything else. It was like learning how to live all over again. I am the type of person who looks at the big picture in life; I like to have a good time and try diligently to not let little annoyances get me down. Brook is the exact opposite; he could care less about the big picture and I swear it will never disturb him to have truly major things happen to him. He could meet the president one day and be attacked by a man eating coyote the next and neither would ruffle his feathers. But try to get him to sleep at a slight incline with his feet a meager inch or two above his head and you just as well could have stabbed the man in the heart.

Every morning I'd drop Brook off wherever he'd stopped walking the day before. There wasn't a single day in his entire journey that he skipped an inch; it was of the utmost importance to him to walk every single step of his route. Then I'd go and pack up the campsite, and drive twenty to thirty miles up the road where I'd look for a playground or another spot to set up camp for the night. If I found a playground, KO and I would play until late afternoon then head on and scout out a site to camp. When we were in the woods and there were no playgrounds, we looked to nature as our provider of enjoyment. Rocks became slides, trees became swings when I hung up our portable hammock and we had a blast learning new ways to play and explore with what we had. When Brook was done for the day I'd pick him up at the arranged meeting spot. Then we'd drive back to camp where I'd cook dinner while he tended his wounds and rested. Then, if the weather was good we'd pile into the tent to sleep. As the weather was never good in Oregon, we would put all our stuff in the tent and climb into the empty truck to sleep. The next day we'd start the whole process over again.

One of the worst plagues we came across in our early days of the trip was security lights. It seemed like every single time we'd go to sleep in a hotel parking lot or campground; we'd inevitably choose the spot under a security light. It would be daytime when we'd arrive, so I'd forget all about how much of a problem this posed and wouldn't look around to see if a light was nearby. The light wouldn't turn on until late into the evening, which wouldn't be awful except for the fact that the stupid thing was always at just the right angle to shine in and keep Brook awake. If there was a light, it was going to sneak in and be directly in his line of vision. He couldn't sleep that way. Brook's dad, Frank, had even sewn curtains for the car that we would hang in all the windows, but somehow the security light would get in. We were at a rustic state park in the first few weeks; no showers, no sink, just a pit toilet and a very traditional campsite with a picnic table and gravel slab. It wasn't well maintained and there wasn't even a campground host. But there was a big bright security light that we of course parked right up next to and had shining on us all night. The light didn't bother me; I can sleep through just about anything, except a miserable husband who can't sleep and whines all night long. I felt so sorry for Brook because in those early days he was exhausted from getting used to everything, and the lights were like an extra beating at the end of an already excruciating day. Later on in the trip I would just tell him to quit his belly aching and offer to buy him a sleep mask which tended to get him to roll over and be quiet, but it took a while for me to get to that level of impatience.

What didn't take me long to get impatient about during our first few weeks on the road was Brook's newfound fear of being dirty. Brook, being the rational man that he is, had decided to go through a germaphobia and clean freak stage while living out of an SUV with his wife and toddler son during a cross country walk. I would feed KO macaroni and cheese and of course it'd get everywhere. Brook would be incapacitated with discomfort at the thought of mac and cheese fingers coming at him from his little boy. He had to do a nightly routine of peeling off his filth no matter where we were, or how cold it was. This routine involved a mountain of baby wipes, complete nudity, soap, a bit of our precious water supply and lasted about 15 minutes.

The first few weeks I just shrugged my shoulders at Brook's need to be clean, but when we hit our six day stretch of no bathing in the middle of Oregon's national forests, I had to put my foot down. "Brook, you absolutely cannot live out of your car and walk 25 miles a day without getting dirty. It isn't possible and I will have to kill you if you do not get over your ridiculous paranoia! Seriously, stop using the antibacterial sanitizer and wallow in your germs like the rest of us!"

He did get the picture, though he still looked queasy every time I suggested letting KO feed himself. His desire to be clean was completely understandable. I for one did not enjoy being dirty and carrying five extra pounds of filth on my person for extended periods of time. However, there comes a time in your life where you just have to suck it up and get used to it, and Oregon was that place for us.

As Brook walked and walked in that first state, his body transformed. He was plagued with quarter sized blisters on his heels, the balls of his feet and his toes. The blisters came and went throughout the journey, but the large, centimeter thick callous that built up over the entire bottom of his feet took many months after the walk to finally be rid of. He begged me to get him a day pack while he was tramping through Portland (I knew he'd need one!) and even the lighter pack which, when full, usually weighed about 15 pounds, caused his back to ache. His calves doubled in size, and even though it rained all the time in Oregon, his skin got darker each day. One night about halfway through Oregon, while we were trying to get to sleep in yet another parking lot with a spiteful streetlamp shining down on us, Brook said "There's just no way."

"No way? What are you talking about?"

"There is absolutely no way I could do this without you here to support me. Now I know why men that do this alone can take years on end to finish this task and even then they end up hitchhiking. I'm sore, and I'm bored out there, but I get excited knowing I'll get to see you at the end of the day, and that you'll be waiting with rice and beans and a cold one. I look forward to KO excitedly waiting for me to show up. I get so lonely, I'd never have made it even this far without the knowledge that you were waiting for me at the end of the day."

I felt the same way. I never would have been able to raise KO alone back home in sweet Carolina, knowing that my husband was a solitary walker, and we weren't helping each other through. We laughed at how foolish we'd been to think that we could have done our trip any other way than how we were doing it right then. All the struggles we'd had to get used to the road finally eased up after that conversation. It was as if we simply needed to acknowledge our feeble understandings of life, and embrace the walk and whatever it would mean with arms and minds wide open.

Of course, as soon as you embrace your appointed task with all your heart, things are put in your way to steal your joy and to set you off on an unprepared path. We had been at it for about two weeks when we were in the woods (again) when, during his walk, Brook felt the urge to answer nature's call. He hiked off into some underbrush after not having a car pass by him for nearly two hours and assumed all was clear. As he was walking into a thicket to find a place to do his business, a large unkempt and snarling dog ran up and bit him on his thigh. Brook grabbed the dog as it came at him again, and this time subdued it before it bit for a second time. He pulled out his handy dandy knife and, as the dog seemed to be a domestic animal, started looking everywhere for the dog's owner. In the distance he saw a man who appeared to be the definition of a lunatic hillbilly. He was wearing a pair of cut off denim shorts with holes all over, a tank top that had clearly been white once upon a time but was now yellowed after having been drenched in sweat many times over. He had a mullet, and he had a huge machete hanging from his belt. Brook shouted "You'd better call your dog off or I'm going to have to slit its throat!" I hope this was an exaggeration, because I do detest animal cruelty. But the dog had bit him and he was all alone, so who knows? Mr. Lunatic Hillbilly shouted for the dog to come to him, and then hollered back, according to my poor dear husband, "If you'da killed him we coulda eaten him for supper together." I swear that this occurred. Brook had a huge yellow bruise on his thigh for about two weeks, and he said after he got the invitation to eat dog from a machete clad wood dwelling maniac, he ran faster than he's ever run before out of those woods.

Brook couldn't call me to come pick him up after this unfortunate event because there is very limited cell service in the national forest land of Oregon, so when he relayed his story to me that night after he finished walking 25 or so miles I was horrified. The bruise was awful; I was so grateful the dog didn't break the skin and that my husband survived to tell me that there is no way I should be hiking alone in the woods with KO anymore, especially off the trails. I had prayed for safety from those lunatic hillbillies, but hadn't counted on them being in the woods of Oregon; I figured we'd run into them later somewhere closer east like the Tennessee mountains.

One of the hardest things that we faced in Oregon was that, though I had sent out about a hundred emails to churches, community groups and organizations in Oregon, no one had responded to host our little family as we began our trek. It was demoralizing in those first few weeks to think that no one cared about the work we were putting into this journey or at the very least that no one cared about the clean water crisis. We contacted a family outside of Portland who hosted us one night, but beyond that we were on our own until we hit a tiny community called Mitchell.

On another cold and rainy day KO and I were stuck in the car with nothing to do in the middle of nowhere. We had already sung "Row, Row, Row Your Boat" sixteen times, thrown every toy possible at each other and had a few breakdowns. We were getting desperate and stir crazy. At home, I would just take him to any number of indoor play facilities or the mall. Not in Mitchell, Oregon. There, you have to get creative. Mitchell has a population of about 120 people. I think that I have lived in buildings where there were 119 other people residing. Imagine a town that size! It shocks your senses, or at least it did mine. So there we were, wandering around in cold and rain trying to find *anything* to do besides drive each other crazy when I saw a little thrift store that was advertising a bag sale, "Anything that I can fit into a bag for 3.50?! And indoors!? I'll take it!"

We went inside and wandered around. The store was an old converted house that had a big wood burning stove in the front room where the store owner had all her racks laid out. We warmed ourselves and KO charmed the other road warriors that had taken shelter on the cold day in the comfort of shopping (yes they were all women), and we enjoyed the warmth. The store manager came over and started talking to me and I told her about our journey. She asked if there was anything I was looking for. Brook had wanted a foot tub to soak his feet in and I figured I'd try my luck. She didn't have any for sale, but she did have one at home and if I just waited for her she'd be right back with it! The foot basin arrived and Sherry extended another kindness, would we like to pitch our tent in her car port so as to keep our stuff dry tonight?

It turns out that Sherry was the mayor of Mitchell, and she showed us a great time that night. She was almost sixty, tall, had short hair and she wore an angel with a white ribbon pinned to her shirt in honor of cancer survivors like her grandson. She had lines from smiling, and her kind heart was definitely worn on her sleeve. We arrived at Sherry's house and met her boyfriend Stan, who was about the same age as Sherry, with a beer gut and a few teeth short of a set. We were sitting in her living room, letting the warmth of their woodstove heat our cold, tired bodies that night when she and Stan started to tell us their stories.

The two of them had wrecked in a Wyoming snow blizzard once. They were true hippies in the seventies, and Sherry thought marijuana should be legalized to boost the economy. Stan didn't care if it was legalized or not. He was going to keep smoking no matter what. Sherry showed us pictures of her family, a niece who was an editor of a major Oregon newspaper, her grandson who had beat cancer in his teenage years. Stan cooked mushrooms for us that he picked in the woods that day; they were safe and non hallucinogenic (though I was concerned at first). He told us about the yummy rattlesnake that he frequently caught and ate. Thankfully snake wasn't on the menu. They had traveled all over the states, loved adventure and kept offering us boxed wine. We got hot showers that were real gifts from God. Stan and Sherry weren't religious, not even remotely so, but they opened their doors to us and showered us with inclusion. Including us in their lives was a treat, and we were encouraged by their taking us in. Mitchell, Oregon may not be much to look at, and it may have fewer inhabitants than an apartment building, but it is filled with kind and generous Oregonians, and it even has a pet bear that lives in a pen right in the middle of "town." After the connection we made in the Mitchell thrift store, I was hooked.

I went into a hundred or more thrift stores throughout our journey across America. I am fairly certain I went to an equal amount of yard sales. Those really revved my engine. The reason I spent so much time going into these yard sales and thrift stores was because, for starters, it was cheap entertainment. I could get a whole new round of children's books for KO for pennies. Most of the time, it also gave us the opportunity to enjoy some air conditioning when it was hot or heat when it was cold. But my favorite part of thrift stores was this: these places were so full of fellow bleeding hearts I made a network of helpful connections through the country in these little epicenters of discount and dust.

Back home, I always noticed places like the public library seemed to attract the homeless and needy, and I never thought about why until that summer. When you can get free heat or air conditioning and entertainment all in one place it can make your entire world outlook better. It was the same for me; as I was learning how to be homeless in this adventure I treasured the moments of not only immense comfort provided by thrift stores, libraries, and local museums, but I valued meeting my fellow Americans in these places.

I got to socialize all across America with fellow bargain hunters and many needy people in these locales. I'd ask about good places to stay, places to see, and where was the best place to get a burger. They'd share their local history and knowledge and then they'd listen avidly while I explained the trip and the clean water crisis. I was able to share God's love and His mission for our family to more people across the U.S. in these venues than any other way. People responded to our mission when they heard that we would give up everything in order to help out a cause that was consuming a billion people's lives. Often, people would be so moved they'd donate on the spot, handing me a twenty dollar bill or a five dollar bill or whatever they had. Sometimes they'd invite us to their church or their home, where we would be fed delicious home cooked meals and given a shower. Even though it sounds a little weird(let's be honest, most everything I've told you so far is a little bit weird), I prayed for God to provide us with yard sales and thrift stores at least once a day so that I could have the chance to share the walk and the clean water crisis.

When we arrived in Oregon and Brook began walking on June 1st, our family had to learn how to relive. Everything was new, and every action I performed was done in a different way. To spend so much time in thrift stores and at yard sales meant that I was immersed in a community of those who, like me, didn't have an exponential amount of funding at their disposal. Yet it was these individuals, many of whom were far worse off financially than me, wanted, needed, and insisted on helping us.

We were moved that those with little were willing to share in great quantities with us. So many people that were hit hard by the economic downturn offered to pay for our campsite, get us a meal, or even just hand us one of their extra apples. The little acts of kindness that we found among our American brethren was touching, and I encourage anyone who doubts the goodness of the American people to take an extended period of time to live in the land and be immersed in the generosity and genuine love of others.

The first time someone offered to pay for our campsite was a poignant day for me on the trip. That day, we were in a little town called Mount Vernon, where KO was excited to find a dilapidated old play ground. Mount Vernon has a population around 600 people, and its main attractions include a gas station, a post office and a café.

We were all alone at the park, hot and sweaty but having a good time when a little girl and her dad rolled up on their bikes. The little girl had blue eyes that shouted about the wonders of childhood. She had a chin length bob of blonde hair and the evidence of the five year old bragging rights-lots of new grown up teeth. She was about as cute as any human could be, and her attitude was even better. This girl had sass. Already at five you could see a diva in the making.

Kids have always flocked to me; I think it is because I either resemble them too closely in my overly colorful clothes and goofy demeanor, or it could be my Peter Pan complex. Whatever the reason, this little girl wanted nothing more than to play with KO and me and be our friend; and we were fast friends! We chased butterflies, had a water fight, played on the swings with KO and made a daisy chain. When it was time for her to go, we decided to be pen pals. As a parting gift she gave me a four leaf clover charm on an old chain, and I will still wear it for good luck or if I am going to be around kids for the day. I gave her a box of Dr. Seuss stationary to write to me.

When I shared our journey with her father he was insistent on helping us. His leg had been amputated in the past, and was unable to work because of his disability. He called his wife and she agreed that they *must* help us. That night the three of them met us at Clyde Holliday State Park in a beat up older car and I realized how generous people can truly be. They paid for our campsite, even though I have an inkling they could barely afford it. When we let people do these generous deeds for us I struggled with feeling guilty because I never wanted to impose on people who seemed to have so little. But I realized that God sent those people our way so that I could be filled with an all consuming comfort that the world is still swarming with good people and

He was blessing us as we went along in ways that helped keep our focus on our mission. Looking back, that was one of my favorite days on the trip; I learned a lot more from their act of kindness than that family could have known.

Oregon was a month long endeavor for us, and we were almost out of it when we had to sleep in one of the strangest locations to date. Brook's walking had us landing in a place called Ironside, Oregon. Ironside has a box for a postman to pick up the mail, but it doesn't even have a post office. No mini mart, café, gas station, or business at all. There aren't any public restrooms either. There is a cemetery though. The cemetery there is set up on a hill, off of the road, where you aren't in anyone's way. The only people you're intruding on are dead and gone. I arrived and was shocked to find nothing but an old field of gravestones. Reluctantly, I pitched the tent in the gravel parking space in front of Ironside Cemetery.

We didn't have any encounters with the dead, and thankfully, KO wasn't all that interested in the gravesites, though one of them had a gnome on it and he desperately wanted that gnome. KO and I picked flowers off of a desert shrub, because at this point we had entered into the barren, dry portion of eastern Oregon, and placed them on the gravestones. We tried to act as respectful as possible; though using the bathroom was slightly awkward.

That night as we were lying in the back of the truck, Brook and I were chatting about the graveyard and what kind of unexpected events had occurred so far that we still were coping with. "I tell you what Billy; this is hard on a girly girl some days. You know how long it's been since I wore perfume? I miss perfume."

"Perfume? Seriously? I miss the ability to control the climate I am in, it's freaking windy out there. I never thought I would be this cold in late June. I would kill for a heater. The cold makes this even spookier. Don't you think?"

"Yes, perfume. I am tired of smelling like 3 day old car funk. And don't you even start trying to scare me. This trip does a very good job at keeping me on my guard; I certainly don't need your help."

In the darkness I heard his smirk cross his face before he ever said "What was that sound! I swear I just heard a moan!"

"Oh shush up and go to sleep," I barked over at him.

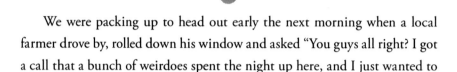

We were packing up to head out early the next morning when a local farmer drove by, rolled down his window and asked "You guys all right? I got a call that a bunch of weirdoes spent the night up here, and I just wanted to make sure you weren't broken down or anything."

We explained what we were doing and his eyes got as big as saucers. He didn't say much after that except wish us good luck and then he drove away in a cloud of dry dust. Even though we were usually met with kind greetings, we also had a lot of people, like this farmer, rub our bizarre noses in the fact that to the rest of the world, we were doing a completely outlandish act. "Man, I love being called a weirdo." Brook laughed as we watched his truck fade away. As the dust from his truck settled back down, so did the realization that Brook and I were going to be "weirdoes" to a lot of people for a long time.

That day I called my parents to tell them about our graveyard jaunt, and my dad laughed hysterically. I actually lost the call with him and when I called him back five minutes later he was still laughing. My mother didn't take it so well. "You slept where with my grandson?! That is gross. No that is worse than gross; that is wrong! And what did you do about the bathroom?! Please tell me you didn't go on a grave!"

It's always good to know that you can still shock your mother, and believe me; it takes *a lot* to shock my mom. One of my best friends love scary movies and all things spooky, and when she found out her reaction was the best "I don't know whether I find this creepy or AWESOME!"

We would get downright desperate for civilization after our long stints in the forest or expanses of empty land. We lost the ability to function decently and normally in public pretty quickly. KO and I arrived in Vale, Oregon, after the cemetery night and I was flooded with appreciation for a town. While I drove through the town scouting it out and getting my bearings I'd shout out, windows rolled down and all "Praise you Jesus for that playground! Oooh, look KO, let's thank God for the gas station-we can get a slurpee later." Then I saw the Dairy Queen. I shouted "Praise the Lord!" like you wouldn't believe and jumped out of the truck to get KO. We were going to get a Blizzard and it was going to be paradisiacal.

I immediately noticed that every man walking around Vale was wearing cowboy boots and a cowboy hat. My son was dressed in a tie dyed t-shirt with a Bob Marley patch ironed on to the front and I too was sporting tie dye that day. We got some funny looks. The first thing KO and I did was go to the Dairy Queen and order ice cream. It was more glorious than I could have imagined it would be. As the ice cream melted down my throat, all my stress melted as well. While KO napped, I drove around and poked into yard sales. I was at one yard sale where I struck up a conversation with the woman running it. I promptly spilled my life story. Though I was able to refrain from telling her most of my darkest secrets, I may have let one or two slip as I was so overwhelmed by human conversation. Either out of fear of me being a lunatic and having a break down or true kindness, she offered me access to her internet and a drink of water.

It was glorious to sit and check my emails after having been disconnected from so many people for so long. She and her husband were moving to Portland where they were starting out on their own new path for life. It was fun to talk to people, share stories and be blessed. Plus I got some of the cutest shirts I own from her yard sale. When it was time for me to leave, she gave me a parting gift and I took down her address so that I could keep in touch if ever we made it back home. These were the moments I treasured.

Treasured moments happened often on the trip, but so did miserable ones. It was in Vale where I first messed up the Yukon. I had never driven a car this big, and it was obvious when I parked, because I always failed to judge the space that I needed and ended up taking two spots. I had pulled into our very first el cheapo motel and had a hard time parking because there were two trees directly in front of our room with about a car length and a half between them and the door. We had so much stuff in our back seats, as we lived in the car, so I had no visibility out of the back window. I wasn't paying close enough attention when I went to pick Brook up and reversed into one of the trees. I dented the bumper, broke one of the taillights and scratched it all up. I called and told Brook and he wasn't happy. My father in-law Frank took it well and wasn't at all upset which was good, because Brook was mad enough for the both of them. Unfortunately for all of us it wouldn't be the only mistake I made in the car, but was just the beginning of a large series of blunders. I came to learn that I am a woman that needs to be behind the wheel of a compact car. Or a tank.

Amidst all of these new chores and my completely altered lifestyle, I crave quiet time. Everyday, KO takes a nap. Getting KO to sleep was never easy, but out here I've had to figure out a whole new way to get him to doze out here on the road. Usually, I give him a stroller ride until he falls asleep or I drive him around until he succumbs to rest. While he rests I pray. I pray for Isaac, and all the kids like him out there, to get clean water locally in their communities so that they aren't late everyday for school from walking for water, and so that they can stop getting sick from the water borne illnesses that they are exposed to. I pray for Brook to make it another day with all those oozing blisters and aching muscles. I pray that KO won't eat poison ivy or toxic berries in the middle of the forest. Most of all I pray that our little family will complete our task.

Oregon has been homelessness boot camp. As we like to say in the south, "We got our butts whooped" as we've forged our way across the miles of cold mountain terrain and hot farm country. Brook has walked a total of 534 miles in Oregon, through rain, snow, cold and hot. His body has begun to adapt to the rigors of walking across America as he completed his fourth week and first of ten states. We've begun to see God's provision to our cause as we exit our first state; people are caring for our needs out of the little that they have to offer. We've already raised enough money to build two wells, and we haven't been eaten for dinner by psycho hillbillies.

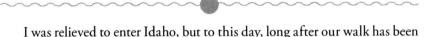

I was relieved to enter Idaho, but to this day, long after our walk has been completed, Brook says that crossing into Idaho was the best border he crossed his whole walk. Once he got through Oregon, his most difficult state, he said he felt more accomplishment than he'd ever had in his own work.

"I can't believe I've walked this far. 534 miles is a long way to walk, I just can't believe that I still have 2,766 miles or so to go! But if I made it this far, I guess I'll make it all the way," he said with a touch of bewilderment on June 27th, 2011 when he met up with me after he'd crossed into Idaho. It was edifying, going into a new place knowing that if we could get through the first month of learning the ropes, we were going to be ok. We were going to make it.

Idaho: The Hot, the Sick, and the Spudly

"As a face is reflected in water, so the heart reflects the real person." Proverbs 27:19 NLT

Idaho has a ton of dairy farms; this is my warning to you that a pungent methane gas odor permeates the air in large tracts of the state. The stink of Idaho was accentuated by the blistering heat we began to enjoy. Nothing makes a big pile of manure smell better than high temperatures and a good breeze. We had been in Oregon for so long that as Brook wrapped Idaho up after only 2 weeks, we were out of our minds with joy. Though his trek in Idaho was shorter, we had a great time exploring Boise, staying with a loving host family, and experiencing our very first radio interviews.

The first few days in Idaho we didn't have a lot happen besides getting used to the stinky cows and hot weather. After sleeping with snow outside the tent in Oregon, the heat was welcome in my case. I was content to marinate in the sun's lovely rays, though Brook could have dealt with the perfect 70's accompanied by an easy breeze the whole way across the country. The heat was hard for him to adjust to initially. He had gotten so used to wearing two shirts and keeping his hoodie on for warmth that as he began to shed the layers in the heat he forgot how important sunscreen is and how much he loathed it.

The first day I tried to get him to put sunscreen on he flat out refused.

"I hate how it feels on my hands and it doesn't go away. That greasy, smelly, residue is going to be on me for days. No way am I putting it on."

He got back that night with the reddest neck I have ever seen. Even his huge wide brimmed hat couldn't keep the sun at bay. The next morning I generously offered to apply the sunscreen for him, if he would agree to wear it. He conceded, probably because I didn't wait for an answer and just snuck up and started smothering him in it. He walked his sunburned self into Boise that day, which is where our Idaho fun began.

Boise is one of the coolest cities I've ever been to. I can honestly say that there are few people living in America right now that have experienced as many parks and playgrounds as myself and my son, so I am delighted to report from my vast experience in the parks department that Boise boasts some of the best community green spaces in the entire country. Ann Morrison Park has a colossal fountain and playground that KO and I were obsessed with, and we spent many happy hours there while Brook walked. While planning the journey we'd discovered a social networking site that connects fellow adventurers like Brook and me to individuals that have opened their home to travelers. We'd stayed with our first hosts we'd connected with via the site way back in Oregon in a suburb of Portland. They were dear hippies that we'd enjoyed, so we anticipated meeting more new people and staying with another family we'd met through the network in Boise.

When we got to the home of Jude and Rita, we were greeted by Rita's 17 year old daughter Lucy and two of the biggest dogs I have ever seen in my life. The family had three pups, but two were Great Danes. Let me tell you, Scooby Doo makes Great Danes seem a lot smaller than the real life version. KO would walk up to the dogs, look up at them, and then run back to me as quick as he could when they made eye contact with their big puppy eyes. We were escorted to the room that was set up for us, and I was not surprised to find little Buddhas, cactuses, and numerous rubber ducks littering the window sill. There was also incense burning. The room was decorated in a style I like to call "Bohemian Mish Mash" because it's just a collection of the 'grooviest' little trinkets you can find mish mashed together. KO kept playing with the little Buddhas. He put one on the back of a rubber ducky and pretended to let Buddha ride the ducky like a horse. Siddhartha would likely have enjoyed the sight. It's possible that my child is not a miniature barbarian but instead is a walking, breathing, enlightened one. Only time will tell.

The Great Danes had these huge dog beds, and KO kept lying down on them. He loved them so much that I decided I was going to get him one of his own for the duration of the trip. They are small enough to fit comfortably in a car, and they aren't all that expensive. Plus I'd been trying to find a way to make him a little bed to sleep on that wasn't attached to my own bed in order to minimize him kicking me in my face to wake me up.

The next day I embarked on a mission to buy a dog bed for my child. I settled on a soft and cushy one with a leopard print. As KO and I picked out a dog bed that I would end up sleeping on more than he would, I felt so much guilt. I battled guilt a lot as a mom on the road with a toddler, mostly because kids are supposed to have a steady schedule and feel secure with their routines. Our poor son was in a different place every single day, meeting new people and never knowing what to expect. Thankfully, my child is resilient like you wouldn't believe. He is built to last, and last he did.

That night Jude and Rita fed us veggie burgers, yummy basmati rice and fresh tomatoes, and we had a lovely time with them. Rita had scored an interview with a local radio station for us the next morning. I woke up super early and took a shower, did my hair, and got all dressed up, or as dressed up as one can get living out of a car. Then I woke up KO and Brook and we loaded out. Rita escorted us to the radio station where we said our goodbyes. Brook was tired, as expected of a man walking across America, but he was chipper and alert when we arrived at the studio that morning in early July. We had a five minute segment in which the dj's interviewed us on the walk and the clean water crisis. The best part of the interview was that we got to bring KO in the studio with us and the only way we could keep him quiet was to play SpongeBob on his portable DVD player. Needless to say, when my best friend Deidre called me later that day to tell me she'd heard the program online, she asked if someone had SpongeBob on in the studio. All the listeners in Boise that heard us also heard the innocuous laughter of a little, animated yellow sponge. We had a great time spreading the word about the clean water crisis to a listening audience and were encouraged to get some press for our campaign. Even little five minute radio spots fueled us because we would imagine a listener somewhere hearing for the first time that kids as young as four walk to fetch their dirty drinking water in impoverished nations. Knowing we may have informed even one person of the crisis was the pick me up we needed to endure.

After the interview, Brook set out to walk. The day he walked from Boise into a great expanse of nothing was his longest day yet. He came across an Idaho state prison, shooting ranges, and he said it was so lonely his heart began to groan by the time afternoon rolled around. To make it worse, he'd gotten lost on a goat path that he thought was a frontage road and ended up having to jump a barbed wire fence that put a deep gash in his knee. After cutting his knee open, he got stopped by a state trooper for the first time. The trooper told him that he'd gotten a lot of calls about a strange man walking alongside the highway and he wanted to make sure Brook was ok (and also not an escaped convict). He ran Brook's license through his database and when Brook explained his purpose the officer relaxed and was even amiable. The officer sent him on his less than merry way after offering him a ride that my Billy of course had to refuse. Earlier in the day, we had scoped out a truck stop that we had planned as the finishing point for Brook's trek that night and our place of rest. Brook finally arrived that evening discouraged, grouchy and exhausted. He had no desire to continue in the walk, he shared, on days like this one. Having to stop was the most debilitating part of his day. "I am so tired of getting looked at like a crazy person. It took a lot of patience not to get real angry about having my license checked simply for walking."

We crashed that night in our body odor, miserably hot, before the sun had even set. I woke up about five hours later tremendously sick. I was burning up, and my stomach was in agony. I went inside the truck stop and bought a can of lemon lime soda and some crackers. I didn't have a thermometer, but I would guess my fever was spiking at about 102 degrees. My throat felt like I'd swallowed a rose bush and the thorns had stuck around to keep me company. I had the worst aches I'd experienced since I'd given birth to KO. I rotated between shivering and sweating the night away all the while praying for good health and for our burdens to be lifted.

"God, this is so unfair. Here I am with feet in my face that have already walked over five hundred miles and smell like hot garbage. I've got a fever and no idea how to find a doctor that will be on our route. Don't you see that we are doing good things here? Don't you see that illness is the last thing we need to lift morale and persevere? Please, release us from this agony!"

I am unsure of what agony I was praying to be released from; whether the commitment to the walk or the sickness I can not recall. It was probably both. The next day I went into a little town where I found a motel room and tried to rest off my pulsating pain and stomach flu. This seems like an opportune moment to discuss motels of the cheap variety; I'm talking 30-50 bucks a night. These are the places with unmistakable ceiling stains, funky smelling sheets, and 'eclectic' furniture choices. The definition of eclectic here is "a random collection of bed frames, coffee tables and TV stands gathered from yard sales, street curbs and the salvage yard."

When you enter the office of a cheap motel, you first are overwhelmed by the smell of curry. I do not mean this in a stereotypical way, I honestly only went into two motels our entire trip that weren't owned by someone of Indian heritage. I know this because I always asked the motel owners where they hailed from; it often got them friendly and would help me weasel a few dollars off of our bill.

Once you have made friends with the curry odor, you must then search out a sign on the counter that instructs you how to find the "office manager" which is just a term that refers to a little man with a thick accent who has a shifty eye. My personal favorite cheap motel experience happened in a tiny town called Mountain Home at a place called the Thunderbird.

I was very sick. I hadn't slept at all in that stupid truck stop parking lot and I had a high fever. I was throwing up and I had KO while Brook was, you guessed it, walking. I pulled up to the Thunderbird, yanked my hollering wildebeest out of his car seat and walked into little India. The office of the Thunderbird Motel was a wood paneled, cluttered, smelly room but I was desperate to lie down on some musty sheets. I located the bell on the counter amidst a freaky golden cat and a stack of restaurant coupons that had expired months before. An itty bitty man came out after I rang the bell on the counter about ten times. He was approximately 75, had four teeth and couldn't hear a jack hammer going off five feet away. He handed me a piece of paper to fill out and the fun began.

The piece of paper asked the normal questions you get asked at motels; license information, plate numbers, number of guests per room. I filled it out in about a minute in a half. Then I handed it back. He proceeded to ask "Do you smoke?"

"No sir, I don't."

"Does the other person who is in the room smoke?"

"Nope."

"We don't like smoking. This is a no smoking room."

"Shouldn't be a problem for me, sir."

"No smoking?"

"Sir, I haven't *ever* smoked a single cigarette in my entire life, I don't plan to start tonight!"

"Good Girl. You are good girl."

"Thanks, can I get the key now?"

"Listen, I give you good rate, cheap room. When you leave the room, turn off the air conditioner okay. You save me money. Okay?"

"Umm, sure, not a problem."

At this point I was about to throw up all over this winky eyed, toothless, miserly, old, curry smelling fogey. And keep in mind he was so deaf that everything he said was yelled. By the end of the question and answer session KO had found a sprinkler attachment on the floor and was banging it into a glass cabinet filled with dusty old artificial flowers and began to make the old guy angry (I love my child) so he started wrapping up his interrogation with a series of rapid fire queries.

"Your name is too long for paper, what is name? Out of state, no I don't like that. I go look at license plate to make sure you get it right. How long you staying? You have to leave by 11 tomorrow, I have cleaning lady, they do good job."

Just as I thought this guy was about to hand me the keys; he had checked out my car, interrogated me like I was a hostile enemy, hollered at my sweet monkey of a son and driven me to the point of complete insanity, a woman's voice hollered from the back room in a language that I could not understand. Curried Rice Man shrieked back, and the hollering continued for about three minutes before I let KO bang on the glass cabinet again. That got his attention. "Here, keys, you pay for double, room 19. You can't swim until 4, I clean pool. No smoking?"

If I hadn't had strep throat, a fever of 103, a stomach bug, a sweet buffalo of child that needed to be played with and Jesus as my example I would have slammed the gas on the truck, driven to the closest convenience store, bought a pack of cigarettes and burned them all in room number 19 just to spite the man who had made my life a curried smelling misery for the past 20 minutes. As I was completely overwhelmed with my illness and child, I literally ran to room 19, locked the door and blasted the air conditioning as high and long as possible.

That day had been another scorcher for Brook with the temperature hitting the high 90's. The roads were in awful condition. I had to pick him up early from his walking because I was so sick I couldn't handle KO alone. He was frustrated because he was behind on his schedule and feeling sorry for the lot of us. The day was not turning out to be a good one for our little family. After he'd rested and showered he went to find ice. The Thunderbird had an ice machine, so he went to see if it was working. Mr. Interrogator was waiting in the office for him. "What room you in?"

"Number 19."

"Oh, with lady and baby."

"Yes, my wife and son. Does your ice machine work?"

"Oh, it works."

"Then I'll just get my ice and let you be."

"No ice in machine today."

"Excuse me?"

"It costs too much to run the machine. Nobody want ice for a week so I turned it off."

"Oh. OK. Thanks."

"You good boy, I get you ice."

"Really? I could get some?"

"Oh, you got some? Good, have good day."

Brook returned to the room ten minutes later after having gone to the corner store to get ice. He relayed his experience with the ridiculous old man and we both laughed. Unfortunately, this was a typical cheap motel experience for us.

Our patience, endurance and dependence on God was necessary on the journey more so than it had ever been. While Brook was being challenged physically and mentally to complete his walk, I was being equally challenged to make it to the other end of the country without losing my mind over the nomadic lifestyle and the wretched people I sometimes had to deal with. There are days when we just wanted to be left alone, but on our mission, privacy was non-existent. Our life was a public one. We had out of state plates and were in small towns where strangers were detected almost instantly and we often stuck out in our different clothing, accents, and lifestyle. Not to mention one of us was simply walking alongside of roads all day long; that is bound to attract attention.

One of the greatest gifts that the trip gave me personally was a heightened awareness that the people I just called wretched in the previous paragraph were not so unlike myself. They had the same basic physical, spiritual and emotional needs. They were Americans, living in the same nation as myself, experiencing much of the same culture and language that I experienced. We ate the same foods, shopped at the same places, and lived under the mystical concept of American freedom. Concluding that I was surrounded by wretched little people, and that I too had a pension for wretchedness, I cancelled my pity party and invited some of the other wretches into my life in order that they might change my outlook and help me perk up. Often this was the key to my endurance, and I noticed that it was for Brook as well. As the hideous old cliché goes, misery loves company.

We left the Thunderbird the next morning hoping to find a less invasive place to stay and found another motel. This motel boasted a pink bathtub and a pink toilet; our room at the Thunderbird only featured a pink toilet. Brook took a day off to help me out with KO so that I could recover. While he and KO played, I shivered, suffered and firmly decided that I needed to see a doctor. There was a family scheduled to host us beginning the fifth of July and I figured I could get to a doctor through them, but Brook's walk was going to prevent me from getting that far on our route if we stuck to his no forward driving rule. I mustered up the energy and asked Brook if he would make a concession for me on his walk.

He had been perfectly clear that he didn't want to drive ahead of where he was walking at all throughout the trip. We'd already had to drive a few miles ahead on numerous occasions because of camp placement in the evenings, but I asked in genuine fear that he would say "No" if he would consider driving the 60-70 miles on July fourth, the next day, with us so that I could see a physician on the fifth. He wasn't happy about it, but he conceded. And so on July 4th, 2011, he walked until noon, and then we set out to drive the 60 or so miles to meet the host family who would be nurturing us for the next four days.

One of Brook's uncles is a pastor and he had sent out a mass email to his friends and colleagues throughout the country about our journey and asked for host families on our behalf. John and Naomi answered the call. When we arrived at their home on July fourth they greeted us with open arms and lots of hospitality. Their two sons were 12 and 13. They didn't roll their eyes or act like it was totally uncool to help out with KO like I figured they would; rather they were excited and eager to play with my little cub.

Later that night we joined John and Naomi at their friend's home for a community cookout and 4th of July celebration. Steadily, Brook and I had been becoming ever more patriotic the past four weeks. As we were immersed in America we grew to love our land deeper and more completely than I ever thought possible. Our love of our nation had only just begun as we sat down with burgers and bratwurst that Independence day. As we gathered with other Americans who shared our values, our culture, and our love of God that evening, we told our stories of the road, ate the American way (big, flavorful and artery clogging), and enjoyed the fellowship of our countrymen.

We were informed that the town we were in did not have a fireworks display because the rural community that presided there preferred to travel to the closest city for the show or blow stuff up on their private property. We were bummed we didn't get fireworks that year, as it was the first year that we truly understood what it means to be "Proud to be an American," but we were so exhausted we probably couldn't have stayed awake long enough to see them had they been offered in that small town. We retired early that night and as Brook put KO to sleep I lied down in John and Naomi's bed (they had offered it to us while they slept on the floor or on the sofa in the living room). After having been so sick and sleeping in such questionable beds the past few nights, I cried.

The tears that I cried were of joy to be in a clean and comfy bed. I was intensely grateful to be blessed abundantly. I was also pierced with the tragedy that there are people all over the world who don't get to sleep in the luxury of a clean, comfortable bed for their entire *lives*. The tears, I am sure, flowed out of exhaustion and illness as well. Our hosts had already booked an appointment for me with the local doctor for the following day and I felt absolutely cared for as I breathed deep of refreshment that evening. The next morning we woke up and my heart nearly burst when I smelled bacon frying in the kitchen.

Naomi and John were fantastic cooks. While Naomi made us bacon, John blended these green smoothies each morning. They looked disgusting but were surprisingly tasty. I think that all the fruit and veggies he pumped into those smoothies, partnered with the antibiotics the doc gave me had me up and on the road to recovery way faster than I could have been otherwise.

John had moved his family from Charlotte, NC to Idaho. He felt that the church there needed his leadership and was excited about the prospect. His wife was an educated artist who adored the culturally elevated life. Naomi was used to museums, theatre, galleries, live music and being around other college educated people. She opened up to me about her aching loneliness as we sat across from each other one day while KO napped. I asked her how it felt to be the wife of a pastor, and she explained that though she loved her husband and sons, she felt more isolated and on display than she thought possible. She said that she felt she couldn't go out without people knowing her and watching her, and she couldn't easily relate to Idahoans.

She continued to share that she loved the people she was befriending in Idaho and wouldn't have made it without her new friends, but she still felt so distant and alien. I have met few people with as much sadness as Naomi. This woman was no dairy farmer, and never would be. As the population around her was born and bred with an agricultural mindset, she found it impossible to fit in. She was drowning in her misery, and it was obvious from her deeply sad, exotic eyes that she needed a lifeguard to pull her up out of the water and help her onto some dry land; preferably somewhere with an exhibit on display of an impressionist painter's workmanship. I invited this woman to go shopping with me in Twin Falls, which was the closest 'big city' and we had a fun day on the town. She is a gorgeous woman. If I have a figure like that when I am her age I will be shocked and overjoyed! We tried on shoes and looked at jewelry displays, most of all we laughed a lot.

I did my best to encourage her that life isn't a boring dairy farm, but that God clearly had a reason for their move there. I have never felt so nervous leaving someone. I felt like I was abandoning Naomi when we said our good byes after a few days with her, John and the boys. Naomi's loneliness and tragic sadness over her physical location taught me a valuable lesson: It's not where you are but who you're with. If you are with those you love, even if you are sleeping in a cemetery, you are blessed because there are people there that love you, which is more than a lot of people can say about their lives. But I understood her pain out there on the road. Home sickness is debilitating at times, and while I was out there in Idaho and beyond, I missed North Carolina and the things that it meant to me more and more. When we interviewed Isaac many months before, I had asked him if being in America made him homesick. He didn't understand what I was asking and looked at me like I had a third eyeball until I explained it to him. When he understood the question he simply told me that though he missed his favorite food (jackfruit) and his family, he was happy where he was, with his friends doing what God wanted him to be doing. Between Naomi and that memory of Isaac I was inspired. The two of them impressed upon me the value of home, but also the value of doing the greater good and how important it can be to lean hard on Jesus for His blessed assurance when we feel our loneliest.

Naomi had scored us a second radio interview in Twin Falls and we enjoyed the opportunity to speak with another dj in Idaho before we left.

This time, we were pre recorded and the dj edited the piece a bit so it was a lot more polished. We also got about twenty minutes of air time, so more people were able to hear about the walk and the need for clean water. I adored John and Naomi's sons. They were a lot of fun and the two of them wandered around the local pool, parks and Twin Falls together with myself and KO while Brook walked. They are awesome kids! Usually middle school age kids overwhelm me with their "whatever's," mood swings and unbearable awkwardness. Brook and I were happy (and surprised) to find them agreeable, enjoyable and interesting. On our last day, John joined Brook in his walk and became the first person to trek with our water walker.

Brook said John kept up well, and he enjoyed having the company for the time John walked with him. I saw John before we left, after he'd walked with Brook and he said he was exhausted after the little bit of time he'd put out there; he couldn't imagine walking all day, every day, for months on end. Hearing John's description of the walk made me crave being able to join my husband as he put one foot in front of the other. After our four day stay with John, Naomi and their sons, during which Brook had walked all day each day, we headed on. KO and I toured the Shoshone Falls while Brook continued to walk. The falls are stunning. I loved all the adventuring I was getting to do with my son. Since both he and I were so silly, we'd sing and dance as we hiked along trails and some of those moments will be forever smiling back at me as they are recalled. Though the three of us had finally gotten into a groove after our six weeks on the road, we were anxious for the company that Brook's parents would bring as the date of their arrival to join us inched nearer and nearer. The impersonal road had been rigorously giving Brook a trial of his ability to mentally and spiritually look beyond what his body was telling him, which was of course, to pack up and head home. He had overcome the blister stage for the most part, but the new found heat left him evaluating his water intake, the unavoidable chaffing of his skin in certain spots, and wilting.

Brook desperately needed his breaks, because getting a good night sleep seemed impossible the closer we got to Utah. One night, I found Murtaugh Lake State Park, cruised in and set up camp. The state park was a mile out of Brook's way on a side road, and as he is always the fuel conservationist, he was determined to hitch a ride from the corner of the road to camp rather than have me drive the two miles round trip to bring him back to camp myself. He barely made it to the turn when he got offered a ride by a couple of stoner hippies in an old van that reeked of cheap beer, marijuana and funk. When they opened the back door to let Brook in he laughed at the shag carpet that was accompanied by a few lawn chairs, set up for sitting in the 'back seat'. He declined their offer for beer, and any other substances that they were privy to, and when he walked triumphantly into camp with a smirk on his face he said "Now that is why I haven't accepted any rides from strangers so far. Remind me not to do that again."

He told me that the guys that had given him a ride were headed across the lake to a music festival and motorcycle rally, and that when he'd told them about his walk they were stoked. However, when he turned down the beer they shut up real fast and didn't talk much more. "I think I offended their hospitality, so I am really glad it was only a mile of awkwardness."

The music festival that the guys had been headed to seemed to be quite the event for this part of Idaho. Traffic got heavier and heavier, and the volume of Aerosmith cover bands did as well. There were party animals jamming, drinking, carrying on and revving the stupid engines on their motorcycles all night long. The night was not shaping up to be a good one as we got into bed.

Our neighbors at the campground were a bunch of college kids who apologized in advance when I arrived. "We are having a going away party tonight, and we are having a bunch of people come out, so it might get noisy. Sorry about that."

These students knew how to throw a party. They brought coolers and coolers of booze, wood for a big fire, and get this: a full size trampoline. They let KO jump on their trampoline and he became obsessed. When I tried to get him away from it he was furious and threw fit after fit as he watched the college kids enjoy the "jump jump" while I tried to get him to play with me with his toys, sticks, rocks and whatever else I could think of. As Brook and I settled into our tent that night, we tried to fall asleep to the soothing sounds of our neighbor's trampoline springs being stretched over and over, their beer pong matches, and a "COOLEST TATTOO CONTEST!" that was happening across the Lake at the music festival. My poor husband growled and threw himself a much deserved pity party on his side of the air bed while I laughed and cringed at the horrors of it all. I fell asleep long after Brook once the trampoline party had calmed down and a woman sporting some kind of dragon/phoenix tattoo had won the contest at the festival. Though sleep evaded us countless nights on the road, there weren't many nights as eventful as our evening spent at Lake Murtaugh.

On the day before Brook's parents were planned to arrive, I got to Burley, Idaho where I found a few motels. I chose one with a good location and cheap rate and checked in. The room they put me in neighbored a room that was under construction. I was bringing stuff in with KO when all of a sudden the owner of the motel and the repair man got into the loudest cuss-out I have ever heard. They told each other all sorts of ways to go to the lake of fire and they did it right in front of my son and me. To say I was offended is to sugar coat the anger I had erupting inside. I went into the motel room with KO to stop fuming and said a prayer "God, please let those two men pay for their inappropriate behavior and ridiculous anger." Literally a second after I finished praying, the motel owner knocked on the door and apologized. He also asked me to move to a different (much larger, nicer and quieter) room because his hired help had just informed him that the hot water heater was broken for the room I was in. I forgave the guy, but was sure to let him know in the sternest voice I could muster that no child should ever have to witness that behavior from him again. I changed motel rooms satisfied that my God is a God that answers prayers.

While I was giving lectures to foul mouthed motel owners, Brook was having a much more relaxing moment under the shade of an old tree in the yard of a man named Brad. Brook had walked up on Brad's property and saw him digging in the front yard. Brook described Brad as a scrawny guy with a big beard, but no mustache, wearing a straw hat with the overall appearance of the Amish. Brad had apparently been at a yard sale over the weekend and bought an underwater camera shaped like a fish and was digging up worms to go fishing with. When Brad saw him walking by he hollered out and asked what Brook was doing.

"Just walking," replied Brook.

"Where to?" Brad asked.

"Well, eventually North Carolina, but just to town for today." Then Brook shared his mission.

When Brad heard Brook's explanation his reply was "You wanna cold one?"

Of course Brook said yes. Brad got Brook a beer and they sat and chatted about the walk and life. Brook learned about the family history that Brad revealed with pride. Apparently, all the walking Brook had been doing that afternoon had been through land that Brad's family had cultivated and worked for generations. As Brad shared his life, Brook sipped on his cold one and pondered. When it was time for Brook to keep walking, Brad handed him twenty dollars and told him that it was the first time he had ever donated to a charity in his entire life. "I don't trust all those people you see on TV, but I have a feeling you're a good guy and will see right by me here." We made sure that charity: water got the twenty dollars in Brad's name, and Brook enjoyed his first free cold one on the road. When he got back that night, after he'd told me all about Brad and his visit, he said that he wished he'd had more time on this journey. Brad had invited us all to stay with him for a while, and Brook had wanted to take him up on it.

"It's hard to keep pressing on with all these cool people to meet all over the place. I know I have to finish because we can't live this way as a family forever, but it was a welcome change to just take a break under the shade of an old family tree and learn a bit about the land I'm walking through. It makes the land more personal, more special."

Across the country, whether I was walking with Brook, caring for KO or attempting to be a campaign manager that procured interviews, lodging and food, I often had *The Little Engine That Could* chug into my thoughts. I caught myself chanting "I think I can. I think I can. I know I can. I know I can" more times than any college educated, adult woman and mother should. I even tried replacing my chant with Philippians 4:13 "I can do all things through Christ who strengthens me," which helped me at times, but did not diminish the constant mental recall of the chant. It seemed as if God had sent me the little engine's words and they were sticking around. I like things to be succinct, easy and simple, and *The Little Engine That Could* chant certainly met those requirements. Which is important, because when you're trying to look past an illness and a little Indian man wreaking of curry is giving you the run around, while your toddler son is needing more attention than you can possibly give him and your crazy lunatic of a husband is *walking* across the country and is currently located feet from a state penitentiary in a state you know very little about, you need to find inspiration that will strengthen you in a simple way. Thus, God's provision of *The Little Engine That Could* chant was a blessing of great proportions in my life on the road.

We made it through Idaho in good spirits. Though I was sick half of our time there, and we got behind because Brook had to take a day and a half off to help me, we were encouraged to get through the state quickly. Our time with John and Naomi, their sons and community was a healthy release from our normal routine. We will never stop being appreciative for the time and help we were given in their little town. Boise was jamming and I can't wait to go back. Most of all, God saw us through yet another state, another couple hundred miles, and we were gaining confidence every day that He would help us to the very end of this. We left Idaho with me muttering "I think we can, I think we can, I know we can, I know we can!"

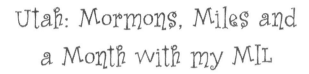

Utah: Mormons, Miles and a Month with my MIL

"Do two walk together unless they have agreed to do so?" Amos 3:3 NIV

Having muddled through Idaho, we figured Utah would be a better experience for us because we were going to have reinforcements. Brook's parents, Wendy and Frank, arrived during our last two days of Idaho. After spending six weeks basically alone with my son, I was in desperate need of an adult to talk to and Brook was looking forward to having someone along to break the walking cycle that was beginning to bore him. When Frank and Wendy arrived we were ecstatic to have them.

About a year before our pow-wow in Utah, we'd had an unfortunate falling out with Frank and Wendy. Families full of passionate, opinionated people tend to have moments such as these. We'd all worked so hard that year to repair the damage done, and though I felt as though the healing had happened, I had my worries about spending so much time alone and in isolated terrain with my in-laws. However small or large my worries were, I had prayed for peace, joy and rest during this month with family. I was determined for it to be a time of lasting happy memories and uplifting change, and blessedly, so did everyone else. I was so excited when the day finally arrived for them to be with us that I actually had butterflies in my stomach! I'm a lucky gal to be able to say that about the arrival of my in-laws.

Frank and Wendy had picked up a shuttle from the airport in Boise that had a stop where Brook had finished walking the previous day. Brook waited to walk until his parents met us, so we parked at the travel station they were getting dropped off at a few minutes prior to their arrival. The bus pulled up, and my beloved father in-law Frank jumped out and immediately started hugging us, meanwhile my sweet mother in-law bounded out of the bus like all perfect grandmothers and had KO in her arms about as fast as the pungent smell of cow hits you in Idaho when you walk outside. Then, Frank proceeded to gather up their bags and I was incredibly impressed at how little they had packed.

Between the two of them they had two big packs and two daypacks, and Wendy had one tote bag. Frank could live out of plastic grocery bag for the rest of his life and function perfectly fine in society, but Wendy; that woman can accessorize. She always has the cutest outfits, which are perfectly complimented by shoes and jewelry that fit the occasion. And though I'd not call her high maintenance, I was impressed at her ability to just say "No" to the excess for the month she was going to be with us. I cried a bit and we all laughed as his parents told us their travel stories and then Brook and Frank prepared to walk. They were going to try and make it at least 10-15 miles that day, even though they were getting a late start.

Frank is in his early 50's. He has a full head of medium brown hair, brown eyes, and a brown mustache. He also has smile lines deeply embedded around his eyes that he passed onto Brook, for which I am eternally grateful. Those smile lines are Brook's secret weapon. They are the key to talking me into ludicrous things such as living out of a car for an undetermined amount of time in the wilderness. But back to Frank. He's about 5'9 and his calves don't grow any hair because they've been stifled in cowboy boots for many years. His skin is dark from years spent outside working on a farm. When he walks he is slightly bowlegged and is the definition of purposeful. Frank's presence exudes action. When I first met him, before Brook told me what he did for a living, I just knew Frank was a sheriff. He looked straight out of the Wild West with a big moustache, boots, a deep tan and locked jaw. I was wrong, but secretly I still call him "the Sherriff."

Wendy's love for the outdoors is obvious, especially in the summer because her skin is the color of cinnamon and brown sugar. Thinking on it, this is probably what her soul smells like to God. She has blonde hair that graces her shoulders and blue-green eyes that twinkle. Wendy is all kindness and accommodation wrapped up in a delightfully curvy frame. Unlike Frank, Wendy moves more like a meandering stream; slower and more relaxed without a definite pace. She is the deputy to his sheriff and watching the two of them together is often like watching an episode of the Andy Griffith Show; they are cohorts like only Andy and Barney can be. Wendy brings all the fun that Barney does, and Frank, though try as he might to get frustrated, generally ends up cracking a smile at the adventures they endure together.

Before they had flown out, Frank and Wendy had visited the running store in their hometown, as well as REI and some other outdoor and athletic stores. They came bearing a bounty of fancy powders, energy supplements, top of the line socks and foot creams. I only wished for their sake that they'd also gotten a prescription for some high dollar pain meds, because they could have used some on certain days. Brook looked skeptically at all of the new equipment.

"What's that you're putting in your socks?" he casually asked Frank. "It's cooling foot powder. It's like icy hot for your feet. Only without the hot," Frank explained patiently, while he puffed two more clouds of it into his fancy socks. "Would you like to try it?"

"Maybe tomorrow. I don't figure if I've made it this long without it I need it today." I rolled my eyes, knowing that the foot powder Brook was turning down was like cocaine for feet: highly addictive and worth its weight in gold. I made a mental note to try it myself the next time I got the chance. Brook gingerly explained how he filled his water bladder, as well as displayed the proper peanut butter foldover preparation techniques. Frank was ready almost instantly. He never forgot that Eagle Scout training that he received as a boy and arrives prepared to everything. The man is going to put on his Sunday best, have lined up the hearse for the correct pick-up time, and neatly checked off the last item on his bucket list the day he drops down dead just so that he arrives ready at his own funeral. But Brook is not that way. He takes his time to get prepared, so when he was finally ready, we dropped them off.

Wendy is a photographer, not by profession but by true calling. She takes the most poignant and moving images, and she was snapping away as the two of them departed. Frank and Brook were rolling their eyes. Both of them have been privy to her Cyclops pose for over 20 years, but I think that both of them have a framed picture of walking together on their desks today.

Brook and Frank "The Sheriff" Hinman Walking
in Utah. Photo Credit: Wendy Hinman.

And then I was alone with KO and Wendy. Brook's parents wanted to treat us to a hotel room that night, so our first goal was to find a room. We were in Burley, Idaho where there are only a handful of places to stay, including the fantastic motel where I'd witnessed the near fist-fight the day before. Wendy marched right on into the fanciest joint in town and booked adjoining rooms on the ground floor (so that no tired walkers would have to choose between waiting on ridiculously slow elevators and taking the stairs) and we checked in. The air conditioning was glorious. If ever you are feeling blue in the summer time and you are blessed enough to have air conditioning., you should just stop feeling sorry for yourself and be grateful for the wondrous chilled air that you are blessed enough to have blowing on you. At least that's what I tell myself now that the walk is long gone and my eyes are opened to the joy of things such as air conditioning.

Once we'd procured lodging, we considered dinner. Burley had a Wal-Mart, so I eagerly offered to go and pick up dinner if Wendy would enjoy some one on one time with a certain wild buffalo boy. As I walked through that Wal-Mart, I took my time. I ogled the freezer pizzas, considered the neon yellow nail polish, figuring it might be cool to look at and good for signaling help if we got lost in the desert in Utah (though the logic there failed so I settled for some tamer orange). I even sat down and did the blood pressure machine for the heck of it. I was so dazed and unaware of what I was doing that it finally dawned on me that I was supposed to be getting food for dinner. When I looked at my phone to see how long I'd been waltzing with the mass commercialism that is Wal-Mart, an hour had gone by.

I quickly grabbed a rotisserie chicken, a pre-made salad and some salad dressing. I also grabbed a two liter of coke. Frank and Wendy love coke. As I paid, I chatted with the clerk and she asked how my day was.

Yet again, my reserve escaped me and I told her all about how my in-laws had arrived and my husband was walking across America and I was excited to paint my nails orange. The explosion of information from my mouth had the woman looking bewildered but she was genuinely kind and congratulated me on making it that far into our trip. I left Wal-Mart feeling that creeping relief that can seep into your body ever so slowly after a difficult time in your life. It was as if I was a cup of hot water and the arrival of Frank and Wendy was a bag of sealed herbs that had just started to blend into a peaceful swirl of hot tea. As I walked out to the car I noticed that there was some heavy cloud coverage, and it was starting to get very dark, very fast.

I was so relaxed that I didn't call Brook to make sure he was ok and beg him to let me pick him up before the bottom dropped out of the sky like I normally would have if I noticed a serious weather change. I figured it'd be a cooling rain since it was so hot out and that he and Frank would be able to handle it together. I returned to find my sweet child playing with his grandmother and happy as could be to have someone different to interact with, and then I got the call.

All I could hear was rain and wind pelting onto the receiver in torrents. "BABY! Come Get US! WE ARE BEHIND THE BLUE TRACTOR."

Wendy, KO and I piled into the Yukon and were soaked in the few seconds it took to get from the hotel to the car. The car thermometer read 54 degrees. It had been 89 degrees when I had walked into Wal-Mart two hours earlier. I had just finished reading the book *A Walk in the Woods* by Bill Bryson. His hilarious book about hiking the Appalachian Trail was full of interesting fears that he had as he walked. One of these fears was of catching hypothermia. People can get hypothermia when their body temperature drops rapidly, or when weather changes in a flash from cold to hot or hot to cold. It was actually more common for people to get hypothermia in the summer on days just like this one, I thought I'd read, than it is in the dead of winter. Thanks to Mr. Bryson, the whole way there I was praying that Brook and Frank were safe "behind the blue tractor" and wouldn't catch hypothermia.

Wendy drove and I just sat in the passenger seat wet and worried. I was exceptionally grateful Brook wasn't alone. Then it dawned on me that this could happen at any moment, anywhere and Brook was alone all the time. I was having a hard time being comforted as we drove through sheets of cold rain and hail. It took us thirty five minutes to find the blue tractor, which Brook and Frank were not under. However, we did see them off in the distance, running toward us. I was so relieved when they jumped in the truck all soggy and stinky I nearly cried. Through chattering teeth Brook muttered to his father "Welcome to the road."

Once they defrosted, and I obnoxiously made sure that neither of them felt a loss of feeling in their extremities due to hypothermia, we laughed as Brook relayed the story of the storm coming down on them:

"We were walking along and making good time when we saw a dirt bike headed our way. So we turned around and when we did we saw how black the sky had gotten. The bike rider rolled up to us and said through a thick Hispanic accent "You are going to get wet." We then turned around again and looked at the impending storm. We looked at him on his bike and said the same thing right back. He laughed at us and simply said "Yes. But you are going to get *really* wet." Then he puttered away. Five minutes went by after that and the storm caught up with us. The temperature plummeted, the winds picked up and the rain started. The wind had to be blowing between thirty and fifty miles per hour, and it was pelting rain into us. Then, it started to hail. We saw this tractor, so we ran to get behind it to hide from the hail. The tractor blocked most of the hail, but we still got whacked by a few good ones. The worst of it was the cold though. It is so bad when you go from being hot to freezing cold. Thank God for that tractor to block some of the hail. I only hope and pray we won't have any more storms like that one."

When we arrived back at the hotel, Brook took it all in and gave me a look that said "Thank the Lord my parents are here to foot the bill for this place." Brook's eyes were jumping from one 'luxury' to the next in rapid movement. There were fresh baked cookies in the lobby (which is the very best part of hotels), and the staff was courteous. No one challenged us about our out of state license plates and when he said "I don't smell any curry," I knew he'd realized ecstasy.

We walked by the door to the pool and hot tub and I think Brook became overwhelmed at the sight. When we arrived in our room he didn't say much, but he gingerly threw off his beloved purple shirt and rushed to the pool before the rest of us could get there. We all took turns hot tubbing and playing with KO in the pool. It was the ideal first night together. We ate the chicken and salad in the lobby, and Frank, Brook and Wendy destroyed that bottle of coke. We all went to bed well fed, and though Frank was limping, we were all joyous to be together.

For two nights we stayed at that hotel. It was a glorious feeling, just to be in the same place for more than one night. The next day Brook and Frank walked a full day together, while Wendy, KO and I played at the hotel and around Burley. When Frank got back that night I was reminded of our first few days of the trip because he was limping, blistered and incredibly sore just as Brook had been. Even though we'd only been at it six weeks, I had adapted to Brook's routine and forgotten how physically demanding it is to walk for eight hours a day or longer. I remembered to say a special prayer that evening for the water walkers around this world. I also made sure I worked out a little bit in the hotel gym because the next day was going to be my first day of walking with Brook and I was so nervous! I was ready to see what all his bellyaching was about, and hoped I could hold up to the challenge.

The next morning we filled up on continental breakfast and hit the road. Frank and Brook were going to walk while Wendy and I set out and found a campsite. Then I planned to switch places with Frank about halfway through the day. At this point in the walk, desert surrounded us. I tried to prepare Wendy for where we were heading, explaining that there weren't going to be any stores to get coke, or even bathrooms for that matter. She looked at me in disbelief, and I imagine she made the same assumption that I had made back in June when I embarked on this thing that there had to *bathrooms;* I mean this is America for goodness sake.

We drove and drove and drove trying to find a site that wasn't private cow herding land and we finally came up on a state "forest" strip of land. It led to no forests, and to more cows. We were starting to get a little worried when we spotted a sign for a state maintained campground. We headed down this road for about 30 minutes, and after climbing through dusty, rocky, shrub covered road that looked as if it hadn't been driven on in a decade or two, we arrived at a primitive campsite. There was a developed site lower down the road, but it had been shut off due to flooding earlier in the season and was impassable. I delegated baby duty to Wendy and set about putting up the tents, some chairs, and our table.

I went to check on KO after a little while and noticed a bunch of bones about three feet from where he was playing. It appeared that some larger critter had tried to bury a smaller critter and the rain had washed away the dirt that had covered the thing. I thought it was weird but wasn't bothered by it too much. Wendy, however, quickly moved the play site away from the bones. She also walked down to the closed off campsite and snuck in to use the pit toilet that was there on site. I laughed to myself as I realized this was going to be a fun month.

Once camp was set up I prepared to walk with Brook. I got dressed in clothing items that weren't likely to cause chafing, per Brook's advice, and put a knee brace on my bad knee. I slathered myself in sunscreen. Brook was about as brown as a man could get, excepting the awesome sock lines he had and the farmers tan from his t-shirt, he was a picture of bronzed manliness. I however, am not so fortunate as to tan. I look like a tortured piggy when I get too much sunshine, with pink skin that automatically peels after a day of painful misery. I felt ready, so we made the switch and off I went; my nutty husband leading the way. The first thing I offered to do on our walk was carry Brook's pack for him.

His pack was usually about 12-15 pounds, but I added extra weight with my water bottle. I figured he could use the break so on the pack went, and it wasn't long before I regretted offering my services as a pack mule because my back ached within an hour. It was about 93 degrees and smoldering hot that day; there was a strong breeze that was increased every time a vehicle whizzed by. The first agitation I noticed while walking with Brook was the wind. It was so loud in my ears! I understood why Brook was getting hard of hearing the longer he walked. I soon discovered the second difficulty of the road.

The first time Brook saw a truck off in the distance he warned me, "You're going to want to close your eyes in about 20 seconds when that truck gets real close." I didn't listen. I was too busy goofily waving at the trucker to heed his cautionary remarks. I quickly learned my lesson as a large dust cloud filled the air and joined forces with the truck's exhaust to make a full frontal attack on my wide eyes.

These semi trucks weren't just hauling regular old cargo like boxes of corn or shoes or something. Instead, they were hauling manure by the ten ton loads. Their company was about as pleasant as having your own personal IRS auditor as your only companion on a long car ride. I was trying to be friendly though, having been raised in the south, so I continued to wave at all the truckers as they drove by. The fourth time I waved I was in for a treat when the driver honked back at us. I nearly jumped out of my skin. The horn on a semi-truck is so loud to the naked, unprotected ear it is excruciating. I stopped waving after that. Brook just grimaced as I learned the rules of the road.

It was mega hot and I didn't want to get dehydrated, plus I was trying to make the back pack lighter so I was drinking a lot of water. About an hour into the walk, I realized I needed to go to the bathroom.

"Billy."

"What?"

"I need to go."

"Seriously? It's been an hour."

"Seriously."

"Well dear, there isn't anyone around right now, you might as well go."

"Right here?!"

"Well, yeah."

"I'll hold it."

We were walking about a 3.5 mile per hour pace. I had made it about six miles when I couldn't hold it any longer. I walked off the side of the road and prayed a truck wouldn't come whizzing by. Thankfully, there was a lonely bush for me to hide behind. Of course, as soon as I pulled my pants down I heard the far off rumble of a truck. I was trying my hardest to beat the semi, and I had just pulled up my pants as it passed. I realized that this walking thing wasn't the easiest in the world.

After awhile, to Brook's annoyance, I got the urge to dance or do anything to break up the monotony of putting one foot in front of the other. I turned some dance music on Brook's iThingy (my word for all of the Apple gadgets that exist) and I started dancing down the road. He was laughing at me and wincing at the changed routine at the same time. When I calmed down a bit and we settled back into our pace, I realized we'd only gone about 7.5 miles. Our goal was 12. My back hurt from the weight of the backpack, and my hips were beginning to ache from the pounding of pavement. Brook had already walked 10 miles before I had gotten there. I had been at it for only a few hours and I was bored and sore.

I didn't comment on my boredom, and we made it another couple miles before we saw, to our excitement, the 'Welcome to Utah' sign up in the distance! I was so stoked to get to cross a border with Brook that I cheered the whole time I could see the sign. I think I was annoying Brook with all my hooting and hollering, but I had walked 9 miles to get to that sign and he had walked about seven hundred so I felt the occasion deserved some cheering. We took our picture and then we kept on walking. A little while later we saw an abandoned shack to the left of the road up ahead. I was excited because I had to go to the bathroom again and it was about time to call it a day. I couldn't believe how tired I was after only a few hours.

We walked up to the shack and called Frank and Wendy to come retrieve us. While we were waiting I used the bathroom in a lonely corner of the building and then proceeded to explore. There were old rugs all covered in dust and animal poop, and there was some ancient looking furniture that had been weather beaten and trashed inside the ruins. It was a solemn, spooky place. I realized how many of these we were going to see all over America. It haunted me that evening to think about the people that must have come and gone by that same spot we were standing in earlier. Perusing that rickety old landmark opened my eyes to the beauty of the history we were getting to experience. Though I considered Brook an incredible man at the end of that day when I slipped off my dusty shoes and tried to rinse the road grime off my face after just a few hours, I realized he was fortunate too. He was getting so much exposure to moments to be in awe of the world, God and life. It's no wonder he was exhausted every night.

We had two tents: one was a regular two person sleeper that we were able to fit our double bed air mattress into and all curl up and rest in, the other tent we picked up for twenty dollars to use more as an extra storage compartment and play room than anything else. The box of the second tent read "Scout Junior" which we just figured was the brand. We didn't quite understand that it was called the "junior" version because it was meant for smaller sized people. We felt pretty stupid when we realized the error we'd made the first week on the road when we took it out of the package in Oregon.

That night, as we were preparing for bed we offered to let Frank and Wendy sleep with KO in the larger tent. Brook and I were willing to squeeze into Scout Junior together, but they refused to let us. As the three of us nestled snugly into the big tent as usual, we were surprised to hear bursts of laughter coming from the other tent. Then we heard:

"Wendy, just hold still, only one of us can move at a time!" and

"Well, I am trying to straighten out!"

"You can't sleep straight because you are too tall, you have to sleep diagonal."

"Oh. Bahahahahhahaha."

As the two of them attempted to get comfortable, Brook and I laughed in our tent at the absurdity of two fully grown adults trying to squeeze into a child's tent. Then all of a sudden the dreaded thought occurred to us that Ol' Junior had no rain fly. It advertised that it did on the box when we purchased it, but what it called a rain fly was actually a piece of cloth that was about the size of a hand towel and far less absorbent. We hollered over to them that if it rained we'd grab the tarp and place it over their tent for them, but we all figured since we were in the high desert it wasn't very likely it'd rain…

…we were wrong.

At about five in the morning we heard thunder and I started to drowsily become aware of the pitter patter that could only mean one thing. I jumped out of the tent and dragged Brook with me, and we got the tarp and brought it down over his parent's tent. A few minutes later we heard more laughing.

They had woken up completely stifled in Ol' Junior because the tarp cut off the cool air supply and they had to smell each other's morning breath, stinky feet, and body odor from the day before in a cramped hot box that they'd been lying diagonal in for the whole night. Needless to say, we got an early start that morning.

Frank and Brook predominantly walked together that week because Frank was only able to be with us for seven days. Frank's feet took a beating, just as Brook's had his first week. The Sherriff sported gaping blisters, aching knees, and his back was in agony. Every night that we were in a hotel, he'd eagerly limp into the hot tub and try to ease his suffering. It was Brook who figured out after the third or fourth night in a hotel that week that the hot tub was actually causing as many issues as it was curing. "Dad, I was trying for the life of me to figure out why I've got another blister forming, but I think that it is all the soaking in the hot tub. It's making our skin soft so the blisters aren't able to dry out." From then on, the entire trip, Brook eyed hot tubs suspiciously and would only allow himself five minute soaks followed by rigorous feet drying techniques involving towels, blow-dryers and at times barefoot walks around the hotel parking lot in order to toughen up his calluses.

The week that we'd had with Frank and Wendy was flying by. We cracked up every time they went to sleep in Ol' Junior, and they were great at feeding us delicacies like pizza whenever they found a place that sold it. Truly, both of them were remarkable at roughing it, especially since they didn't have to and they were doing it out of love for us.

I asked Brook that week about what it felt like to have walking companions. He said that it was refreshing to have a change, but at the same time, it threw his entire pace, routine and system off track. Brook explained that "My dad walks faster than I do, my mom walks slower, and you dance around like a dopey ballerina, so I have to adjust to all of your different paces and it is difficult at times to remember to share the road."

I also asked him what he and his parents would talk about as they walked down the road together. He said that the first full day his dad walked with him, they "talked about everything. God, politics, life, liberty, business, the past and the future. After we had covered all the topics that are possible to cover, and as the week wore on, Dad got more and more tired. Conversation lagged some. But I liked it that way. It was nice to have the company, because even though all we were doing was putting one foot in front of the other for miles and miles, we were still doing it together. I was happy to not be alone."

Brook laughed when I asked him what it was like to walk with his mom. He said "It's got to look funny to people who pass by. Here I am smelling like cat pee (his body odor resembled a litter box that summer) and old sweat, stomping along with the purpose of a man on a mission, with a jolly sidekick wearing a cute little green sun hat and skirt thingy (he meant skort) meandering beside me taking in all the "wonders of nature" as she calls it. We are a walking juxtaposition but I'll give her credit, she surprised me by keeping up."

Frank and Wendy were unanimous when I asked them how they felt walking with Brook. They both said "Proud."

Brook and Frank were walking one day near the end of the week when they came upon an interesting detour. There, in the middle of nowhere, was a gate with a small sign that warned passersby (all two that passed by each year!) that behind the gate was a missile and ballistics launch and test site. The two of them peered through the gate down the long road that looked as though it led to nowhere, and kept on walking. A few miles later they came upon a rocket ship.

"We were walking along, when all of a sudden I saw a rocket off in the distance. I blinked my eyes and asked Dad if he saw it too. When he did I was relieved. At least my mind wasn't lost to the desert heat. But then we were both really interested. Why on earth could we see a rocket ship?"

Why on Earth indeed. It turns out that there, on Brook's route, in a remote location from civilization, was an aerospace and aircraft development site with a historical rocket on display out in front of the facility. While Brook and Frank explored the rocket display, Wendy and I were busy at the Golden Spike National Monument, which is a historical landmark that features two of KO's most favorite things, "Brmm-Brmms" (trains) and a gift shop. The Golden Spike monument had a lot of historical information on the transcontinental railroad and was tucked away in what I like to call the middle of nowhere. Utah is a strange place.

Later, Wendy and I drove off to pick up the guys and saw the rocket ship for ourselves. We stopped and took pictures, and laughed at the strangeness of what we'd seen so far that week.

It was our next to last night with Frank when we stayed at an awesome campground in Snowville, Utah. Snowville had about fifty inhabitants, a truck stop, two diners and a playground. Wendy and I had played with KO at the run down playground that day and had eaten lunch at one of the little diners. While we were eating, we chatted with the waitress about the walk and she got excited. "You ever see the movie about the guy who rode his lawn mower across the country? He came and ate here too! We got our picture taken with him and everything!"

You wouldn't believe the things that get people excited in certain parts of this country. I had decided to walk with Brook again that afternoon, so Frank and Wendy were responsible for finding a place to stay.

There we were tramping along only this time it was way worse than the first day I'd walked with Brook. I had to go to the bathroom within thirty minutes of walking, and we started out on a frontage road that sidled up to the interstate, which meant that I had a large audience of Salt Lake City commuters if I tried to go so I had to hold it. That frontage road was louder than any rock concert and I was not a fan of all the ugly glares and honks we got as we walked along. Thankfully we were able to get off the frontage road after an hour or so and walk on a secondary highway, but there still was too much traffic to risk using the bathroom. On we walked, and on I held it for three more hours until we reached the campground which was right on Brook's route.

The best thing that could happen was for Brook to walk into camp at night. We tried so hard in Oregon to perfect this technique, but it's a tricky beast to tame. It was so fantastic when we could make it happen because it meant that the next morning he could wake up, eat, use the bathroom, pack up and go. There was no waiting for me to break down camp so that when I dropped him off I could drive thirty miles down the road to the next stop; it meant we could all take our time. We were excited about the extra prep time we'd have the next morning as we marched into the Snowville campground where there is, you aren't going to believe this, a driving range. You can pay five dollars for a bucket of golf balls and a club on loan, and whack away at the range. The only catch is that you have to pick up your balls fast because there is a large black crow population in Snowville that like to try and eat the balls. They obviously can't swallow the balls, but they had choked on them in the past and scared some of the other campers so we were instructed to avoid the ugly mess by grabbing our balls before the winged idiots beat us to them.

Not only was there a driving range where you ran the risk of choking local birds with golf balls, but this place had showers. Hot, lovely, spider crawling up the wall sort of showers. And flushing toilets. There were even other campers which was a pretty cool new thing for us since we hadn't camped around other human beings lately.

The next day we said our good byes to Frank. He was taking a shuttle bus from a hotel to the airport in Salt Lake City. When the bus pulled up we wished Frank safe travels and said good bye. Then it was just the four of us. Brook looked at his mother, then KO, then me. I could almost hear him thinking "This is going to be a long three weeks."

As we got further into Utah, the first thing that got our attention was the presence of the Church of Jesus Christ of Latter-day Saints and the Mormon population in the community. We grew up in the Bible belt, so we were accustomed to church on Sunday, seeing Christian bumper stickers and even were aware of businesses that closed Sunday. Brook and I had driven up to Chick-fil-A many a Sunday only to be reminded that the company doesn't serve their addictive chicken sandwiches on the day of rest. Utah Mormons and the LDS church put the Bible belt to shame. We arrived in Salt Lake City on a Sunday and wanted to go to the Children's Museum for the afternoon while Brook walked but it was closed. We wanted to go out to eat but the restaurants that we wanted to try were closed. For a major metropolitan area to be so quiet on any day, let alone a weekend day was shocking to us.

I'd always wanted to see the Great Salt Lake so I was enthralled as we got our first glimpses of it coming into town. The stretch of Salt Lake City and its suburbs, Ogden, Provo, and Orem took us about two weeks to get through because not only do they cover a lot of ground, but Brook took a few days off for some sightseeing and fun. It is also much harder to navigate major cities than it is stretches of desolate road where there is only one way to get anywhere so Brook's time got delayed as he trekked through Mormon country's capital and its bustling roadways. Our first tourist destination was Antelope Island, located in the Great Salt Lake.

Antelope Island can be summarized in two words; serene and smelly. When you arrive at the gate to get in you are welcomed by friendly staff and given all the tools you need to find the points of interest on the island. Just beyond the gate you see a stunning landscape accentuated by rocky hills, and the lake tenderly caressing the shore line. The Salt Lake mischievously duped this east coast girl into thinking she was about to arrive on a beach in the middle of a land locked state.

The tranquility permeated my senses; I could feel myself slipping into realms of relaxation at the sight of the lake. The sound of water lapping against a beach has always eased me into peaceful surrender, but then my nose kicked in. The island confronted us with its frightful stench from the moment we arrived and rolled down our windows to pay to enter the Island,

and it was our faithful companion the duration of our stay. I have never been as overwhelmed by an odor as I was by the stench of the Great Salt Lake. It smelled like raw sewage, bird poo and rot. Wendy and I arrived on Antelope Island and promptly set up camp. Then we took KO down to the lake to 'play in the water'. I don't know what I was expecting, but it wasn't what we got.

The sand on the beach was hot as we stomped down the long slope towards the murky shore. There were vacationer's sun bathing, and there was a group of Europeans ahead of us who had just removed their clothes and walked down to the water in their underwear. As we walked down the sand, a whiny teenage boy thundered past us shouting over his shoulder at his mother "I WILL BE IN THE CAR! COME SEE ME WHEN YOU ARE READY TO LEAVE THIS HORRID PLACE!"

Wendy and I gave each other a look of wonder as we neared the water line. There, on the shore was a battalion of flies. There had to have been a million there. They were disgusting. I finally understood why the Old Testament story of the plagues was so horrid, especially the plague of flies. No wonder the Egyptians were ready for the Hebrews to leave. There were Seagulls flying about, trying to eat the flies, and flies were eating on some dead seagulls that had fallen prey to the elements. The only way to get to the water was to walk through the fly army. KO hated it, and whimpered in protest as we passed through the pests. I certainly didn't blame him. Wendy was the best though! She tip toed up to the fly army, and then charged through them at full speed. She held her breath a lot that first day at the lake trying not to let the stink fill up her lungs, and she kept letting out these great big huffs! She and I were in stitches at the filth and our lack of pristine femininity here.

Once we got to the water, those of us stupid enough to come bare footed (that'd be me) felt oozy, squishy, slimy silt engulf the space between our toes. The salty water immediately started drying out our skin. There were hundreds of sharp jagged stones littering the sand under the water, but I couldn't see through the brown liquid so I kept poking my poor feet. KO did not like walking through the water, even though he was wearing shoes. He plopped right down after about fifteen feet and just started to splash. Wendy and I joined in which was a lot more fun than wading through the lake of torture to get where we assumed it'd be cooler and have less stagnant water. Then the water ended up in our eyes from the splashing. Having the burning salt water hit my corneas was the extra push I needed to exit the Great Salt Lake. There is nothing like burning salt water, swarms of flies and seagull cadavers to endear a place to your heart so quickly.

Later, we went and picked Brook up from his trek and returned hoping to see the wild bison that Antelope Island is famous for. We didn't see any wild bison right away but later in the evening we took KO for a drive to get him to sleep and we had to stop in the road to let a lone bison pass.

I was so excited I texted my friends and family a picture (it's crazy where you will find cell service in this great country of ours) with the tag line "We got stopped on the road for a bison to cross." My best friend texted me back "where on Earth are you now?" My dad called me and all I heard when I picked up the phone was roaring laughter. I told him to call me back when he was done laughing.

Watching the beast trudge across the road in the dusk was a sight I'll never forget. I felt aligned with nature as this rebellious animal that had kicked tradition and wandered from his herd on a quest to find something meandered past us. As KO had already fallen asleep, Brook and I just stood outside the car for a while and watched as it walked away, enjoying the deafening silences that the blessed Antelope Island provides.

The next day, Brook took it easy and we all went back to the water. Now that Wendy, KO and I knew what to expect, and Brook had been forewarned, we had a great time. It turns out that if you stick with the water long enough, and wade out much further than we had the day before, it becomes much cooler, less salty, and almost like swimming in the ocean, minus the sharks.

After our swim we went to the incredible visitor's center where there was photography on display from individuals that had visited in years past. It also had a vast array of history and information about the lake available to guests posted on plaques, boards, and in videos. I was intrigued to find out that historically, the lake was formerly the place to go for 'health spa' treatments. There used to be thousands of visitors to the lake in order to experience the health benefits of the salt water. There were even spa-style lodges that used to thrive off of unsuspecting people who wanted to be healed by the magical effect of the lake. If I'd booked a room at a fancy pants spa lodge for a long weekend, and ended up having to wade through a merciless sea of flies to just get into the water, I'd have felt pretty ridiculous. I could see why the lake no longer boasted the lodges.

The center also featured a tank filled with tiny shrimp that can live in the lake, which I learned was what kept the seagulls around. Those itty bitty shrimp are the only living critter that can survive in the Great Salt Lake because of the salt content. Not having to worry about sharks, sea monsters from the deep, giant squid or snapping crab is a pretty big advantage that Salt Lake goers have over the rest of us ocean fans.

My favorite part of the visitor center was all the information on the bison. We were shown videos of how they are carefully and meticulously cared for. The farmers that help them to thrive explained the importance of letting them live as naturally as possible in their habitat. Armed with the map of all the roads in the park and a good idea where these fluffy giants typically hang out, the group of us piled back in the Yukon for a buffalo search.

We drove until we found the whole herd, lounging about and eating grass not too far from a main road. We piled out of the truck, Wendy wielding her third eye and snapping as many pictures of buffalo as possible. KO kept looking at them, pointing, and giggling. Even kids a year and a half old can laugh at the poor ugly things. They are the weirdest looking animal that I have seen up close, and though I don't doubt God had a purpose in his design of them, I do kind of wonder if that purpose might have been to make people like KO and myself laugh.

I began taking photos as well; Brook seized this moment to carefully walk towards the herd with KO in tow, without my knowledge of it. They were about four feet from a sleeping bison when I realized where they'd gotten to. "Brook! Bring him back here!" I whisper-shrieked, as only the most annoying of wives can, "If our child gets trampled by a bison I will never forgive you!" "Oh hush," he said. "Just take a picture." So I did.

I guess you might be wondering why it is called "Antelope Island" rather than "Bison Island" or "Island of 80 Million Flies." Besides having the largest free ranging, protected herd of bison in America, Antelope Island is also home to antelope.

We saw some of these runners scurrying away from the road a few times while we were there. They had magnificent horns and looked almost like the images of the Devil in medieval books. But my favorite wildlife we saw on the island is what I fondly refer to as Jackalopes. As they were jack rabbits from Antelope Island, what name could be better?

The first day we arrived at the campground, Wendy had gone to use the pit toilet and had come back wide eyed and asked "Have you seen any hares?" She explained that she had just crossed paths with the largest jack rabbit she had ever come in contact with. Though I am not an animal kingdom fan normally, I am a sucker for animals in the wild. When I am in their territory, I want to know everything about them and see them peacefully about their business, in the distance of course.

I absolutely loved knowing that all around me were wild species. I started asking Wendy about the rabbit. I only hoped I'd get to see one myself while we were there. I got my chance on my way to the horrid little pit toilet later that night. In the dried out shrubbery that grows right by the bathroom shack, I saw a movement. So I wandered over and my proximity scared the poor thing. He leapt out of the bush and hopped away; he was huge! It was bigger than a lot of dogs I've encountered. I guess it was about the size of a small beagle, or at least it looked that big to me as it was bounding away. Its feet were so long! I was mesmerized by the Jackalopes big feet.

When I was a kid, I roller skated a lot at the local rink. Every forty five minutes or so the staff would come out on the rink and play games with the crowd of kids that was there. Glorious games like "Red light, Green light, Go" or "Simon Says." The winner of these games always got a prize. They had the prizes on display in a little case as you walked in, and I was determined to beat out the other fifty kids one of these days and get a lucky rabbit's foot. There was a neon pink one that I wanted ever so badly, and it dangled alluringly in the prize case. I never ended up winning any of the games, so I saved up my allowance for a few weeks and went in and bought the awful thing. I treasured that neon pink lucky rabbit's foot. I kept it in my box of treasures. I don't know what happened to it, I'm sure it got tossed by my poor mother who found the thing to be entirely too weird for me to treasure. I never wondered about where lucky rabbit's feet came from until I saw that Jackalope, but once I saw it's incredibly long appendages; I was shocked that I had once treasured an animal's hacked off, dyed, preserved foot. Poor little rabbits. My new friend greeted me almost every time I dared to enter the realm of the pit toilet; either his burrow was right in that shrubbery or he was a glutton for punishment as horrid smelling as those stalls were.

The only other remarkable moment we had on Antelope Island took place when the sun sank low and the citronella candle was lit. The three of us adults were sitting at our picnic table laughing and telling stories as well as making a plan for the rest of the week when we realized that the flies were beginning to swarm. In a matter of minutes, we had what felt like thousands flying around, landing on the table, trying to get near the light. They were biting flies! All of sudden, we were chased into our tents by the nasty, nipping things. It was gross. As we all huddled into our tents, that night, I again was grateful for the incredible amenities that I had been blessed to experience my whole life and would be privy to for the rest of it, God willing. As I was dealing with nipping flies I couldn't shake the images I'd seen of children from Africa sleeping under life saving mosquito nets every night. I can't imagine having to fight off that incredible enemy day in and day out, as our American ancestors did, and as many people all over the world do today. I was made grateful for what I have when I realized what horrors I'd been fortunate to miss out on the majority of my life.

Leaving Antelope Island was bittersweet because we'd all been enchanted by its charming atmosphere, stink and all. It was tranquil; we all agreed that it was a place you just felt at peace in nature, until the sun went down obviously. We left Antelope Island and entered into about a week long period in which Brook walked through Utah's capital and all of its suburbs.

Salt Lake City is, as previously mentioned, a devout place. It is filled with LDS Cathedrals, LDS headquarters and even stores that advertised "Missionary Clothes." I went into one of these, just out of curiosity. Women's, or "Sister's" as they are called by the LDS church, clothes cannot be too baggy, too tight, or too trendy; no leopard print or pleather, that's for sure. They cannot include t-shirts, peasant skirts, shirts with any logos, and most importantly: they can not be wrinkled. It was very obvious that wrinkles are a big no-no for Mormon missionaries as everything that was for sale was marked as "anti-wrinkle" or "wrinkle-resistant." It turns out that just about every clothing item I own is inappropriate for doing the mission work of the Mormon Church, and my signature "It's cooler wrinkled" excuse that I always gave my parents was not one that would fly in these pious circles.

But it wasn't just the mission work that my clothes weren't cut out for. I started feeling self conscious about my attire almost as soon as we hit the Salt Lake City area. Don't get me wrong, not everyone in Salt Lake City was dressed in a bonnet and floor length dress, but there were modest people everywhere, more so than anywhere that I have ever been. Walking through Utah's capital's streets was sort of like walking through a large, traditional church on a Sunday morning. The men had on slacks, dress shirts and ties, and the ladies were well covered. I don't walk around with everything hanging out, but it was July, and it was hot so I was wearing tank tops and shorts everywhere. I didn't see many other women wearing tank tops. I've never been to the Vatican City, but I have inkling that it has the same effect on an everyday sort of person, like me, that the epicenter of the Mormon Church did.

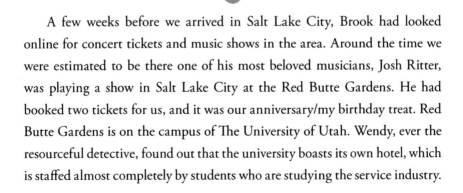

A few weeks before we arrived in Salt Lake City, Brook had looked online for concert tickets and music shows in the area. Around the time we were estimated to be there one of his most beloved musicians, Josh Ritter, was playing a show in Salt Lake City at the Red Butte Gardens. He had booked two tickets for us, and it was our anniversary/my birthday treat. Red Butte Gardens is on the campus of The University of Utah. Wendy, ever the resourceful detective, found out that the university boasts its own hotel, which is staffed almost completely by students who are studying the service industry.

It was one of my favorite hotel stays of the entire journey because it was such an original outfit that was marvelously operated. She booked a room for us so we were able to walk back from the show. Wendy dropped Brook and me off at around 5 o'clock and we waited in line for about an hour and a half to get seats right up front.

While we were waiting in line we got to tell all the people waiting near us about the walk. We asked the locals about the Gardens and what the venue was like. Everyone raved about it, and as we inched closer to the beginning of the concert our anticipation rose. When we finally got inside, it was everything the Utahans had promised and more. It was an outdoor arena, with a well manicured grassy lawn. We got a spot on the lawn about ten feet from the stage where we set out our picnic blanket and basket of food. We ate, laughed and were mesmerized by the opening bands, both of which I'd never heard of but now adore. When the man of the evening finally came out Brook looked the most excited I've seen him look in a very long time.

Josh played an incredible show, and we danced, laughed, and loved the performance. When he played my favorite song of his, Brook asked me to slow dance and we dorkily stepped all over each other's feet as we enjoyed the harmonies. The sun set over the great Red Butte which was a fantastic sight to see, and we treasured our evening. As we were walking back to the hotel after the show, I asked Brook what he thought of the concert. He thoughtfully communicated "Well, I listen to Josh all day some days, so it was sort of like meeting one of my road buddies, by watching him play live. I sing along with him on my iPod all day, so it was cool to be able to sing with him for real."

Brook had spent more time that summer listening to Josh Ritter, and a slew of other musicians, than he had conversing with any other human being, me included. They were his buddies, cheering him along the open road. As far as pals go, Josh Ritter delivered. His show and the Red Butte Gardens provided an epic night on our journey. Utah rocked our socks that evening.

Wendy is a wonderful mother. I think her greatest strength as a parent is that she diligently works to understand her children by reading the books that they read, listening to the music they enjoy, talking to them and actively seeking ways to relate as a mother. It is honorable to work so profusely in order to grasp your child's reality. Which is why, when it came time to shoe shop again in Salt Lake City, and I had a near panic attack at the idea of going through the horrors again, Wendy looked at me and said "I can understand why Brook is so picky about his shoes. They are the most important thing he wears throughout the day and no one likes uncomfortable shoes."

She was wrong of course. I have about fifteen pairs of painfully uncomfortable shoes that I vastly enjoy wearing because they are stylish, match a certain dress or they sparkle. Anyway, she offered to go with him this time, and I almost let her, but then I felt so guilty about sending her on such a terrifying endeavor that I figured I better come along and try to expedite things with Brook.

But Brook is not a man that can be expedited. We were in the REI in Salt Lake City for over two hours. During those two hours, Wendy and I took turns playing with KO, attempting to convince Brook to try this shoe and that, and giving each other eye rolls at his painstaking methods of shoe shopping. We ended up leaving without a single pair of new shoes. Wendy and I talked about it later, and she said "Well that was a little ridiculous. I can see now why you didn't want to go. I understand why he is so picky, but at the end of the day he needs a new pair of shoes. I just wish he'd pick out a pair and at least try them. But we can't force him to do something he doesn't want to do so I guess we will just have to wait until he is ready." I thought to myself "Easy for you to say, you aren't the one who has to keep shopping for shoes with him until he is 'ready'." I did try to learn from Wendy though, and even though it was strenuous work, I aimed for patience and understanding in the great shoe debacle.

While Brook continued to walk on, Wendy and I took turns walking with him and exploring Utah together. We laughed, played with KO, and spent a lot of time discussing life on the road. Had it not been for Wendy's company in Utah, I think I would have lost my mind at some point on the trip. She was helpful with KO and came up with some brilliant ideas that we kept using long after she'd left us. One of my favorite parts of the month we spent together was watching her haggle with hotel staff for a lower price on a hotel room and searching out coke. This woman could find a 32 ounce, ice cold, fountain drink in the middle of nowhere as if by magic. Most of all, she was resourceful. Wendy makes me look like a walking disaster with her ability to find out information. She and Frank both came to Utah equipped with iPads and iPhones. Between the three of them, Brook included, I was so overwhelmed by all of the I-thingies and the information that they can generate I was a hopeless dud. Wendy found many a park, historic site, lodging opportunity and stellar restaurant through her ability to ask good questions and use technology.

Though I appreciated her wealth of information, I most of all just thanked God for her company. Two is better than one, and I had a refreshing month with her as our companion. Brook and I couldn't have financially afforded our trip without Wendy and Frank's assistance, especially in Utah, but I am certain that I would've lost my marbles had I not had the company of my MIL as we trekked through the land of Mormons, both of us equally ignorant of the LDS religion, the Utah landscape and the ever changing life that was Water Walk America.

The very best thing I learned from Wendy that month was something I have taken with me everywhere and will try to for the rest of my life. Wendy loves comfort. Who doesn't, really? Though we all love the comforts of life, many of us, I especially, don't take the time to make our lives as comfortable as we can no matter our circumstances. Attaining comfort has to start with acceptance of the hand that we are dealt. In order to get any level of comfort on the road we had to work hard! It wasn't easy to make a tent or sterile hotel rooms feel like home.

Wendy brought her tiny pillow, her signature comfort item, wrapped up in a pretty pillowcase. This seemingly insignificant item turned her air pad into a sweet little spot in Ol' Junior and made many a hotel room into a homey atmosphere. She would stock up on ice so that her water would stay cold longer, and she took advantage of every amenity a hotel offered. If it offered anything complimentary, she would graciously accept it; and she always sought to lighten the mundane feeling of the road by little treats like a candy bar for me, a bag of peanuts for Brook, or a new brmm brmm for KO. She taught me to work at making my life comfortable by using the beautiful things that I was blessed with to their fullest potential, and utilizing the options I had by finding out exactly what those options were. For the duration of the trip and even now, after the walk is over, I am diligently seeking to create comfort in uncomfortable places.

I had been living out of my car for almost exactly two months when the uproar began about the debt ceiling needing to be raised. We were still in the Salt Lake City area so were unfortunate enough to have easy access to TV and newspapers. I wish I had been in the woods when all the drama went on and what seemed to be every politician in America got on TV to discuss the problem. Brook and I were disgusted by the whole media circus and perpetuation of fear issued by the ridiculous coverage, and I don't think we were the only ones.

Ben Franklin probably rolled over in his grave on July 31st when we raised our debt ceiling again. George Washington and Thomas Jefferson couldn't have been far behind. I have seen more of America than most Americans, and I do believe that our founding fathers had a bigger dream for us than the rampant debt we have accrued and the nation being divided in half between two political parties that won't get along. After seeing my fellow Americans at work, play, and at home, I wanted to take an active approach to my American citizenship. This prompted me into writing the president about what I had been seeing on our journey, in order to encourage him and to remind him of all the uniquely wonderful people he has depending on him to make wise and careful choices. Have you ever thought about what it must feel like to be a president? I bet it is horrible. Trying to make decisions with a small group of individuals for the other 300 million people in your nation, half of which are going to disagree with you no matter what you do simply because of party affiliation; it doesn't sound like a job any human should have to endure.

It may sound silly but I wanted to have an address for him to write me back, so I waited long after the walk was over to mail it from my own home. As I placed it in the mailbox, I prayed over it in the hopes that the words within would bring encouragement to whoever read it. I doubt that the president will ever read my letter, but I hope that if he does, he feels refreshed. All this negativity that we hear reports of all day: the party division, the awful debt issue, protests and general frustration needs to be met in equal measure with encouragement, the knowledge that we can get through this, and that we need to fix our problems through surrender to Jesus and His teachings of peace and love, and through hard work, personal sacrifice, and prayer.

My birthday is July 24th. We were in the heart of Utah that day, and we were nearing the end of our month with Wendy. I would soon be headed on an airplane to Florida for a mini vacation with KO while Brook would be traipsing through the desert while his poor mother would have to wait all day under a highway overpass for him to complete his walk for the day. I wasn't expecting a lot for my birthday, but Utah rose to the occasion splendidly and planned their beloved "Pioneer Day" to land on July 24th as well. You may be wondering what "Pioneer Day" is, and though I am no expert, I gathered that it is the day that Utahans celebrate the Mormon pioneers who settled the state and established the Church of Jesus Christ of Latter Day Saints.

The entire population of Utah seemed to be outdoors that day enjoying the summer weather. Wendy and I dropped Brook off and headed to Robert

Redford's Sundance resort. Words of praise at God's workmanship could litter these pages. America is phenomenally beautiful, but I don't have words for how I felt as my big browns engulfed the aspen groves and snow topped peaks in the panorama of our windshield on the way to where the sun dances.

When we arrived at Sundance, we unloaded KO and began to wander around. Sundance is lovely in a wild sort of planned way. It has the most unassuming buildings and is rustic and understated; but if you look closely, you can see that every single tree, building, stone and plant works in unison to create an atmosphere of the wild that is far more manicured than what Brook, Wendy, KO and I had been experiencing. There was a group of people from (what I guessed to be) Los Angeles holding a conference there; they looked like they wouldn't last one hour on the road with Brook or out in the real woods with KO and me. I saw a lady trying to walk one of the trails through their pristinely manicured woods in seven inch heels and what appeared to be a Dolce and Gabbana silk dress. She looked uncomfortable, to put it mildly.

Wendy and I chatted as KO ran around exploring. We found a creek with rushing water and decided it was the perfect backdrop for birthday photos. Wendy and I took turns taking pictures with KO in front of the water and I basked in the peacefulness of that morning. We departed chattering about the history of Sundance, the people around us, and the landscape at the resort. We stopped at a bookstore on our way to camp and I got some notebooks and stationery for myself from Brook, as he told me to get a present for myself that day.

Utah Lake State Park was our destination, and we stayed there for two nights. It was packed with redneck boaters out enjoying the holiday. I laughed to myself when I realized that just like anywhere else in the country; a holiday meant drinking cheap beer and grilling out for a lot of the people in Utah. When we picked Brook up he was in a foul mood. His foot was aching and it appeared that for my birthday he wanted to give me the gift of misery. He was sore, tired, hot, stinky, and blistered, and he wanted the whole world to know it. I banished him to his hammock where he listened to music and ignored the rest of us. It was hard to be away from my family and friends on my birthday, and this was compounded by his inability to look past his suffering to help me have a good day. I wasn't exasperated though, I remembered the fun we'd had at the concert and reminded myself that it was just a day.

While we drove KO to sleep that night we talked. I asked Brook why he was so cranky, what had happened to him that day, and what his deal was. In his slow southern drawl that comes thickest when he gets introspective, he revealed what was bothering him.

"Well, it's your birthday and normally we get to hang out all day and do fun stuff together. We get to wake up in our bed and I make you breakfast, then we go out and swim or lounge at the beach. We get to come home and take a shower, and I get to take you out to dinner or cook for you at our place. We get to see your family, you know? And it didn't happen like that this year. I'm out there all day, tired, lonely, bored, stifled, and you get to go see a cool place without me. And I'm so ready to go home some days, you know? I don't know if I can do this."

He had his moments, when he was so overwhelmed, tired, discouraged and burdened that summer. We all did. But the remarkable thing is that we never had these moments at the same time. If he was down I was up and if I was down he would help me. Ecclesiastes 4:9 NIV says wisely that "Two are better than one because they have a good return for their labor." This was proven true countless times on our trip; we needed each other to get through this ordeal. If any state had a theme, this verse certainly summed up the time we shared in Utah with Brook's parents.

During our bedtime drive, we prayed. We asked God to help us on our journey, to give us the strength to keep walking and roughing it, and most of all, to help us know we were doing the right thing; to carry us when we couldn't get ourselves through the pain, suffering and exhaustion. When we finished praying, Pioneer Day wrapped itself up with a grand display of fireworks. To Utah, for the lovely fireworks and celebratory hearts all over your grand state: thanks for a swell 22nd birthday. To my wonderful mother-in-law for turning a blind eye to my husband's and my arguing, and for suggesting the lovely Sundance and making my day special, I am forever grateful.

We got back to camp and KO was still awake. I coaxed him and my Billy to sleep and then I lied there, crying. Before the walk, I rarely cried, but the pressures of the lifestyle we were enduring brought the liquid purity from my eyes as often as I needed to purge myself of my emotional weariness. Tears of joy that I'd made it this far and had such awesome years behind me fell. There were also some tears of woe streaming down my cheeks, and fear. I lied there wondering if we could make it. We'd been at it for 54 days and we weren't even halfway done.

The next morning we woke up and had cake for breakfast since I hadn't gotten to eat it the day before. Wendy surprised me with some presents; a pretty top and some hair pins, and best of all a nail file! Sometimes getting a gift is the best pick me up I can get. Knowing that she cared and realized how hard it was for me to feel so grimy all the time helped me realize I wasn't alone in this; she too was a woman who had been feeling out of sorts for a few weeks. By giving me tokens to help me feel beautiful she succeeded. I did feel more beautiful that morning as I slipped the top on and pulled my hair back in the pins. But it wasn't just my outer appearance that felt more beautiful. Knowing that she understood my struggle lifted my spirit.

There was a general feeling of resolve at camp that morning to pick ourselves up and dust ourselves off. We all bustled about like it was new day filled with new opportunities. When we prayed for Brook that day before he set out I said a special blessing for Isaac as it was his birthday. Just the memory of his little frame carrying our Jerry can back in April kept both Brook and I focused on our mission and I prayed that Isaac would be lifted up that day.

We left the campground and headed into the great unknown that is the desert between Utah and Colorado. There was nowhere to sleep, no towns even for about 70 miles. As Brook set off Wendy and I both hoped furiously for a safe and simple place to set up camp for the night. Our hopes were met in the form of a brand new rest area located just about 25 miles past where Brook had started walking that morning, which was the ideal distance because Brook could simply walk into camp. There were signs posted all around that said "No Camping, Overnight Staying Allowed," but we figured that as the place was fairly isolated and had minimal traffic we'd be all right. It was a unique state of the art facility, with history information on large boards posted outside. It also had a fancy (for a rest stop anyway) sitting area with a TV that played info movies of Utah and its park systems. There were bathrooms, an outdoor spigot and it backed up to a railroad that was still in use.

As Wendy, KO and I played throughout the day, we all got excited every time a train would arrive and wait at a signal where it was required to honk. Honk it did. These trains' horns were painfully loud. KO loved them. As we got ready for bed that night, clouds formed and the last of the road warriors started to leave, sending a slew of weird looks our way for pitching the tent in the picnic area.

Black clouds had filled the sky hours before, and thunder had been booming about for the afternoon, but we prayed against all hope for the rain to hold back. Night fell and it became clear that our pal the rain was coming. And it wasn't coming alone. It came with its friends, who collectively I like to call "Super Loud and Obnoxious Trains." That night was one of the worst on the entire trip. Rain fell in sheets and it was freezing cold, which was surprising for late July. As soon as we'd fall asleep, a train would arrive at the signal and toot its horn, waking us all up again. Well, not all of us. Wendy and KO slept soundly in the big tent, the both of them snoring throughout the night. Brook and I turned and tossed in Ol' Junior until we faced facts and both crossed our arms across our chests and fumed quietly as we lay there diagonally in the pint sized tent all night. With morning came more rain, more weird looks from the onslaught of new visitors and a keen awareness of our acute pains and aches. Poor Brook limped around that morning like a wounded soldier. He could barely make it to the bathroom he was so stiff, and watching him try to put on his shoes and socks was pitiful. A good night's sleep is so necessary for good health, happiness and success. I can't imagine having to walk twenty some miles alone day in and day out after yet another crappy night's sleep. I was so inspired everyday that Brook embarked on eight or nine hours of walking so that people thousands of miles away would have access to clean water. My Billy put it best "I am choosing to do this, and it isn't always fun or what I want to be putting myself through, but I chose this path. The other water walkers might not have to walk so long, but they don't have a choice. They *have* to walk, which is why I will keep putting one foot in front of the other."

After the train station stop of nightmares, we pressed on to Price, Utah where we were treated by Wendy to yet another incredible hotel stay. It was in Price that our anniversary arrived. I walked a half day with Brook on our anniversary. We walked 14 miles; it was the longest I'd ever walked with him. The road we walked was busy with traffic, deafening with noise, and it was exceptionally hot outside. There were blind curves which were scary to have to walk since we didn't know if a car was going to round too fast and not see us in time. There also was absolutely no where to use the bathroom. I had to hold it for the five hours we walked. Talk about suffering.

There was a deep ravine that ended in a murky river to our left, and all around us we saw the evidence of coal mining. We stopped for a rest at a historical landmark that told the story of how, one hundred and fourteen years earlier, Butch Cassidy and The Sundance Kid stole 7,000 dollars worth of gold from the Pleasant Valley Coal Company a stones throw from the spot we were standing at. We laughed as we recalled the previous four years we'd spent married and all the crazy things we'd done.

Obviously we agreed that we never thought we'd be standing at the sight of a Wild West robbery after walking on the side of a highway for 2 hours on the day most couples go out to eat at a fancy restaurant. I begged him for jewelry next year, a dozen roses, or some Godiva. Anything besides semi-trucks flinging junk in my eyes and having to abstain from bathrooms for painful durations of time! We made it the 14 miles, and I about passed out when I finally got access to the bathroom at the hotel that was waiting for us. "Bless Wendy and Frank for all these hotels. Bless them," was all I could pray when I reached the lodge that afternoon.

Later that night we decided to go out to dinner and left the hotel at about 8. We arrived at a high quality chain restaurant that takes pride in beer, deep fried chicken wings and their signature sauce. This was the nicest place we could find at the hour. Needless to say; Price didn't have an abundance of romantic hotspots. We did have fun and we were blessed to be together and still in love after such trying events had taken place in our lives over the four years we'd shared a last name. When we prayed over our nachos and chicken wings (like I said, not the grub of Shakespearian lovers!), we gave God all the glory for our love of each other and for our future together. It was a special anniversary, chicken wings and all.

After Price, Utah, there is basically a bunch of dust and road until you hit Grand Junction, Colorado. Grand Junction is where KO and I were flying out of for a much needed vacation. I had dreams of lying on the beach in my swimsuit while my delightful family took turns playing with my son. I could barely stand the wait to get there and the journey was making it easy to want to leave to road, especially when I experienced what I remember as one of the scariest night's I had on the trip. After which, there was nothing that could keep me from hopping on that plane to the sunny, humid paradise that is south Florida.

As we were checking out of our hotel in Price, Wendy was chatting with the hotel clerk and asking about camping or lodging in the direction we were headed. He mentioned a few places that had camping, and then she asked if there were any bears to be afraid of. Up to this point, nearly eight weeks, I had not even considered the blasted ferocious beasts of the wild, in the hopes that if I didn't acknowledge them, then they wouldn't acknowledge me. It sounds ignorant, but it kept me at peace for quite some time. The clerk laughed and said that there were no bears to fret about, but that mountain lions weren't uncommon so packing out food was a must.

Wendy proceeded to tell me about the mountain lion threat as we drove away from the hotel to find camping for the evening. When we arrived at a campsite, a sign greeted us that said "Beware bears and lions: pack out food." I didn't think much of it at first, but Wendy mentioned the lions once or twice more so I got a little worried. That night, as we cooked dinner in yet another rain storm, I imagined that the lions were hidden in a burrow or cave somewhere trying to stay warm and dry. Wendy decided to slumber away in the truck that night, safe from the beasts. She offered to take KO with her, but Brook insisted that we'd be fine and so KO and I went into the tent with him. As I crawled into our feeble shelter I was worried. Fear overcame me as the wind picked up and I began to hear scratching sounds all around. I told Brook I was scared and he just laughed and rolled over. So I lied there, all night long, straining my ear to determine if each little sound I heard in the wild was originating from a hungry mountain lion that had arrived to eat me. I knew I was the one that would have to be dinner for the beast, because I couldn't let Brook get eaten before he finished his walk and obviously I am going to do whatever it takes to keep my baby from being a voracious carnivore's supper. I finally fell asleep a few hours after I'd worried myself to exhaustion. Soggy, disgruntled and twitchy, I joined the others for breakfast the next morning. Brook and Wendy asked why I was so grouchy and tired and all I could mutter was "Stupid lions kept me up all night."

Florida: Ahhhh...

"Peace I leave with you, My Peace I give to you..." John 14:27 NKJV

We had to drive a long way to make our flight to Florida. Brook almost didn't come with us because he didn't want to drive into another state before he walked into it, but when he realized he'd get to shower and sleep in a hotel after two days spent in the flaming heat, he complied. The day before we were scheduled to fly he walked a little over a half day and then we drove to Grand Junction. Wendy treated us to our own hotel room as a late anniversary gift and she kept KO with her that night so Brook and I got to enjoy the privacy and king size bed without our little wild man. We got to the airport the next morning and I put KO in his child harness. Yes, I am one of those cruel parents that puts my son on a leash at places like an airport where he could easily bolt and leave me hysterically searching for him in a crowded terminal. I get eight thousand dirty looks every time I pull the thing out and you know what, I don't care what people think about it because they don't have to live with a child that thinks it's fun to climb impossibly high furniture, play in ashtrays, crawl out of bathroom stalls under the door, and go anywhere with anyone, no matter how sketchy. My son's monkey leash preserves both his safety and my sanity.

Wendy would be gone when I got back, so I tearfully hugged and thanked her for all she had done to keep KO and me alive and well over the past few weeks. I laughed then I most of all wished her luck as she was going to be in desolation for the next few days. My heart was in a conflict when we had to leave Brook. I wanted and needed a rest with KO, but I was tinged with guilt that I was getting to relax when he wouldn't be for months longer.

We said our goodbyes and then Wendy drove Brook back to where he had stopped the day before. KO and I boarded our plane and the airline fiascos began. The first flight was torture. KO was miserable, tired and he wouldn't go to sleep. He screamed, fought, fussed and couldn't be comforted. He was also teething. When we unloaded in Houston for a plane transfer, I had forty five minutes to navigate to the other end of the airport and feed him some grub before we boarded our second plane, which was absolutely not enough time.

When we unloaded from the first plane, I put KO in his stroller, put my diaper bag and purse on the stroller handles and held my suitcase in one hand while I pushed the stroller with my other. My back was breaking and I was sweating profusely as I rushed across the airport. I had picked up these cute vintage suitcases on the road and had packed for Florida with them. Unfortunately the locks were busted, unbeknownst to me, so in the middle of the airport my suitcase exploded and all my underwear, clothes and books were being hopped over, shuffled around and touched by strangers from around the world.

KO continued to scream and holler while I frantically scooped up everything and shoved it back in the suitcase. I then proceeded to our gate with the suitcase in a football hold under my one arm, not wanting to repeat the clothing explosion amidst a crowd a second time. I grabbed some pizza for my overwhelming 20 month old and just made it in time to board. As we walked on the plane KO lunged out of my arms and I had to react so quickly the strap on my dress tore and my chest was nearly exposed. Then after I'd tied the strap back together and sat down, KO reached over and rubbed his pizza hand all over the poor lady sitting next to us who, of course, was wearing a crisp white blouse. I offered her some baby wipes and tried hard not to cry, knowing I was only a few hours away from tanning my body on the beach and turning my wild boar of a child over to his grandparents. She seemed upset for a moment, but then she looked at KO and looked behind us to the seats in the following row where her almost grown grandson sat with his father (her son), and she smiled at us. She didn't speak English, but I could tell she was remembering a time when she had been in my shoes. As soon as the plane took off KO clonked out. I just praised the Lord the whole flight as he slept until we landed. Getting to Florida was one of the toughest days of travel I have ever endured thanks to my beloved buffalo boy, but we made it!

As we arrived, I searched for my family. When I saw my Dad and sister Caeley the tear ducts opened up again. I was so happy to see them after being away for so long! Then we walked out into the humidity, and I cried more than I had when I saw them. Many people hate the feeling of the wet, sticky air, but I have always loved it. I had missed that moisture for so long that I wanted to drink it in. I had longed for the east coast entirely more than I'd like to admit. And as my tears mixed with my dewy face from the air, I knew I'd done the right thing by booking our flight.

I had so much fun with my parents, sisters and my sister's boyfriend, cousins, aunts and uncles, and grandparents while in Florida. My mom and I found this abandoned grocery cart in my grandparent's neighborhood. I pushed it back to their house and we had grocery cart rides, which were hysterical and as immature as you are imagining. We played card games, swam at the beach, and we went to an awesome children's museum. Amidst all of this laugher, fun and games, I felt guilty that Brook wasn't there and I was having so much fun without him.

The guilt must have kept poking me because, even though I knew I needed the constant access to a.c. and showers for the few days I was there, my husband wouldn't know what this level of relaxation felt like until November. That was a long time for him to suffer without a break. For me to have such a smashing one, well of course I felt guilty! But only guilty enough to monitor how happy I sounded when I talked to him so that I kept my elation at bay and didn't rub my joy in his poor, sun burnt face. I was determined to capitalize my blessings to their fullest potential that week, no matter how sorry I felt for Brook.

Every night once KO fell asleep, which took forever because of the adjustment back to Eastern Time, I'd nestle into bed with a little book light and take part in quiet time. On August 2, 2011 I wrote a journal entry about how far my little family had come:

"Brook and I are already changed...God always answers. My life is good and I am happy. I might use the bathroom outdoors more than the average person, and I might not eat as many vegetables as I'd like, but living in my car on the road is a thing that I'm supposed to be doing and it is superb to be in God's will. Nothing can be better, except for being in His presence, which I'm not quite ready for yet as I'm still here on Earth."

In the room that my Dad played in as a child, I resolved to do everything I could to stay in that place of peace that is God's will, so long as I retain my life here on Earth. Though I missed Brook those nights that I lay alone in bed with my snoring baby, I was comforted by thoughts and meditations of peace and God's love. "My life is good and I am happy," I muttered to myself as I cuddled KO and drifted off to sleep. I returned from my vacation in Florida to Brook in the same sleepy peace that I felt each night in that guest bedroom at my grandparent's home, and the sticky humidity of Florida was something I tried to carry with me back to dry Colorado in my suitcase.

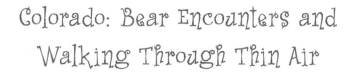

Colorado: Bear Encounters and Walking Through Thin Air

"Watch, stand fast in the faith, be brave, be strong. Let all that you do be done in love."

1 Corinthians 16:13-14 NKJV

When I was in college, I took a semester off to travel and work. Brook and I spent an entire month bumming around Colorado and snowboarding back then and we had fallen in love with the state. We knew that it had a lot to offer us and we were excited about spending some time in our home away from home. After we'd made it through Oregon, Idaho and Utah, I didn't think that there was much that could catch me off guard. This trip had given me encounters with people of the psycho hillbilly variety, kind strangers, sleeping in a cemetery and everything else or so I thought. Colorado had a different plan in store for Brook and me than the scenic and relaxing one I'd imagined. Instead it was one of wild adventures, ridiculous blunders and a whole lot of difficult miles covered.

Brook entered Colorado while KO and I were on vacation in Florida. That week was a little slice of heavenly joy for KO and me but Wendy and Brook seriously roughed it. Wendy had to wait for Brook under a highway underpass for two days. They slept under it one night and both of them agreed that it was the most miserable rest they endured up to that point. The temperature had blazed them for the entire week, though Wendy contended that the boredom she faced under that lonely underpass was more stifling than the temperature.

The desert Brook and Wendy endured while KO and I soaked up the Florida rays.

I was immensely grateful that KO and I were in Florida and didn't have to suffer with them. When KO and I flew back into Colorado, we were excited to see Brook and get back to our 'normal' routine. Thankfully, KO flew back from Florida without any breakdowns. When we touched down in Grand Junction around nine at night, we were thrilled to see our beloved daddy/ husband waiting for us.

Grand Junction is where Brook landed his first TV opportunities on all of the major local stations. He was filmed and interviewed while I was in Florida, so I wasn't there to see what it was like to be interviewed firsthand, but he did a great job and I loved watching the segments online the day before I flew back to him. I had been trying diligently for our entire trip to get TV interviews for Brook so that we would be able to share more about the clean water crisis. When I got the call that he was actually going to be interviewed I was excited! I remember calling and making him promise that he would wear deodorant and brush his teeth and then begging Wendy(who hadn't left yet) to make sure he did. He said he enjoyed the opportunity to share the word about the clean water crisis and that he had a good time, although it bothered him to stop walking. Gaining TV coverage as soon as we entered Colorado was the best way to start off in a new state. We felt refreshed by getting the wider audience through the media and figured that if this was any indication, the duration of our time in Colorado would be a pleasure as it had always been for us. The good feelings kept coming when we received an email from Scott Harrison, the founder of charity: water, the day I returned from Florida. A brief email from him was all it took to add that vote of confidence that Brook needed for the week. When someone you highly respect gives you even the most simple of encouragements with their acknowledgement and support it can mean the world.

In Grand Junction, where we stayed for four days with a host family, KO and I acclimated back to the life on the road. The family that hosted us cooked some of the best food I have ever eaten. Joy, the mom of the family, made a breakfast casserole that I still crave every time I think of Grand Junction. We enjoyed the fellowship of Christians during our stay with them through our visit to their church, their Bible study and a cook out. The intimacy of their home was a fantastic place to share our mission and make new friends; it was times like those four days that Brook and I felt the most comfort on our journey. As we left Grand Junction all of the wildness that is Colorado began to take over and the next few weeks were a blur of adventures gone very wrong. Thankfully God was there, to see us through all of our mishaps and keep us safe.

The whole of the trip, because Brook carried a back pack and was walking on the sides of roads, people looked at him like he was a dirty vagabond. He repeatedly got stopped by police officers just to have his license checked through the system. Even when he would tell people what he was doing they'd look very accusingly at him. Brook met a lot of other travelers as he walked, mostly men, that looked like your typical bum. But their stories are real ones; many were homeless, but many others had families waiting for them to return after a short journey of hiking and trekking in an old fashioned way. Walking has become an action that we not only practice far too little, but also think of as a last resort. It became apparent on the road, to Brook especially, how unimportant people can feel walking is to their life. He understood this through the absolute rudeness he experienced in the way people would treat him for continuing to place one foot in front of the other in areas that it was not typical to see a man walking. For me, it was a big thought to ponder how important and undervalued walking is, as well as how harshly the majority of habitual walkers in America are judged.

It was a huge realization for me when God opened my eyes to the fact that not every guy that I pass by on my way to the mall that is walking on the side of the road with a back pack is a homeless bum. I began to wonder about every single person I saw walking. Who were they? Where were they from? Why were they walking? What was their name? What was their story? It can be overwhelming to realize that you've looked down on people your whole life up until you've become one of those people. I was certainly taken aback by my newfound understanding of the old cliché "Don't judge a book by its cover."

God worked on me about my judging of others throughout our trip, and as I read through the book of Acts, I was struck by Acts 10:15 NIV, "Do not call anything impure that God has made clean." I was reminded that as Jesus sacrificed for me, He sacrificed for everyone else too. God has evened out the playing field, so the judgmental people who assumed Brook was a dirty bum just because he was walking with a backpack were wrong. But so was I for allowing myself to judge people who I saw walking on the side of the road up until that point. The longer Brook walked, the more lessons we learned.

One of the biggest changes I saw in myself on our journey was a carefree attitude about what others thought of me. When you are in such a new environment every solitary day and your life is in a constant flow of change, there is no point fretting over how you look to others. Firstly, because you will never see them again, and secondly because you realize it doesn't matter what other people think about you so long as you aren't offensive or hurtful. When I arrived in Delta, Colorado, this newfound carelessness helped us out in a way that I hadn't anticipated.

I had plugged lodging into our GPS and it came up with a Young Life location. Young Life is a Christian based ministry that shares faith through fun, with camps throughout the country, so I figured that there was a camp nearby. I had heard about Young Life growing up in the Bible belt, though I had never actually been a part of its work. I figured I might as well check it out so I drove to the location and ended up in a church parking lot. As I was clearly not at a camp, I asked a group of little girls that happened to be walking by at just that moment where the Young Life camp was. They looked at me like I was a crazy person, and told me there was no Young Life camp. There was, however a Young Life house right behind the church where the offices were held. I drove over to the house and there, in the front yard, was a team of guys doing some sort of yard work. Not caring how I looked (which was good because my hair was greasy, my clothes were dirty and I had two days worth of filth on my skin), I shared my story to the guy who seemed in charge. This fellow told me who I could contact that might be able to help me out.

I took the number from him and left, wondering what could come from this phone call as I dialed the number of a man named Bob, who was the area director for Young Life. Bob was excited to hear our story, though surprised, and offered to meet KO and me at the Young Life office to see how he could help us out. When I met Bob and his wife Sue, I was touched. They were the definition of accommodating and offered to let us sleep at the Young Life house for the few days we'd be in the area.

That night, they took us out to dinner at Pizza Hut where we met some of their friends who ended up taking us out to breakfast the next morning and having us over for dinner later that same night. One of their companions was a massage therapist and offered to give Brook a complimentary massage, which he received after a huge spaghetti dinner the second night we were in Delta. Brook was very awkward getting the massage, "I was torn because it felt so good, but at the same time I felt so weird having a complete stranger try and massage my body. It was like taking your beloved car that just broke down to a mechanic that worked in another state that you met by sheer luck. Awkward, exciting and terrifying."

I made a friend while playing at the park in Delta and our sons got to play together at the city pool on our second day there. This community fed us, housed us, prayed for us, and loved us as we shared our stories and adventure, as well as our mission for the clean water crisis to see positive impact through our efforts. Our stay in Delta was an outpouring of blessings from Christians in the community, and we were very moved by their love and provision to our little family. We would not have been so greatly blessed had I sat around caring what these strangers were going to think of me in my unfortunate state of travel funk and nappy hair. I realized how pivotal the help of others was to our journey.

We needed help from God everyday to make it through the walking, traveling and camping. He usually provided that help through others that were available to do His will. It's important to ask for help, which I accepted as truth more and more as we crossed this huge country. It's also important to just make yourself available to help others. If the community in Delta hadn't done all they had for us, we would have made it through but love wouldn't have been there, just survival. They showered us with excessive love, letting Brook and I yet again see God's hand at work when we weren't expecting it. By being available, they turned what could have been just another faceless town on our trip into one of our most beloved locations

We departed Delta with newfound friends and refreshed bodies. From Delta, we passed through Hotchkiss and Paonia, Colorado on our way up to the Cottonwood pass. We then took two days to go see Black Canyon of the Gunnison National Park. Black Canyon is our favorite national park. It is breathtaking and spooky; the sheer size of it dwarfs us and our humanity seems so feeble each time we are there. The canyon isn't as popular as the other national parks out west so it is quiet, and there are animals everywhere. I saw foxes and wild deer as well innumerable rabbits and chipmunks. Seeing wild life makes the outdoors so much more real to me; it's like I'm being hosted by the woods and the homeowners and neighbors are all coming by to meet us and say hello. Brook and I were deeply captivated by the Black Canyon the first time we visited, to the point that we had picked out the name Gunnison for our son before he was born. Though we didn't end up naming KO after the park, taking him there and letting him peer over the gorge down into the canyon was a moment I will always remember. We had him strapped to his leash as we hiked. We were laughing and following him as he led the way into the wild woods. My little boy is so strong and fearless at just over one and half years of age. I am thrilled everyday that I wake up and get the pleasure of watching him grow.

The three of us at Gunnison National Park.

I have resigned myself to the fact that the name Gunnison would have suited him fine had we stuck by it, but our little knockout will have to do with the name he was given. He was at home in that national park swinging from his hammock in the trees and looking over the cliff down to the rushing river below. I was reminded yet again at how perfect he was for Brook and I. God gave us a whirlwind of energy dressed up in cute brown eyes and curly blonde hair. We were going to fight him all the way through the next 18 years, but we were blessed that our son was exciting, adventurous, hilarious, and felt at home in the great outdoors. He drives me to the brink of my sanity a lot more than I'd like, but I know that he will never bore me, which is my biggest fear in life, being bored I mean.

Brook and I loaded KO up in the car seat our only night at Black Canyon and drove until he departed to the land of Nod. Then we parked the car next to a great spot for free climbing, locked the doors and cracked the windows and took turns climbing up the rocks and peering into the great canyon below us. Though we both mentioned in words how small we felt on those rocks amidst such an encompassing surrounding there was no verbalization of our marked insignificance in that canyon. Though it was surreal to understand how minute we were in this great big world, we were content because we knew God, and He knew us. No matter how many other people, places, and spirits He knew, we were at peace on those rocks knowing that our existence was recognized and cherished. On our walk back to the car, we talked about the beauty of God's land here in America.

"I love Colorado," Brook said, serenity cloaking his words with its quiet peace.

"I do too Billy. Is it your favorite place to walk so far?"

After a minute, he responded "That's an impossible question to answer. Oregon was the hardest so far, but it was beautiful climbing through The Cascades. And Idaho's green hills which are cut apart by waterfalls and gorges made me feel like Frodo wandering through an uncertain landscape. Utah was stunning in its desert peaks but it was way too hot. I guess I don't have a favorite yet, but I'm happy to be back here. Though I tell ya, walking through all this thin air is going to be tough."

Tough it was. After our brief stint at Black Canyon we pushed onward. Brook continued to wear the tread down on his shoes and climb up into the high altitudes. Up in the sky as we were, the temperature was cool, even though we were well into August! Brook was sporting a hoodie or flannel jacket in the morning when he would set out, he would shed it later in the day when it warmed up, even at the warmest, and we were feeling high seventies to low eighties during the day. This is a foreign concept when you grow up in the South. We arrived in Crested Butte, Colorado, and were enchanted by the cohabitation of ritzy country club types and granola crunching, vegan-sandal wearing hippies.

Though charming, Crested Butte was also a place where the wild things roam, and it was where we had our first ever run in with a bear. When we arrived there, the couple that was hosting us warned us to lock our cars and the door to the house when we went to bed at night because the bears in the area had been trying to get in to eat food. While in Crested Butte, we decided to take advantage of happy hour at a Mexican cantina, which featured discounted food and drinks. We forgot to lock our car when we returned because we were having such a good time goofing off and being merry. That was not the brightest thing Brook and I have ever done, and we dearly paid for it the next day when we got a knock on the door around 7:30 in the morning. Our host had some exciting news, "I think a bear got in your car," he said as his warm breath filled the cold air with rapid, visible puffs.

We threw on sweaters and went out to survey the damage that had been done. The first thoughts that crossed Brook's mind were obviously concerning numbers. How much it would cost to fix the car, what would have to be replaced, how far this could set him back; these pesky little questions about quotients were far from my little pea brain however! All I could think about was how awesome it would be to have captured a picture of the big bear in the back of the truck.

The first thing we realized when we surveyed the truck was that the bear had done a lot more than simply get in our car, test out the leather interior and lumber off after sitting in the captain's seat. When we opened the door our nostrils were attacked by the sticky smell of sugar. Mr. Bear had gotten in, found our laundry basket of food, gingerly opened every granola bar and eaten each one, demolished all our peanut butter, thrown Brook's vanilla protein powder all over the entire car, spilled KO's canned peaches everywhere and consequently created the nastiest, slobbery-ist, sticky-sweetest mess I have ever seen. He also sat right on Brook's guitar and crushed it to bits. To say that the Yukon was in disarray is to add another layer of sugar to the already well coated car.

Besides the mess and the broken guitar, there wasn't any damage to the vehicle; we were just out the majority of our food. Brook was irate. He hates waste, and he was wearing his germaphobe cap that day so the mess was overwhelming him. I thought it was the funniest thing I'd ever seen in my life and couldn't stop laughing or taking pictures of the aftermath which irked Brook more.

"How can you laugh when your entire existence is covered in bear slobber and vanilla protein powder!?"

"Honey, just leave the mess to me and go get ready to walk, I'll take care of it while KO naps."

Unfortunately the mess had to wait in the car for a few hours until nap time rolled around. When I finally entered the bear zone five or six hours after the initial attack, I was armed with a fresh pack of baby wipes, some Febreeze and a vacuum. That was it. I left the truck with an entire trash bag of stuff covered in bear slobber and hair and the feeling of true enlightenment amidst my filthy exterior.

"Never again will I get the chance to clean up bear slobber, and chances are I'll never meet enough people who have done this kind of cleanup to count on my two hands. I am so grateful for this opportunity to laugh. And to appreciate the shower I get to take after this. Thank God this happened here and not in the wilderness." I laughed the whole time I scrubbed protein powder and squished peaches out of the leather and upholstery. The moral of this story is to never leave home without a plethora of baby wipes and lock your car door at all times, especially in bear country.

That next night, I was determined to get a picture of our furry culprit. I hatched a scheme to stay up late with snacks and soda and wait for the bear to return to the scene of the crime. I told Brook my plan, he took a long look at me, let out a deep breath, and then he turned around and went to bed.

"Do you want me to tell you when he gets here?" I called after him.

I had the TV on and was working on my writing and the campaign, trying to keep myself awake. The clock said 11:23 when it happened. The bear had arrived! It lumbered up onto the porch and I tip toed to the front door with my camera to get a picture. As I inched closer I could see the brown fur that I had cleaned vigorously out of the car earlier that day. My heart was beating so fast I heard it in my ears, and my palms got cold as I made my way to the bear. I arrived at the front door and peered through the window. Then, to my stunned surprise, the bear stood up on its back legs and stared me right in the eyes! I was so shocked that I forgot to take a picture and I ran to get Brook to come see.

The bear was gone when I got back with my sleeping oaf and with it my chance to get a picture of the illicit creature. I was peeved at myself for not hitting the little button on the stupid camera. Brook went back to bed but I got in the truck with a flashlight and drove around trying to find the thing. I did lap after lap while I angled my head so far out the window my neck screamed in pain, trying to catch a glimpse or hear a trace of the bear. I had accepted failure at 12:45 and headed back to the house. I climbed into bed and as I fell asleep I heard the bear again! It was nosing through the neighbor's garbage cans, but I was so mad at the thing that I didn't get up. I just yelled out the window

"You win you big jerk!" I punched my pillow a few times before succumbing to rest.

We reluctantly left Crested Butte. It was a sleepy little place that made us so comfortable, bear break in and all, that we didn't want to pursue our goal. We knew that our route was taking us into some gnarly territory. We went to a crazy expensive grocery store in Crested Butte and restocked our laundry basket with grub before heading out. Brook was less than amused. "I knew that this bear thing was going to come with a price tag," he grumbled as we drove off into the Colorado woods.

Brook's mood didn't improve when he looked at the map that morning and the sheer heights he was facing became clear. My Billy had chosen to hike the Cottonwood pass in order to reach Buena Vista, Colorado, the next community with a populous on our route. The Cottonwood pass is renowned for its beauty and freshness. Drivers had raved about it to us all through Colorado up to this point. I'd like to stress the word "drivers" in that previous sentence. When we got to the Cottonwood pass, I drove up while free range cattle walked into the road over and over again. It took me what seemed like hours to climb and do all those switch backs, and though it was stunning, I couldn't help but wonder how Brook was walking this! My calf muscle hurt on my right leg from having to press the gas pedal so firmly at that incline, and I was simply driving. I can't fathom how that man kept on walking through all of those miles on his own two feet. I truly admired my husband as I drove up, up and up to the top of that pass.

The Cottonwood pass boasted the highest elevation point for Brook's entire journey, and when he summated at 12,126 feet, he said that breathing in all that thin air accentuated his feeling that he was on top of the world.

A few days after Brook summated the pass I found a campsite off the road in the woods with KO. I lied my son down to sleep. As I knew he'd be snoozing for a while and I hadn't felt pretty in a long time, I did something I am almost ashamed to write about.

I pulled out my makeup and put on a ton of it. I did smoky eyes, deep blush, and red lipstick. The lipstick was tricky because it had melted and re-hardened so many times in the heat and cold that I had to use a q-tip to apply it, which meant I had to find a q-tip, which I had a limited supply of in a bag that was buried deep in the storage box we had on the roof of the car.

Eventually, I succeeded in looking like I was a high fashion model wanna-be. Then I pulled out the designer dress I had scored at a thrift store in Oregon and my only pair of high heel shoes which didn't match the dress at all but were a lot of fun to walk in. And yes, I know how superfluous it is to have a pair of high heels on a five and a half month long road trip. I was told it every time my husband saw them in the Yukon.

I proceeded to paint my nails with that orange nail polish I had hidden away. Then I royally paraded around the camp site all dolled up, just because I wanted to feel like a queen. I am so embarrassed to admit this, but I even practiced my beauty queen wave to the trees and squirrels who were my loyal subjects that day. I turned on the only radio station I could find, which featured old gospel music, and danced around pretending I was in a far away land of comforts, delights and climate control.

For whatever reason, as I fluttered around in my shoes and dress and ten pounds of makeup feeling not completely sane, I sensed the sheer miracle that is spontaneity. That was one of my favorite moments on the whole trip. It was unplanned but completely necessary. I finally felt feminine in such a cold environment. Those woods weren't friendly and welcoming. They were harsh, shaded, and secluded; this was my chance to tell them to get over themselves. Sure they could be tough and cold, but I could be pretty and dainty and still survive half a year living in them.

That was a special moment, my rebellion in the woods. It was my breaking point. I broke free of my mountain woman exterior and filled myself up with some of the joy of being a lady, which for me includes designer dresses bought on bargain and bright red lipstick. I never told Brook about that day, and I cleaned all the makeup off my face before he walked into camp (that took a lot of baby wipes, let me tell you!), but when he got back I was in good spirits that lasted a long time.

Brook climbed and climbed in Colorado, he went through so many mountain passes and high peaks I teasingly called him Frodo. I imagined him up where we still could see snow in August, carrying this heavy burden on his back on an endless walk. He was my Bobbit; on a quest to destroy a problem that he knew was harming and even killing people all over the world each day.

Though his body was well adapted at this point for his walking, Colorado was tough. He didn't have a lot of blister issues at this point but his joints were constantly sore. The mountain terrain put a lot of pressure on his knees, ankles and hips, and he was always limping at the end of the day. On he walked, knowing that he had to keep going to finish his appointed task.

I prayed for Brook every day before he would leave for his walk, and most days I simply would ask for the strength of body and mind to keep him putting one foot in front of the other. But about twice a week, I'd remember

Isaac, and in my prayer I'd thank God for all the people that this walk was helping. Those days, Brook always had more strength. It was the reminder that his sacrifice was for the benefit of someone else that kept him going the longest, hardest and strongest.

On August 20th, 2011, I was in the middle of the woods in Colorado about to dismally screw up the Yukon. We were in the national forest outside of Colorado Springs, where the elevation had ducked down a bit and the air wasn't so thin, when I arrived at a campground in the forest and decided to drive straight into the site as opposed to reversing in. Apparently the site was designed to be reversed into; somehow I missed that memo. I drove in a few feet and ended up climbing over a rock that was about a foot and a half tall because I didn't have the truck angled right. Then, and I still have no idea as to how I managed this, I reversed and picked up another rock that could qualify as a small boulder, depending on who you ask. I then proceeded to drive with the heavy rock on the underside of the truck and climbed through the field next to the campsite dragging said boulder about six feet. Then I was stuck.

The campground host ran over hollering and freaking out at me, yelling like a maniac until I gave him one look of pure helplessness mixed with fury, and said

"Sir, I don't need you yelling at me right now! I clearly didn't do this on purpose."

He backed away looking like a scolded child. I recruited the assistance of a competent looking man from the neighboring site to help me build a ramp out of some more small boulders. Our plan was to climb up our ramp high enough to free the truck of the huge rock that it was tangled up with. Our plan worked, and in very little time the truck was parked nicely where it would remain for the next few days.

Just in case you were wondering, going boulder climbing in the national forest in an ill equipped vehicle on a Saturday isn't a good idea. We were stranded. I had texted Brook as soon as I wrecked the truck, to let him know what had happened. But, in the excitement of freeing the Yukon from the boulder, I had forgotten to call him back with more details. He had very limited phone service, and since I couldn't pick him up he had to walk the entire day fuming mad. When Brook finally made it to the campsite, he was not only his usual exhausted self, but he was also still irate.

"Angel! What were you thinking!? This is going to put us so far behind schedule!"

He looked under the car and found a cracked transmission oil pan, a busted muffler, and some other damage he thought could be harmful to the frame of the truck. He was angry, disheartened and completely overwhelmed. Brook is mechanically inclined and knew that the damage I had just done was going to cost him at least three to four days of walking while it got repaired. He also hates to spend extra money, so he immediately started whining about the cash we were going to have to dole out to stay in a hotel in Colorado Springs, not to mention the insurance deductible. He was upset because he had absolutely no control over what was going to happen to us, we were in a foreign place and he had never once considered this type of catastrophe occurring. We were arguing about the car and KO, who always gets upset when we argue, was standing between us yelling his little lungs out. I was defending myself, explaining that something like this was bound to happen on the trip since I was constantly having to drive in new areas with a huge car that I wasn't ever going to get used to, and Brook was saying over and over again "I can't believe this!" At that moment, almost instantly, the sky grew gray and it began to thunderstorm. We retreated into the truck and as the rain fell, we looked at each other and began to laugh.

"I am still mad at you!" Brook said as he chortled at our unfortunate circumstances.

"Oh my gosh. It smells so nasty in here with all your road funk and bare feet mixing with the leftover sugar-bear smell and mildew stench from this rain. The car is the least of my worries right now. I'm more upset about having to sniff this stink all night," I replied. This made us laugh uncontrollably.

The rain fell all night long. The next day Brook didn't walk. Instead, he made plans to get the Yukon towed and figure out all the logistics of the car. We had to get towed into Colorado Springs. That proved more difficult than you might imagine, even with our AAA membership, because tow trucks are limited in their time when they are the only ones for hundreds of miles around. Two days after I'd wrecked the truck we were able to get a guy to come out. Brook ended up walking towards Colorado Springs, while I rode in the tow truck with Kiernan O'Malley.

The man that showed up to tow our car was a lanky, Levi's clad, mustache and cowboy hat sporting westerner straight out of a Toby Keith song. He wore sunglasses while he rigged up the truck even though it was barely necessary under the shade of the forest canopy at the early morning hour. I wondered why. He also seemed agitated when he arrived; all of his movements were snappy and rapid, like he was about to fire off at anyone or anything. I was not happy about the prospect of being in a car with him for two hours or longer.

Brook wished me luck and set off on his trek. KO and I climbed into the rig with the frustrated cowboy. I actually asked the guy if he'd mind if I prayed over our trip because I was so uncomfortable. He was respectful and even took off his hat while I said a quick prayer for safety. Then we embarked on a ride you wouldn't believe.

Long ago I accepted the fact that I have a sign hanging over my head in bright fluorescent letters that says "Great Listener and Free Therapist at Your Service" that everyone else can see but I can't. The cowboy had at least enough education to read the sign and settle down into that leather bench seat for the therapy session of a lifetime.

It turns out that this guy had just gone to his wife of ten years, right before he came to pick us up, and told her he wanted a divorce. He had met another woman, was tired of all the fighting and wanted out. He had wanted a few things from the house, but while he was trying to get them, she popped him a hard one in the eye, hence the sunglasses. Later, when he took them off I noticed the bluing area, but he said "I am a lot faster than her, so I slipped away before she could *really* get me."

This guy had a slew of women in his life; two daughters from different women, one ex-wife and another soon to be ex-wife, as well as a new girlfriend who had a little girl that apparently was already calling him dad, and he was close to his mama. He was clearly infatuated with his newest love and didn't stop talking about how mistreated she was by *her* husband and how he almost killed the guy when she came into work wearing her big sunglasses because her spouse popped her a good one.

"My daddy used to hit my mama and it'd make me so mad I just about killed him a few times. Aint no man supposed to treat a woman that way. I only have one domestic on my record and it was a real accident that I still feel bad about today."

As he explained how he got that domestic abuse filed onto his criminal record it actually did sound like an accident. I shyly asked if that was the only thing he had on his record, praying to God he would say yes, but of course he didn't. "Oh, I've been in some fights here and there, nothing any normal twenty something guy hasn't gone and done when they were drunk at a bar. Nothing serious though."

All the while he was spilling his life's drama to me he was erratically switching lanes and cutting people off. He swore a few times as people would honk or he'd have to break rapidly, but he always apologized to KO and me, which was a thoughtful gesture all things considered. I thought we were going to wreck at least three times on that drive, but I kept on praying for safety and knew God would get us to our destination. The real therapy session began when one of those medical helicopters flew over us on their way into the city hospital. "I've had to be air bussed two times already. See this here thumb-it was completely severed at one point."

Judging by the scars all over, his thumb did appear to have been sewn back onto his hand. It turns out that he had tried doing a crazy back flip on a dare from his cousin while on an ATV out in Utah on some dunes and failed his stunt. The failure of his trick landed him unconscious for a few days. He broke just about every bone in his body and he lost his thumb which they were able to locate and return to its proper place on his hand. The second time he got air bussed he had a stove blow up in his face and all the hair was burned off of his head. This guy was surprisingly attractive considering all his hair had been melted off in a fire and he'd been in a near fatal accident on a dune buggy. I could see why all the women were fighting over him, what a catch.

Seriously though, I did try to talk some sense into this rambler. He had two daughters to think of, and a whole gaggle of other women who, whether he liked it or not, were in his life for the long haul. I found myself asking him why he felt like he needed so much danger and why fast living was so necessary for him. When I found out he didn't have insurance for each of those air bus trips, with medical bills that totaled over 100,000 dollars, I couldn't help myself; I started lecturing him hard.

"You're not getting younger you know. You've got two kids already; you need to think about all this dangerous stuff before you take the plunge. Seriously, who can afford another air bus trip or expensive thumb repair job? Not you buddy; you drive a tow truck for a living. Remember that you need to act like the man you want your daughters to bring home to you sir, that's what my dad always told us he was doing, acting like the man he wanted us to bring home to him. And what are you going to do with all of these women mad at you? Nothing is worse than a mad woman. Trust me. You need to seriously think before you make another decision. Think about whether it is going to be good for all those girls you have depending on you, not just if it is going to be good for you. You could use some serious guidance don't you think? You ever consider going to church?"

"Yeah, I know, you're right," he begrudgingly said as we maneuvered through traffic. Though he dodged giving me straight answers, I knew that he was processing the challenge that had been issued to him. At the end of the drive he had calmed down, was driving much safer and was hopefully going to go and get insurance the next day after I had berated him. Ultimately, I prayed he would at least consider not being such a lunatic, and that Jesus would catch hold of his dangerously wild life. I tried to make this clear to him as I shared that Jesus was the backbone of our walk and relationship, which is why Brook and I were actually happily married on this crazy adventure. For two hours he was happy to share his soap opera with me, and when we pulled into the dealership that would be repairing our truck, I was happy to get my son out of the tow cab onto solid ground and get out this man's vicinity as fast as I could. I'd had enough!

Even though he was idiotic in his life choices, I still found myself oddly compassionate about his circumstances. I continue to pray for him a lot, whenever he crosses my mind. God puts some strange people in our paths, and though we can't often help them in any major way, I think acknowledging that they need something from us and saying a prayer that someone with more time or better resources can reach them is a gift to that person in its own right.

The Yukon on the bed of the tow truck. What a day!

When Crazy Tow Truck guy left us at the car dealership, I had a task on my hand. I had to somehow pack up everything we would need for the time it took the car to get repaired, load it onto the stroller with KO and then *walk* in the huge city of Colorado Springs until I found a hotel to check into. I laughed hopelessly, to avoid crying, as I packed everything onto the stroller and assumed my role as bag lady extraordinaire. I had a huge garbage bag full of dirty laundry that I was going to wash at the hotel, detergent, our toiletries, toys, our laptop and my reading books, as well as all the cameras, electronics and things of value I didn't want to leave sitting in the car. Luckily for us there was a huge hotel a few buildings down from the dealership so I didn't have to walk far (that I wish I had seen before I packed everything up as I could have made a few extra trips and not been so heavy laden). Thank you Jesus!

As I walked to the hotel, pushing the overflowing stroller with garbage bags full of everything you can imagine hanging from it, I got a lot of looks from people passing by. None of the looks were compassionate or kind. Most were accusatory and rude. I was stricken by how dehumanizing it must be to get looked at that way all day long. I resolved to stop giving dirty looks, period. Except to Brook when he had a serious case of Numberitis. I reserved the right to give him dirty looks during those moments.

The hotel we arrived at was built in the fifties and was very retro with architectural details that reminded me of the Jetsons. It was a building that was trying to be modern 50 years ago and had come up awkwardly lacking. I could have cared less though, I was just happy it was so convenient to the repair shop. As I walked into the lobby I was eerily reminded of the retirement community I worked at during my college years. There were floral arrangements everywhere, about 18 cushy seats, and chess tables. When I saw the grandfather clock I began to worry I'd misread the sign outdoors and had actually walked into an old folks home. I went to check in and as I was pushing my bag lady stroller contraption to the front desk I almost got run over by a little old lady on a motorized scooter. This was getting weirder by the second.

I asked the clerk if I was indeed in a hotel, and when he assured me that I was, I paid for the room and headed upstairs. I noticed a bulletin board in the elevator that mentioned 'residents meetings' and I wondered if people lived in the hotel. As we exited the elevator and walked down the hall to the hotel room, we passed three different rooms with wreaths decorating the door and welcome mats set out. Never had I been in a hotel that allowed guests to place wreaths on the door to the room. I was thoroughly convinced that God had decided to send me on what felt like a journey through the twilight zone that day. KO and I got comfy in the room, unpacked everything, started to play and jump on the bed and then, all of a sudden the sink exploded gross goo everywhere. I packed all the stuff back up onto the stroller and went back downstairs to get the situation sorted out. While poor KO and I were in the elevator, heading back down to the lobby, I got down on my knees and held his pudgy little hands. "Please, Jesus, don't let any more bad things happen to us today."

While I was being assigned to a new room, I asked the clerk about the resident thing. "Well, when the building was built in the fifties it was half hotel and half apartments. The people who bought the apartments rented them out until pretty recently when they all retired and moved in. So it may seem like a retirement community, but it's really just retirees living in apartments mingled with hotel rooms." Yes, this really happened to me.

The building had everything a retired person could want. The ground floor contained the office of a CPA, a small grocer, a gift shop, and a restaurant and bar. There were also conference rooms where I was told bingo tournaments and bridge games were played. The few days we were there, KO actually got his cheeks pinched, was given a ride on numerous scooters, and told he was too pretty to be a boy by all the little old ladies. While we were in our room, we had the joy of hearing the TV programs of all of our adjoining neighbors who were so deaf they had to turn the volume up to extreme decibels in order to hear their shows. It was the strangest hotel visit of our lives. Brook thought it was hysterical. Every time an old person whizzed by on a scooter he just laughed and said "Only you, Angel. Only you."

I wasn't as amused as he was, and I prayed ceaselessly that they would get the truck fixed at super human speeds. I had learned my lesson. I was determined not to wreck the Yukon again. Because when I do, I not only have to ride with a crazy tow truck driver and counsel him on how not to be an lunatic, I also get stuck in a hotel that smells of mothballs and features a shuffle board court for the joy of residents and guests. I can only imagine God got a roaring good laugh out of that four day span of my life.

On Brook's way into Colorado Springs by foot, he had some interesting adventures of his own. For one, the stretch from the national forest to Colorado Springs was filled with the worst drivers he experienced his entire trek. Congrats people of Colorado Springs! Apparently people there aren't used to individuals walking on their roads and neither cared that there was a human being sharing the road with them nor acted as if he existed. "I definitely almost got hit four times today," he told me as he got into the old folks hotel the second night.

If you are familiar with Colorado geography, you are probably wondering how Brook made it by foot all the way from the national forests outside Colorado Springs into the city in one day, in order to make it to the hotel that first night. Interestingly enough, he didn't.

Brook arrived in Woodland Park on that Sunday evening after having walked 32 miles from camp. He started going around to all the churches in town, looking up the numbers on the signs in the front lawn and calling to ask for help. Sadly, he was met by "No" after "No." One church leader even challenged Brook calling him a scammer, dangerous and lazy, and that Brook should be ashamed for calling to ask for help! Brook was irate and discouraged. He knew if he didn't get a ride we'd have to either shell out fifty bucks for a taxi or he'd have to sleep outside somewhere in town and run the risk of getting ticketed by the police. We prayed for a ride over the phone, we reminded God of His promises to the faithful by reciting James 1:6:"But let him ask in faith, with no doubting, for he who doubts is like a wave of the sea driven and tossed by the wind."

Brook gave one last church a call and a sweet older gentleman and his wife responded in true heroic fashion. They didn't pick Brook up until close to eight o'clock, and didn't arrive at the hotel until nearly nine thirty. It was late for them and you could tell they weren't used to this kind of adventure, but they both had a twinkle in their eye and I could tell that they were enjoying the prospect of helping a brother in need. I greeted them with thanks as they returned my road warrior to me that evening.

That ride from Woodland Park to Colorado Springs meant the world to Brook and me. It was another answer to prayer, and a miraculous one at that. It was an inconvenience to that couple, but they did it out of the utmost generosity they could muster. Just as we had answered the call God had made to us, in faith, so did these genuine believers in Jesus. And to top it all off, they refused the money we offered to pay them for the gas they had used.

There are a lot of jerks out there. When I am at my grumpiest and most selfish, I sometimes wish I didn't have to share my oxygen with a large majority of the people I come into contact with. Then there are folks like this couple that remind me it's not impossible to find goodness in others. That is when I give thanks. Obviously, I still need a lot of work in the compassion department, but the further Brook walked, the more frequently I was privy to seeing God's answers to our prayers and the better I understood the need for genuine kindness.

The next day the dealership provided a complimentary shuttle from the hotel back to Brook's starting spot for the day. He called me a few hours later to tell me about his latest roadside treasure.

"Hey baby! You're not going to believe this!"

"Ok, then tell me so I can be in disbelief."

"I picked up a lottery ticket today, and on my break I took it into a gas station, and it was a winner."

"Funny."

"No, I'm not kidding you! It was a winner!"

"How much?" I asked, expecting all my wildest dreams to come true. I had already purchased wells for villages in Africa, a gorgeous YSL Muse bag (a fancy purse to all wondering what the heck that is), fed as many children as humanly possible, taken KO to Disney World, and given Brook a condo on the beach where he could surf and calculate all the days of his life, in my mind of course, when Brook excitedly said

"A dollar!"

I swear this man is the only person in America who can get this excited over a dollar.

"A dollar?" I asked sheepishly.

"Yes! A dollar! I went and got a chicken sandwich with it, and it sure beat those peanut butter foldovers."

It was then that I realized how cool it was for him to find that winning lottery ticket. He'd been playing a treacherous game of Frogger all day on what he swore was the scariest road he'd walked on, and had already eaten well over 150 peanut butter sandwiches by that point in the trip. To have a reprieve on one of his most stressful days of walking from his loathed peanut butter foldovers was a blessing to him. I guess it truly can be the little things in life that get us by on our rough days.

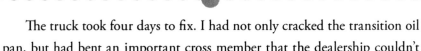

The truck took four days to fix. I had not only cracked the transition oil pan, but had bent an important cross member that the dealership couldn't find a replacement for and needed to re-bend back to its original shape. The exhaust system had to be ordered from another state and replaced. We were blessed to retreat from the old folk's hotel to the comfy home of a host family the last two days we were in Colorado Springs. The family that welcomed us into their home had two school age kids, and when we joined them that first day, we were shocked to find that school had already begun for the year!

Early the next morning, we watched as they bustled about grabbing books and lunch sacks and brushing their teeth. Our attention was grabbed by this school time hustle because we realized we'd been at it for the entire summer. One entire season we'd spent walking and traveling. It was unnerving to us both how much time we had spent on our mission. Brook thought it was frightful because he realized how much walking he still had left. We weren't even half way done at that point, and if I incited any further disasters on his poor walk, he was nervous he wouldn't make it back by Christmas! I promised him I would be more careful and that he'd make it back by KO's birthday, which is November 19th. Meanwhile, I reminded him that had I not wrecked, we wouldn't have had the pleasure of staying at his most favorite hotel where we got to watch a bunch of WWII veterans fight over the last pretzel in a coffee table bowl.

We left Colorado Springs once the truck was fixed. Thank God for insurance because I did about two thousand dollars worth of damage with that stupid boulder. I silently pleaded with God for no more car blunders. Later on I'd find out that God had answered my prayer with a resounding "No."

Right before we headed out of the Springs, I stopped at a Target and geared up for potty training. KO was showing interest in using the bathroom and was nearly two, so I figured I'd give it a go. I bought a few packs of underwear and a training potty that was made to look like a frog. We named the new addition to the family "Frog Potty" and began the horrific experience that is potty training. Though I purchased the potty about halfway through our journey, Brook and I quickly realized we had been missing out on the most useful piece of gear we could have had for the trip.

Frog Potty was a Godsend because Brook and I both ended up having to use it over and over again as the trip progressed. We'd end up camping in a church parking lot on a rural road, without access to a bathroom and not wanting to be disrespectful. So we'd shut ourselves in the car while the other adult played outside with the baby and take care of our business and then we'd dispose of the evidence. It was wholly degrading having to lower oneself onto a child's training pot knowing that you put yourself there by choice, but whenever we had to use the potty, we would laugh off our feeling of shame and remind ourselves that this lifestyle would end. I yearned for flushing toilets more in the five and a half months I lived on the road than I ever thought possible. Thanks be to God for running water and indoor plumbing!

When we left the big city, we headed into no man's land on highway 94 east, which turns into old US 40. It was a historical highway, and the evidence of this was clear in the abandoned gas stations, old restaurants and spooky homes that we passed, all nudging us passerby's to consider glory days of old. While walking this path, Brook's first pair of shoes, which he had bought way back in N.C. busted open in Wild Horse. It was also here, in the burning hot desolation, that I had the pleasure of spending an entire day on the side of a highway playing with my child, as there was nowhere else to go. When you are so disconnected from the everyday world of civilization, as noted previously, you just do whatever makes you the most comfortable. As it was 105 degrees without any shade except what our tent offered, KO and I slathered up in sun screen, and not only hung out on the side of a county highway for a day, but we did it in as little clothing as possible. That's right, he was stark naked hiding out in the tent on the side of the road and I was in a tank top and a pair of Brook's underwear. I didn't care about what people driving by thought because I was so miserable.

Looking back at the entire trip, that day was by far the most trying for KO and me. I wanted to pour all of our water out and sit in it with KO. I wanted to drink it down, all of it. And I wanted to cool my poor baby off with it, as much as he wanted. But I couldn't. I had to conserve water so that we would have enough for Brook's pack the next day and for all of us to drink and cook with that night. I didn't know how fast I could get the Jerry can filled the next day, and so I had to fiercely push aside all desire to swim in the little foot basin with KO, and accept my cotton mouth and heat stricken body. No one should have to live that type of day. And people do it all over the world, every day of the year. I cried when I saw how uncomfortable my son was that afternoon. It wasn't fair to put him through this kind of weather. But the nearest town was forty five miles away, and that would put me a dangerous 60 or more miles from Brook, which was not something we could risk in this desolate locale with temperatures soaring above 100 degrees. I kept scooping a handful of water out and cooling KO off with it, but it wasn't enough. Though we suffered, I kept telling myself it was all worth it if just one woman didn't have to look at her babies and see the discomfort that KO had in his eyes that day.

All day I prayed for Brook. I prayed that God would keep him safe, and that the heat wouldn't drive his body into some sort of stupor that could endanger him. Brook walked 30 miles in that debilitating heat. That morning I had grabbed a bag of ice to cool a Gatorade for Brook. I drove the Gatorade to him after he'd walked for about three hours, and he sat in the car while I blasted the a.c. for a few minutes. When he was ready, he got out of the Yukon, set his jaw, gave the road a look of pure determination, and started walking again. Coming into camp on the side of the highway wasn't a welcome ordeal to him after thirty miles on his feet in 105 plus degree heat that evening. When I saw him off in the distance walking towards us I grabbed KO, buckled him in our stroller and ran as fast as I could to my Billy, trying to give him the biggest welcome we could muster in that lonesome place.

Though I thought the day was misery, if you can believe it possible, that night was even worse. Throughout the entire day only about 30 people drove by, but that night, it sounded as though 15 went by and hour. The trucks passing us were so loud I could barely concentrate on the fact that our bodies were the primary target of every biting fly in a fifty mile radius. I had flies trying to get up my nose, all over poor KO and even in my ears (though those were almost welcome if they could block out the sound of the traffic.). As it was 85 degrees at the coolest, our bodies were sweat plastered to each other in the back of the Yukon in the way a glue trap adheres to furry things. And to top it all off, the air mattress lost about half of its air that night, so our weary bones were touching the floor in the most painful of angles. KO fell asleep fitfully, and Brook and I watched a heat lightning storm that was one of the most visually crippling sights a person can see when they are exhausted and miserable. The entire sky would light up with white and yellow streaks while purple and blue haze filled the space the crack had made an instant before. Brook dreamed of lightning that night. We all woke up laughing, whether from the sad humor of such a pitiful night or from sleep deprivation I cannot tell, but it was a blessing when that sunshine finally announced itself and we could stop trying to sleep under such horrible circumstances.

That was a truly awful experience for all of us. Though I hope to never repeat such angst when my body needs rest, I will tell you that all over the world there are people sleeping in far worse conditions every single night. Thankfully my little band of misfits only had to suffer one night's 'rest' while being attacked by heat and flies. The women and the children that Brook was walking for, that I was playing on the side of the highway in eastern Colorado for, and that KO was potty training in the middle of nowhere for; these individuals were always in our minds. The ones we suffered for helped us remember that though we may sacrifice a night here, a month there, or even our bodies for a while, there was always a comfy home to return to. For the real water walkers, that may never be the case unless those of us who have the means can help them. Some of our last nights in Colorado were spent at a motel for free, because the owner of the place was a truly generous man. Brook was walking away from Colorado Springs towards Kansas when this man drove up on him and stopped to ask what on earth Brook was doing. Brook told him, shared a business card and the manager said "If you're ever in Cheyenne Wells, come stay with us on the house."

At this point in our journey we could either go through Cheyenne Wells, thus taking I-70, or take our originally planned route through 'rural' Kansas. Never turning down an offered blessing, we decided to take the 'busier' of the two paths and take this generous man up on his offer. When we arrived in Cheyenne Wells, Brook went inside to book the room. The man was so excited to see Brook and give us the room he couldn't contain himself.

"Today is a Jewish holiday, if you do something good for someone else; you are supposed to be paid back 30 fold. So you just made me 1,800 bucks!" I've never heard of whatever holiday he was talking about, and I was so hot and tired I didn't think to ask more about it. We were delighted to be blessed with two great nights resting and recuperating after our long hot days in the 100 degree heat of eastern Colorado.

Suffering for the benefit of others is the purest form of love. This fact made me respect, rely on and crave Jesus all the more. As He had sacrificed Himself for me, I was given the purest love there is. Mimicking our God in order to give a better shot at life through clean water to other water walkers was what kept us fueled many days on the road.

Kansas: Welcome to Small Town America

"I rejoiced greatly that I have found some of your children walking in truth, as we received commandment from the Father." 2 John 1:4 NKJV

Originally, I had intended for the chapter on Kansas to just contain an empty page. I was going to have the next chapter start out "Yep, that Kansas was about 400 miles of nada." I say this because I have driven through Kansas on numerous occasions on my way to Colorado and there has never been much to comment on besides cornfields and truck stops. Once I actually got to Kansas and started getting blessed from the moment we arrived until the moment we exited the windy, flat land of farmers and close knit families, I actually had to pull out my old laptop and start writing.

When we first arrived in Kansas, our halfway point, Brook was overjoyed to finally be in a lower altitude, and to be on the downhill of our journey. That was about it. I'd been in Kansas for a day when I turned on the radio and picked up six stations, four were country music, one was old gospel and the final station was the local university that played classical, jazz and NPR. I figured "When in Rome" and tried listening to country, but I couldn't take it after the third time I heard the exact same Taylor Swift song. So I rolled into Sharon Springs, Kansas listening to smooth jazz knowing full well I was far removed from my comfort zone.

Sharon Springs has a population of about 750 people, all of which seem to know each other and are aware of each other's goings and comings. It was here that we first got a glimpse of Kansas community; the nosy closeness that ensures the safety and interest of everyone in town. Brook had the sheriff called on him from Sharon Springs after being in Kansas for a total of 2 hours; some woman wanted to make sure he was all right and not a trouble maker.

In Sharon Springs we stayed with the daughter and son-in law of an older couple that had hosted us in Kit Carson, Colorado a few days before. Jonathan and Crystal were not much older than us, and had two daughters that KO loved playing with. Jonathan was a volunteer firefighter and had heard the call go out over the radio earlier about the strange guy walking into town. He knowingly drove out and greeted Brook before he even arrived that evening. Jonathan and Crystal and their daughters lived right next to the football field in town. Jonathan worked for the local electric company and Crystal stayed home with the girls.

I asked Crystal if she liked being a stay at home mom, because I had this feeling that if I wasn't to work outside of the home I would have been bat crazy most days. She didn't seem that way at all. She smiled a knowing smile and said there was nothing she'd rather be doing that playing with her girls. She also informed me that here in small town Kansas "Women can only work a few places; the restaurant, the grocery store, the salon, or the school. There isn't much else and I don't want to be doing any of that."

That isn't to say that that is all that women can do everywhere in Kansas, it's just one woman's observation of her community. However, I found her summation to be surprisingly accurate as we continued through the state, and I realized that I would rather be a stay at home mom with KO than any of those other things as well if it came down to it. At least at home you'd be able to write and read and play music and impact the life of your child closely. I saw the allure, but realized that I was a long way from becoming a happy housewife, which is okay since we didn't have a house and lived in our car; I guess I was a happy car-wife.

Jonathan got us an interview with the local paper and by the time we left, every person in Sharon Springs that we walked by knew who we were, or at least reminded us that we weren't local. Though I did feel as though everyone in these small towns had us under a microscope, I must say that some of the most generous and kind people live in Kansas. I was getting a slice of pizza with KO in Sharon Springs and an older woman asked me where we were from and what we were doing in Kansas. When I told her she pulled a ten dollar bill out of her wallet and was so excited to give it to us to make an impact. This happened countless times throughout our small town visits everywhere in the country, and I can't thank small town America enough for their generosity, hospitality and even their nosiness. Without all the invasive questions I answered I wouldn't have been able to raise money for charity: water, oftentimes find comfy lodging or know where to get the best burger in the county.

I got strep throat again when we left Sharon Springs. Just like the first time I had a fever, the white spots on the back of my throat, was in agonizing pain, and I had the worst back and headaches. Unlike the first time, we couldn't afford for Brook to take three days off, so I toughed it out, took entirely too much Tylenol, and tried not to spread my germs to my boys.

In a house or apartment, you have a sink with hot running water to wash your hands in and prevent spreading germs. Not so much when you live in a car. Brook and I shared a toothbrush up until this part of the trip, which you may think is disgusting, but was just one way to keep up with less stuff. KO always shared my water bottle with me, and we usually shared a metal spoon to cut on our waste, or shared a plastic to minimize our water usage depending on where we were. And do you know how often you kiss your toddler? I was never as aware of it as I was when I was trying not to kiss him!

Somehow, I absorbed all the strep throat on my own tonsils and my guys stayed healthy again, thank God. We did take a family day one early afternoon after Brook had walked seven miles through torrential downpour and nearly unmanageable wind. We rented a room at a hotel with an indoor pool and hot tub, and oh man it was a much needed oasis! I healed up in Oakley, Kansas, a cute town named for the infamous Ms. Annie Oakley, and we headed on, through more awful weather.

Kansas is a land filled with realists. As an overall population, they are about as interested in philosophy and abstract ideas as your left shoe is. I am aware that there are exceptions to this, but they are few. There is even a town in Kansas called Grainfield, which contains; you guessed it, a grain field and not much else. You don't get any more realistic than that. So when you look, act and live the life of a dreaming space cadet, as I apparently do, you don't fit in very well.

On Labor Day there was a 4-H yard sale advertised in a small town near where we were camping so I headed down to it. I'm sure you've realized the depth of my yard sale experience. I am a true aficionado of other people's old, used stuff. I was exhilarated to be on my way to hunt for bargains and pick through junk. When I pulled up to the yard I realized that nearly every person in this town and the two neighboring communities were gathered for this event. There was nowhere to park so I pulled the truck in front of the fire hydrant imagining that no one was going to catch on fire in the few minutes it took me to make a purchase.

I got out of the car in a flurry, not wanting anyone to scoop up what I would enjoy owning, and rushed over to find piles and piles and more piles of old furniture, tools, kitchen gadgets, clothes, toys and just about everything else under the sun. I pushed KO around in his stroller and grabbed a few things from different stacks and noticed that I was getting a lot of strange looks. I was wearing a fedora, a long paisley printed dress and a vintage black cardigan that day, and KO had on his tie dyed Bob Marley t-shirt. I assumed that the funny looks we were getting were because we were the only people in the entire crowd not wearing flannel, a KU jersey or a cowboy hat. When I was about done shopping, and had a small pile of items collected from all over the yard, a farmer walked up to me and said "Sweet heart, the auction is about to begin, why don't you put that stuff back now and head on over."

I didn't understand and I was embarrassed. "Wait a minute," I sputtered, "You mean they are going to auction off each item?"

"Kind of. That's how it goes around here; the little piles of house stuff get auctioned off as a whole, and the large items like furniture and equipment are individually auctioned off."

There were thousands of items in that yard, I have no idea how exactly they were going to auction off every item unless they were planning on being there the entire Labor Day, which would in fact explain the people with coolers and their lawn chairs, but doesn't explain to me why it was advertised as a yard sale. There was a cake walk and a bake sale there that day too. I understand now that this community, on their day off, had planned to rally together, all day long, to raise money for their kids to have a great year doing 4-H projects, camps and competitions. I was amazed at the power of small town community yet again.

While I was taking my walk of shame after having put all my stuff back in its respective piles, I saw the same junior size tent as ours waiting to be bid on by some other unsuspecting victim. I was consoling myself over my failure at the yard sale by laughing at the idea of a flannel sporting farmer named something like Elmer or Jim Bob nabbing the tent and having to sleep diagonally in it when to my horror I watched a guy that had about 10 teeth, wearing a red checked flannel shirt and a cowboy hat pick up the tent, get excited, then say "Aw, it's a kids tent. Guess that won't do will it?" Apparently I was meant to feel like a complete loser at that moment, so I walked away with KO and headed on to spend our Labor Day playing at yet another park, shaking my head at my own performance of ignorance and wondering at the power of community.

I'm not embarrassed to ask questions; I admittedly have a few screws loose and I am very open when I don't understand what is going on in a situation, so I have the joy of looking like an ignoramus more often than I'd personally prefer. By the time this day had happened in Kansas, I was tired of being educated by the different ways people do things. I was tired of living out of my car. I was tired of moving from town to town every day. I was tired of looking for optimal flat locations to park my car to sleep in, of worrying about my child, and of being so far away from everyone I knew. In a way it was getting harder each day that we got closer, simply because I felt like we were never going to be done. It was KO's nap time after the yard sale disaster, so I loaded him up and drove around until he fell asleep. I parked and read my Bible, hoping God would hear my whining and grant me a pair of ruby red, sequined shoes so that I could tap my heels, say "There's no place like home!" My dream was that I'd end up in my glorious bed with my boys nestled beside me back home in sweet Carolina. I didn't quite have that experience, but I got what I needed from Him when I read "When you ask you do not receive, because you ask with wrong motives, that you may spend what you get on your pleasures" in James 4:3 NIV in my Bible.

That was it. I was asking for my simple 'luxuries' out of the wrong motives. I realized then that I was justifying my whining by thinking "Selfish people everywhere get to sleep on a bed at night, shouldn't I get to sleep in my bed as well? It's not like I didn't work hard to own the things back home. And am I really asking for that much? It's not like I want a penthouse suite in New York City. I just wanted my own stuff and comforts." God told me, in His simple way, that I had a long way to go before I was going to get those comforts back. It wasn't about earning the right to my stuff, or proving myself to God, or even about raising the most money we could and being 'good' people. It was simply that our family was supposed to endure the trials we were facing in order that we fulfill the mission we'd been given. I prayed that God would forgive me for being such a whiner and that He would help me have the right motives; motives that would help and not hinder my light to shine and keep my spirit uplifted as I continued to endure the battles of life on the road.

I put away my Bible and started driving onward, looking for a place to camp that night. I stopped and told Brook about the yard sale on my way past him into the next town and he laughed and said "You're kidding me!" "Nope. These farmers are going to spend all day squabbling over their neighbor's old sofa. I guess there is nothing better to do, though." We both laughed at the sad truth in that.

While I was driving away, I was dreaming about being back home and wondering what everyone would be doing on Labor Day in other towns. It dawned on me how pure it was that an entire community could take a day off and rally together to do so much good for each other's kids. Maybe on Labor Day my family would visit some neighbors or grill out, but they certainly wouldn't be spending the entire day with anyone, let alone everyone in their town. Togetherness at that level was something I have not yet been a part of in a community, and it was a picture of small town America that I will have framed in my mind forever. Maybe I don't fit into the heartland of America so well with my tie dye and fedora, but I do appreciate the kindness shown by others there.

I was writing that last paragraph in the front seat of the truck while KO slept. I'm parked in front of a small elementary school on a 'busy' road in a little town here in Kansas. In the past ten minutes I have had two separate women walk by me during their exercise routines, both made sure to stare at my license plate and check out my vehicle, as I wasn't local and didn't pass their notice. Nosy Kansas ladies, you've cracked me up with your shameless curiosity, but I love you for caring so darn much.

These same nosy Kansas ladies also raise some friendly kids. A little boy, who was about 9 years old, brought us dinner while we were camping out at a park in his town say to me "My house is right over there, it's got the huge 18 wheeler in the front yard. You need anything, knock on the door and ask for me, Ryan. My mom and dad won't recognize ya'll, but I'll be sure to take care of ya."

The award for nosiest person in America goes to a little old man in a miniscule community called Park, Kansas. I had played at the park in Park all day with KO and had asked around to some of the residents about whether or not it'd be ok to sleep there that night. Everyone looked at me as though

I had a second head growing out of my shoulder, but they agreed it wouldn't be a problem. I was setting up the tent that night, while Brook played with KO when I was interrupted by a little old man.

Let's call him George. George was about my height, with dark skin that had grown leathery after a lifetime spent under the Kansas sun, unshielded from trees. He was wearing an old mechanic's outfit, the kind that's one big suit that you step into. He also had on a cowboy hat, and was smoking what appeared to be a menthol cigarette. His house was directly across the street from where we were going to camp, so he had a very good visual of our campsite. When he came over, he began asking me questions about our camping.

"What are you doing?"

"I'm setting up my tent so that my family can sleep here tonight," was my calm reply.

"How long will you be here?"

"Just tonight, we'll pack out early in the morning."

"Where are you from?"

"North Carolina."

"Not Kansas?"

"Not Kansas, sir."

"Well, why are you camping? Are you some sort of vagabond?"

The entire time he was interrogating me he was inching closer and closer to the car. I thought he was staking the place out and was planning on either killing us in our sleep or robbing us blind. Originally I had planned for us to sleep outside in the tent because the weather was pleasant for once but George caused me to reconsider, so I started making the bed in the car in order that we could lock ourselves in.

I was trying not to become alarmed and was maintaining as respectful an attitude as possible. I also didn't stop working while I was talking with him because the sun was setting fast and I needed to finish my job. I had finally emptied out the car and prepared the air mattress pump to blow up our bed when his eyes grew to the size of saucers and he took the last step that he had between himself and our truck. The invasion of my personal space was complete.

He smelled putrid, like menthols and stale body odor, and he was so insatiably curious that he just climbed right on in our car, without asking permission, to watch me blow up our airbed! I realized then that either George's elevator didn't go all the way to the top floor, or that he was so intrigued by strangers he was willing to forgo all societal expectations, manners and respect of my need for personal space.

I said a desperate prayer for words to speak to this man as I was left speechless by his behavior. Very gently, I asked George to get out of the truck; afraid he might be of the psycho hillbilly variety and would come and get us in our sleep if I didn't treat him with the utmost kindness and respect. He finally wandered on home once the bed was made and the show was over. As Brook and I finally rested our weary, sweaty, dirty bodies. Brook asked what on Earth had just happened. He had been watching from a distance while he and KO had played. We both started laughing as I explained how George slowly invaded my personal bubble of comfort with his menthol smoke and funky stench. "I've got to hand it to you; I would have flipped out had he gotten in the truck without asking. Sometimes I think you're crazier than all the whacko's out there darling," my husband said to me as we drifted off that night.

Every morning I end up at a park in a small town and I spend my entire day there excepting KO's naptime. By the end of the day I am so nauseous at the idea of swinging on a swing or sliding down a slide for the millionth time, that I genuinely need to leave KO and Brook and walk away.

I have an unfortunate condition called "twitchy-eye." My right eye twitches when I get excessively stressed or agitated. It isn't a very attractive quality, or one I am pleased to have. By the end of most days on the road, my eye twitches at the sound of children playing tag or goofing off at the park because I am so sick of it I want to scream. I beg Brook to let me walk in his place but he won't trade places, so I just pray that I can bear fruit of patient endurance through my trials.

Here in Kansas, everyone wants to know what Brook's deal is, so he has his own trials trying to finish out his miles each day. He gets stopped by more police officers and local sheriffs to have his license run through their computer system than you would believe. Add to that the curious folks that stop to chat with him the blustery wind that never stops shunting him all over the place, and the expanses of corn fields he has to look at every day, you have the makings of another eye-twitch inducing day. Luckily, I am the only person in our family with the ocular malfunction. Brook needs a good solid hour at the end of his walk to sit, relax and readmit himself to the normalcy of conversation and parenting. That hour is the hardest one of my day. I know he needs his rest, but I also know that if I have to tell KO, "Stop eating the sand!" one more time while I watch Brook sitting in peace and quiet I might possibly lose all fortitude of mind that I have remaining. Plus, I miss Brook's companionship all day. It's weird to have him gone so much knowing that all he's doing is walking. The walking is for an admirable cause but there are moments daily that we both wish this was over.

Having hit our halfway point, we both knew we were going to finish, but there were those times when our desires to be completed with our journey were so powerful we would have given almost anything to be released from our commitment. We were yearning for North Carolina so deeply at times that it felt all consuming. There was one day in Kansas that no distraction could keep me from thinking of southern food.

I called Brook and said "Oh how I wish there was a Bojangles right here. I would get a picnic size fry with extra Cajun seasoning! Oh, and I want shrimp and grits so bad I can't stand it. And your mom's homemade pimento cheese. Heck, I'd even drink a sweet tea (I am one of a small band of southerners that doesn't appreciate the glory that is sweet tea)!" He promptly told me that I had just ruined his day by reminding him that these delicacies existed and hung up his phone.

That day I considered the American pioneers who had originally settled in Kansas. Did they ever crave the delicious foods of their home countries so severely they would catch themselves slobbering all over themselves? I realized then that I had barely considered the strength and unconquerable will power our American ancestors have had throughout our short time as a nation. It is impossibly difficult to be what feels like worlds away from one's own home, without any idea of when you will be returning again. I wondered in astonishment at how ignorant I had been for over 20 years at the plight that so many people have faced in their lifetimes.

I honestly had never once thought about what my great great grandparents must have felt when they arrived here in America from Hungary, Scotland and England. What did they long for, crave, and miss so much that their hearts or stomachs ached from yearning? Would I have been capable, if plopped down in a foreign land with little money and even less education, to make a way for myself? Could I have learned a new language, maintained my old one, and given them both to my child as my great great grandmother did for my beloved great Grandma Audrey? As my stomach roared with an insatiable appetite for cornbread and homemade fried chicken with a side of okra and tomatoes I doubted it. The human spirit is in every way an astonishing thing.

What strength this realization gave me! I was refreshed in the knowledge that what I was doing was a mild challenge in comparison to my forefathers' difficulties. My patriotism exploded within when I finally understood what it means to be an American. It means perseverance through all hardships, community with others in the same position of difficulty, the freedom to worship a God who provides comfort in the worst circumstances and the promise of success in all measures imaginable. My eye may twitch, and I may hold the world record for most community playgrounds visited in a five month span much to my chagrin, and Brook may hurt in every muscle he possesses, but we are blessed to endure this adventure as Americans.

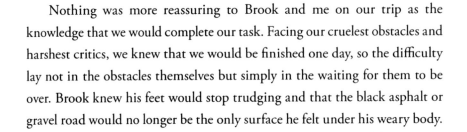

Nothing was more reassuring to Brook and me on our trip as the knowledge that we would complete our task. Facing our cruelest obstacles and harshest critics, we knew that we would be finished one day, so the difficulty lay not in the obstacles themselves but simply in the waiting for them to be over. Brook knew his feet would stop trudging and that the black asphalt or gravel road would no longer be the only surface he felt under his weary body. I kept reminding myself that I would see my family again, I would get to raise KO with full access to an oven and microwave, and I would not have to live my whole life under the microscope of strangers, yet I still forgot this at least ten times a day. We had to constantly remind each other and ourselves "We will finish this, and we will move on."

Knowing that we would finish our expedition was encouraging, but what made us keep living the same day at the playgrounds and walking mile after mile was the knowledge that not only would our plight end, but our deepest hope was that the immensely more challenging plights of others would end as well. We found Proverbs 4:25 early in our trip to be a pillar of focus when we depended on it the most "Let your eyes look directly forward, and your gaze be straight before you."

People always asked, and still continue to, how Brook could keep on walking, mile after mile for so long. He always replies that

"I kept my eyes on the road before me. I lived one day at a time. The challenge wasn't as big when I considered it day to day as opposed to the big picture. The big picture'll surely slow you down, I learned that real fast."

Why is it that people all over America have ocean themed bathrooms? I am here in landlocked Kansas, hundreds of miles away from beaches and I just used a bathroom that had a beach theme. This phenomenon has intrigued me all through the west. Does taking a shower or using the john incite a vacation mindset in so many, or does looking at sea shells while visiting the toilet make your day more peaceful? My parents live about two hundred and fifty miles from the beach, yet for the longest time they had a beach themed bathroom. I always thought it was bizarre. I am so perplexed at the ocean themed bathrooms of this country and why they exist.

There are moments on this trip where my own existence perplexes me, far more than that of an ocean themed bathroom, but I always come around to the resolution that I am here for a reason. Maybe this journey is all I'll ever do with my life, but it's worth it, because it's impacting so many others.

There was a little nine year old girl, named Rachel Beckwith, who died shortly after closing her charity: water campaign. Her death was tragic. But in her death, her mother wisely re-opened her campaign. In that simple act, this little girl's wish to bring clean water to the world became an incredible reality. Her campaign raised over a million dollars! Just as I question ocean themed bathrooms, I question the necessity of death, of life even. However, I realize that when you hear of the Rachel Beckwith's of this world, the cycle of life has so many unfathomable events that we could never begin to understand.

No one should have to lose a child to dire circumstances, but if in your child's memory thousands and thousands of people are given life through clean water and inspiration to think larger thoughts, you must be able to find some solace. Perhaps not enough to make the situation ok, but maybe enough to feel God's order in this universe. I'd love to meet little Rachel's mother one day, to thank her for raising a girl that in such a brief span of life could do so much good for those in need.

KO is sick. He has a yucky cold and is heavily congested. We carry a breathing machine on the road which aids in opening his airways. We use it the most when he struggles with congestion. Tonight, we were at a park in Kanopolis, Kansas preparing for bed. We were eating instant mac and cheese, watching SpongeBob on the laptop and doing a breathing treatment on KO. People were coming over in small crowds asking us what we were doing and we were given an excellent opportunity to share information about the clean water crisis. People were highly intrigued by the weird family that was planning to sleep at their town park, and I doubt they figured they'd get an earful on a global crisis when they asked us about our situation.

One woman was so fascinated by our pitiful display that she insisted that she had to help so she offered to let us sleep in her camper. I am typing this from inside of it right now. She had said that she's never helped strangers, but she just felt like she had to help us, as though there was no other option. As I type I am so grateful for her act of kindness that I can't stop smiling. The autumn weather is creeping in on us, and every night it gets cooler and cooler. Having the camper to sleep in, which is a warmer alternative to the Yukon, is a huge blessing. She also offered to let us shower and use whatever we need or want from her and her husband's home. Though Brook is facing a lot of difficulty out there walking all day long, and though my eye may twitch come evening time due to over exposure to playgrounds, this is a magical life. We get to see all the goodness of the nation firsthand, and truly, it is a wondrous sight.

When we awoke from our glorious sleep the next morning, we went inside the home of our hosts to use the bathroom. Pamela, the wife, had made a delicious breakfast of eggs, toast and sausage for us. It was heavenly and the best way to start out a day for our family. Leonard, her husband told us his stories of travel and asked loads of questions about our adventure.

The breakfast and company was so good that it put Brook out of any sort of walking mood. He decided to take the day off. As we were packing up slowly and without any rush, I noticed an old door on the ground and got so excited you would have thought someone had just offered me the opportunity to get a professional pedicure!

It was an old, traditional tornado shelter and I was determined to get inside it. I have fantasized about being in a tornado shelter since my childhood. I have imagined the conflicting feelings of anxiety and coziness that must come from having to seek shelter in a strong storm from one of these underground nooks. Leonard opened it up for me when I asked about it and led me right on down. It had a flight of ancient cement stairs leading to a domed roof room built entirely out of stone blocks. It was in good shape for its age, and clearly there hadn't been a lot of use for it in recent years because there was a blanket of dust covering the ground. I was enchanted by the space because it felt like a safety zone, where no one or nothing could mess with you, no matter how hard they tried. I wanted to go get KO's dog bed and sit there for a long time just mellowing in the comfort of the shelter.

Brook thought I was the weirdest person in the world when I tried to explain my love of that room to him. He didn't even stay in it but for a second to take a look around before he headed right back up the stairs to the fresh air.

"Honey, imagine who's had to find shelter there and what they were hiding from. I felt all the relief that those people must have felt in the walls, dust, and air."

Maybe I am the weirdest person alive for enjoying being in a tornado shelter, perhaps I was too excited, but I will never forget that security. I hope that if I ever get to live in something other than a tent, I can create that comfort for my son and anyone else who comes into our family.

Brook and I had to leave Pamela and Leonard's house to drive to Salina, Kansas for an interview. We both appreciated Salina in that short day we were there, but we headed straight back to Kanopolis the next day where Brook had left off his walk. I need to comment on one of the most blessed of all American traditions; the potluck supper. KO and I were playing in Kanopolis again, just waiting out the day when a group of people, including Leonard and Pamela showed up at the park again. They were having a potluck after the christening of a baby in the local church. The food scents that waltzed by my nose were so sensational I felt my stomach dancing as fast as it could to keep up. Never has the idea of homemade deviled eggs and potato salad been so riveting as it was that day. As soon as I smelled the food I started praying, "Dear God, if there is any goodness left in this community for my little family, please let someone offer us some bar-b-queue and beans."

I don't think it's disrespectful to take your desires to God for help and I'll tell you, I had an insatiable desire for that potluck lunch. Of course they saw me and let me eat everything I could pile high on two plates. They generously made a huge bag of food to take to Brook which he lovingly devoured that evening. Brook and I appreciated every meal we were given so deeply, that we both hoped to return the favor a hundredfold throughout our lives. Genuine people gathering together to eat delicious food is one of the pillars of the American lifestyle, and we were blessed to be American's that got to participate that day.

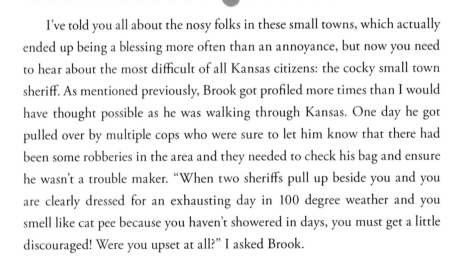

I've told you all about the nosy folks in these small towns, which actually ended up being a blessing more often than an annoyance, but now you need to hear about the most difficult of all Kansas citizens: the cocky small town sheriff. As mentioned previously, Brook got profiled more times than I would have thought possible as he was walking through Kansas. One day he got pulled over by multiple cops who were sure to let him know that there had been some robberies in the area and they needed to check his bag and ensure he wasn't a trouble maker. "When two sheriffs pull up beside you and you are clearly dressed for an exhausting day in 100 degree weather and you smell like cat pee because you haven't showered in days, you must get a little discouraged! Were you upset at all?" I asked Brook.

"Nope, it was just another chance to tell someone about the clean water crisis. Though it did throw off my mile per hour average; that was annoying." I love my husband.

Predominantly, sheriffs are men with portly bellies and big knuckles who want to protect their communities and have decent intentions of keeping their home turf safe. We were awoken by one such representative of the law at 11 o'clock at night one evening in Carlton, Kansas. Carlton actually has a sign in the middle of 'town' that says "In 1986 nothing happened here," but I think whoever made the sign meant to paint "Nothing ever happens here," which is what seemed to be the case to me as I arrived and started looking for a place to stay.

I asked around and found out where the mayor lived, and then went to his house to ask about camping at a decommissioned school on the main thruway. He wasn't home, so I went to a neighbor's who happened to be involved in local politics as well (when your community's population is less than a hundred people, it seems that everyone is a politician). I got the ok from this kind woman and set up camp in the middle of the yard of the school right under the only street light in the entire 'town'.

We were clearly not trying to hide anything as we were directly under yet another obnoxious street lamp. Anyone that passed by could see us in our bright yellow tent. Brook and I were so confident we were ok to sleep there that we even stripped down and cleaned ourselves up behind the car once it got completely dark. We went to bed around 9:30 and were fast asleep when suddenly I awoke to a bright flashlight being shined right in my face.

"Ma'am, I'm going to have to ask you to leave this here spot. You can't camp here."

I honestly thought that the cop had come to arrest me for bathing myself and being nude in a public place earlier in the night. Still in my drowsy frame of mind, I began asking the officer sleepily where else we might be able to camp, relieved that indecent public nudity was not being discussed. He suggested a lake that was some 20 miles away. Clearly this man was not familiar with living with a buffalo boy and a cross country walker. I no more could have gathered Brook and KO up and driven over twenty miles in the dark to an unknown place at eleven o'clock at night than I could have solved a quantum physics problem. In fact, I passed physics with a B in college, so I probably would be more likely to get through the physics than corralling my men folk to an undisclosed camp site in the middle of their sleep cycles.

When I finally realized that the cop wasn't going to leave until either we left or this was resolved, I got up and started pleading our case. I told the officer what Brook was doing, got the local paper article of us out of the car, and explained we had permission from the lady who lived in the big brown house to camp at the school. Finally he called the mayor, told him our story and got the okay for us to remain in our dinky misery at the old school under the overly bright street lamp. The sheriff did make sure he ran *both* our licenses through his systems before he left. I have never had my license checked for anything except for one speeding ticket and I was furious.

Looking back now, it was not that traumatic an experience. More than anything it had royally irritated me to have been woken up. Small town sheriffs don't get the opportunity to wake up strange campers in the middle of the night very often. I am grateful that this was simply a genuine man who was trying to keep his neighbors and family safe from the deranged couple and their Amazonian child that was passing through the town where "In 1986 Nothing Happened Here!"

I don't know how he does it but Brook has stunned me yet again. We arrived in Herington, Kansas where the population is about 2500 people, with few prospects for lodging. I went to the police office to inform them of our whereabouts and asked if they had any recommendations for car camping so as not to repeat the Carlton experience. They didn't offer much hope or help, so I prayed all day that something would come along.

And it did. Brook noticed a church on his walk out of town that was perfect for the needs of our small family. It had no elevation in its parking lot so that Brook could sleep flat that night, and it boasted a play set for KO. It also had an outdoor power outlet that I could plug the laptop into and finally catch up on some writing. We called, got permission, and even got access to the bathroom inside which was a Godsend. I relished in the cleanliness of shaving my legs for the first time in about forever. Washing my hair in the sink was as rejuvenating as a glass of cold water is to someone who's been lost in the desert for twelve hours.

I had just settled down to write when Brook emerged from the church with a handful of crackers. "Want one?" "No thanks," I shrugged him away.

"These were in the fridge. I've never seen saltines in a fridge before. Kind of nice having a cold crunchy cracker after a long hot day. We should keep our crackers in the fridge when we get home."

My neck swung around so fast it hurt the next day. My husband had found what could be none other than communion crackers and was eating his fill of them. Here he was, listening to Bob Dylan, eating his refrigerated crackers and acting like it wasn't a big deal.

"I cannot believe that you can sit there and eat a handful of communion crackers as if there is nothing wrong here! Go put them back! They aren't a snack, they are sacred squares. You aren't King David for goodness sake," I exasperatedly bossed him.

"But I sure feel like him right about now. If God were gonna get mad at me over eating some saltines I found in the fridge after walking twenty six miles towards His goal, I think I'd a felt a little bit bad. But I don't. Besides, the pastor said to help myself to whatever I found in the fridge. The only other thing in there is mustard so I think I'll stick to the crackers."

I love that my husband can eat what are most likely communion crackers out of a church fridge as though its nothing but normal, yet be scared to death to take a soda out of the fridge of a host family who has offered us anything we want in their home. His backwardness is one of the reasons I am going grey prematurely, and one of his most endearing qualities.

I was lying on the beach in this super cute yellow bikini with a dark tan, a tan so dark I could never achieve it unless I freckled so much that all the freckles merged into a darker looking skin pigment, when low and behold Jude Law walked over and started trying to hit on me. I was laughing and being flirty, and Jude looked so dashing in a pair of board shorts.

Then KO sat on my head and woke me up. I realized I was in the back of my in-law's truck in a tiny town that had a population of maybe 20 people and had been up all night getting eaten alive by invisible biting bugs. Being woken up from a dream in which hunky celebrities are flirting with you is not pleasant, and having KO's traditional soggy diaper butt wake-up call to my face is not ideal under any circumstances, so I was less than cheerful that morning. "What's your deal?" Brook asked me.

"My deal is that I am dirty, hungry, itchy, tired and I didn't get to finish my dream in which a handsome movie star was hitting on me. You would have a deal too."

"Was it Hugh Jackman again?"

"No, Jude Law."

"Oh, that's a new one." Brook said looking adorably puzzled. I started to laugh. I couldn't help it. It was so hysterical to me that I had my attitude problem over such trivial things as shortened dreams and physical discomfort that, let's be honest, I had grown accustomed to. Then I noticed that where the bugs had been biting me all night, I had huge raised welts that looked like there were golf balls under my skin.

I freaked out. I can walk to the mailbox and back in the middle of winter with every inch of my body covered and still come inside with a mosquito bite, so I am used to being itchy. But I never have swollen masses that develop after I get bug bites. I am also deathly afraid of ticks, so I wondered if I had gotten Lyme disease or some other horrible illness. I thought I would need to have my right ring finger and my right leg, my most swollen appendages, amputated. Brook said that I was clearly overreacting and that I'd be fine. So I tried not to hyperventilate and prayed that I'd be able to keep my body parts.

The swelling went down after a few days, and I relegated myself to the fact that whatever had bitten me I was very allergic to. What annoyed me the most was that these little pests were invisible. I couldn't see them coming at me. I continued to find little swollen bites all over me as we progressed through Kansas. I overcame my fear of amputation, but I still wasn't convinced I didn't have an untraceable illness from some sort of Kansas bred mutant bug that infected you with a disease that lied dormant until you least expected it.

When I explained this to Brook he accused me, among other things, of being a drama queen. So I shut up and didn't worry about it as best I could. The last thing I wanted was to be dramatic about invisible bugs that caused me to swell and would likely be the cause of my demise, or at least numerous amputations. I did keep close track of how often I got bit, and those little invisible bugs followed me the whole way through the Land of Oz.

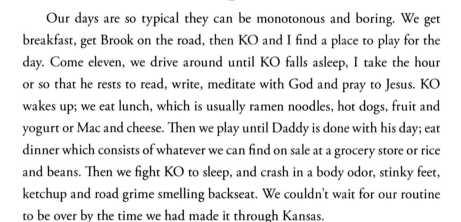

Our days are so typical they can be monotonous and boring. We get breakfast, get Brook on the road, then KO and I find a place to play for the day. Come eleven, we drive around until KO falls asleep, I take the hour or so that he rests to read, write, meditate with God and pray to Jesus. KO wakes up; we eat lunch, which is usually ramen noodles, hot dogs, fruit and yogurt or Mac and cheese. Then we play until Daddy is done with his day; eat dinner which consists of whatever we can find on sale at a grocery store or rice and beans. Then we fight KO to sleep, and crash in a body odor, stinky feet, ketchup and road grime smelling backseat. We couldn't wait for our routine to be over by the time we had made it through Kansas.

In the intimate moments before we fall asleep, we often have a good time poking fun at our lot in life and dreaming. Last night, my husband informed me that I looked like a pigeon lady. A pigeon lady typically has a mass of dirty nappy hair that she has tucked under a knitted cap. Her attire consists of clothes that are also knitted, attained though thrifty encounters and smeared with the fecal matter of her birdly companions, just in case you were wondering. I was wearing a cute cap that I had asked my grandmother to crochet for me, a grey monstrosity of a sweater that I adored because it was snuggly and warm and ten sizes too big and bought for a quarter. The sweater was splattered with KO's snot, food remains such as ketchup and pizza, and I had on argyle socks with sandals. I am 22 years old and a pigeon lady. Perfect. Thank God my son won't remember this.

At bedtime, between calling each other names like "Odorlicious" and "Pigeonette," Brook and I often asked each other the open ended question, "What do you want when you get home?" Brook's replies were always "I just want to sit, and not get up, for a long time." Or "I just want to eat my mom's pimento cheese and crackers, sleep in my bed and pet my Gracie (our cat)." He is a man of simple tastes, but his desires display both of our longing for the normalcy of life. Rest, comfort, our pet cat; we missed the trappings of a stable home. I was usually more specific than he was.

"I want to take a hot shower, then lotion my entire body in my fancy perfumed body lotion. Then I want to blow dry my hair and curl it, just because I can. Then I want to put on my bath robe and pink soft pants and lie on my sofa while all of my family and friends take turns visiting me and telling me how the past six months have been for their lives. I want to have a hundred candles lit all around me and a pile of chick flicks that I watch non-stop while eating strawberry ice cream. I want to play with KO indoors for an entire day."

My "I wanna's" change daily, depending on what I miss the most, but both of us have come to agree that when we get home, no matter what home actually is, we are going to be grateful in every possible way for every comfort and luxury that we are blessed to have access to.

I'm here to share that in my experience, as long as the town has a population numbering near 1,000 people, there will be a Subway restaurant in that town. On top of the ever present Subways, there was almost always a Pizza Hut, and/or a Dairy Queen or Sonic. There was also *always* a Dollar General store, in every small town in Kansas and every state east of that. I have seen the inside of more Dollar General stores than I ever could imagine possible, and am confounded at the ability the store chain has to market their products so inexpensively. Never in my life could I tell you why every thirty miles or so there had to be a Subway, Pizza Hut and Dollar General, but I can assure you that they were the most populated places of business in small town Kansas. Brook commented on it one day by saying:

"It's no wonder with all these Pizza Huts and Dollar Generals America has an obesity problem and every American carries debt."

One of our last days in Kansas, we were in a lovely community called Council Grove. It had a Dairy Queen and a Sonic, as well as the ever popular Subway, Pizza Hut and Dollar General. Beyond the plethora of fast food and shopping options, there was a stately Inn and Motel. Unfortunately it was out of our price range and we were getting desperate for a shower and a place to do laundry. I decided to go around to the local churches and ask if we could camp in the parking lots, hoping against hope someone would take pity on us and find us a place to stay.

I found such a place where a pastor wanted to help our cause. The pastor had offered us the church shower, which was exciting, but also said he'd look for someone to host us. He was giving me a tour of his church when KO decided to be as egregious as possible. While Pastor James was talking with me about all the details of the church, KO peed all over me, even though we'd just gone to the bathroom and he hadn't wanted to go. I excused myself and went out to the car where I sat KO in the front seat and placed my car keys on the dash. I shut the door so he wouldn't climb out while I was walking around to the back of the car to grab a new outfit. It was just then that I heard the unmistakable click of the doors being automatically locked. My son had locked himself in the car with the keys, I had pee all over me, was 2000 miles away from anyone who had a spare, and had already used AAA more times than I'd like to admit that summer.

When you are in a situation like this and you have absolutely nowhere to go but up, you can usually keep a positive outlook. "KO likes to push buttons and will probably hit the unlock button eventually," I thought. I find that prayer is always a good source of resolution so I whispered, "Jesus, please help my child not to be locked in this car for more than a few minutes and please help me not to lose my mind in front of these people that want to help me. Oh, and please let the spare keys that were in the magnet box still be under the car."

I went inside to enlist the forces of the pastor and the youth pastor, who came out and assessed the situation with me. While the pastor and I were under the car searching for the spare key magnet box that Frank had placed somewhere, I considered calling him and asking where he had put it. I decided against this course of action, feeling that it was inappropriate to call and have him worrying about the stability of his grandson's future having such a dingbat for a mother. Then I heard the click again of the locks! The youth pastor had taken a stick and slipped it through the window I'd left cracked. I always leave the windows cracked for such emergency situations, of course. I was never more relieved in my life; and after silently thanking God for his miraculous help, I changed our clothes and we left the church while the pastor and his staff probably all wondered what kind of nutter they were engaging to help.

Later that day, Pastor James called me back and said he'd found a woman who'd host us. We met Ms. Mary and followed her out to her country farm house that night. This woman is true Kansas breed; she'd lived in the same area her whole life and raised her kids there. Ms. Mary had white hair cropped short, walked with a cane and was overweight in the delightful way grandmothers should be. Her eyes were kind and as soon as I met her I knew I was going to like her. When we arrived at her home it was late, almost nine pm and pitch black. She excused herself after showing us inside to go and gather up her hens.

I watched in awe as she climbed on top of her lawn mower, started up the engine and puttered off into the black night without a flashlight, her memory leading her way. "You know what Billy? I think I'm a pretty strong woman but these farm women are a whole different league of tough."

We stayed up until almost midnight sharing our adventures with Mary and hearing all about her own life journey. She was a special education teacher for many years, had retired early after her spouse died unexpectedly from a tumor and began to downsize. She was actively involved in the youth programs in the community, especially at her church, and was clearly a beloved fixture of Council Grove. The thing that captivated me the most about Mary was her role as a matriarchal grandmother. She woke up every morning and went out on her porch to pray for her family. She could see the house she raised her own children in from her seat in that old rocker; the house where her two of her grandchildren had been raised after she and her husband sold the house to their son. She would pray over her grandkids: for tests in school, relationships with boyfriends or girlfriends and friends, their decisions and most of all their spirituality.

"I never pry and I never want to be a pain, I learned that from my own mother in-law who couldn't help but keep her nose in everyone's business. I'm here if they want to talk and I am always praying for them. They know that."

And when I met her granddaughter that night, I could tell that they did indeed know that. This girl was 15, cute and a typical teenager. She looked at her grandmother with love and respect that is uncommon in kids that age, and I enjoyed her kind goodnight to Mary, which was just an "I love you" that most teenagers wouldn't share in front of strangers unless they were serious in their statement of adoration.

Mary calls all of her grand children each day to leave them a blessing. It is a short, thirty second message that she leaves on their voicemail or the answering machine if they don't pick up. She said she couldn't go through her day without making those few calls, "The few times I haven't done it I have been wracked with frustration and it just has to be done."

I've heard a lot of older people say that they aren't leaving an inheritance to their kids. Instead, if they are fortunate to have money in retirement they are going on lavish trips, getting plastic surgery to look younger, or just using the money they might have otherwise left to loved ones to pay bills and survive in this awful economy. Perhaps grandparents shouldn't leave all their money to their kids and grandkids. I certainly commend people for living out their dreams after a life of hard work, but they *should* leave something. Mary's grandmotherly act of selflessness was so deeply moving that I couldn't help but consider what the world would look like if all grandparents were able to show such devotion. Speculating, I could see her small act of love carrying on blessings to her grandkids children. Mary was leaving a lasting gift through her daily calls of encouragement; I was so blessed to have met her.

Casually, I asked Mary if she knew of what origin the abominable bug bites I'd been experiencing might be from. She told me she would need to think on it. The next morning she said "Angel, I thought about those bug bites of yours as I was going to sleep last night and I think they might be chigger bites."

I am not a whiny baby and I wasn't about to freak out, at least on the outside, but the word "chiggers" sent chills up my spine. "Are chiggers dangerous? Are they like ticks? How can you tell a chigger bite?" I spluttered off thirty or so questions in rapid succession trying to wrap my mind around these little gremlins.

It turns out chiggers are little invisible pests that bite but don't cause an awful lot of issues, just swollenness if you aren't used to them and an itch for a few days. Brook was amused by my incessant fear of chiggers. The next few days as I asked him if I should go to a hospital every time I found a new swollen bite he just laughed and said no one in their right mind was going to treat me for chigger bites in a small town Kansas hospital. I tried to console myself by admitting that at least I now knew what the source of my imminent doom was.

As we left Council Grove, we headed towards Ottawa, our last hoorah in Kansas. I felt wiser. Just being with such a matronly woman like Mary had rubbed off on me, and I was filled with peace. Saying goodbye to her was not unlike saying goodbye to my own grandmothers. I knew I'd miss her company and wondered when I'd be seeing her next. I truly believe that if you surround yourself with great people, their greatness can and will rub off on you, and I felt that in action as we meandered our way on to a different town, filled with a different group of people.

Ottawa, Kansas was the land of many major hotels (and a Wal-Mart!) that Brook and I'd been fantasizing about for two weeks. We'd promised each other a grand hotel stay filled with hot tub trips, reality TV watching, continental breakfasts and coziness unattained anywhere else. When we arrived, we were flabbergasted to find all the hotels we went into completely booked because of "Car Show." "Car Show" is an annual weekend long festival of fried food, automobile fanatics and classic cars that people from all over the middle of our nation travel for in order to drink Budweiser and show off their '69 Camaros. It is a very big deal, apparently.

We started calling other hotels in other towns, we were close to Topeka and its suburbs; surely they'd have something! But as our luck would have it, there were two major concerts in the surrounding towns that same weekend, leaving all the hotels booked full, or if they had remaining rooms, they were way out of our price range. Rather than cry and throw ourselves in the middle of the road for an old Model T to run over us, we said a prayer and tried a decent looking motel. The owner, a man of the beloved Indian variety, gave us a great deal and we unloaded into the room right as the heavens opened up and all of the "Car Show" folks around town scrambled to trailer their investments.

The rain kept on falling, all day and all night! Brook hadn't taken a day off in weeks, so he didn't walk that day. We went out to a Mexican restaurant and it was one of the best family days we'd had, just laughing and enjoying watching all of the terrified "Car Show" types fret about the weather.

That night after we'd put KO to bed, Brook went out to the Yukon to get something. One of the "Car Show" guys stopped him to talk. When he heard about Brook's walk, he immediately asked about hail. When Brook relayed that he had had to endure hail in Idaho and Oregon, the man replied

"So you know how bad it is. We're all worried about that hail, we don't have any overhead coverage for the cars and that hail can wreck up a beauty like ours something fierce."

Never in my life has hail seemed as sinister as it did on this journey. We'd been told tales about how it killed bikers back in Oregon, how it wrecks cars that are worth hundreds of thousands of dollars here is Kansas, and learned firsthand how much it can royally annoy you as you walk across the country. How inconsiderate of hail. While in Ottawa, the rain kept on falling; for two days it never let up. We renewed our room for the second day because Brook just didn't have any motivation to go walk thirty miles in pouring down rain. Those last two days of civilized Kansas were mighty refreshing. On our two day break, I talked to Brook about Kansas and asked him if he would be missing anything. He replied:

"I certainly won't miss the harsh winds that beat me around all day. Or looking at all the corn fields. Or listening to crop threshers. The people are nice but it is was so darn hot and flat here for so long I couldn't stand one more second of it. I am enjoying the green I see the closer we get to home, looking at it all makes my day go by much quicker."

As we neared the Missouri line, I began condensing my thoughts on Kansas and our time there into a list on what I've learned about small town America. Here is that list:

What Every Person Visiting Small Towns in Kansas Can Expect:

♦If the population is numbering 1,000-3,000, you can surely expect to find a Subway, a Pizza Hut, a Dollar General and either a Sonic or a Dairy Queen(or both if the town is particularly enterprising).

♦A playground at which you can play with your child. Beware: residents of said town will most likely invade your privacy. If you intend to camp at the playground, expect a large number of concerned citizens to rap on your windows or shine lights through your tent to make sure you aren't a danger to their community.

♦A "friendly" sheriff. Make sure you're on his good side and everything should be all right.

♦Some darn good cooks.

♦A group of friendly and talkative children who are all too willing to give you the scoop on everything and everyone in town (this may apply to all children everywhere if you attract kids like I do).

◆Not a lot of fashion focused folks.

◆Not a lot of literature focused folks.

◆A *lot* of agriculture focused folks.

◆Some tough women who can corral livestock in the black of night without anything to guide them but their instincts and memory.

◆An absolute monopoly of radio stations held by the country music community.

◆Real Tornado Shelters.

And Finally,

◆A neighborhood of kind people, ready to help out whenever and wherever they can; the people that built this nation and have established it as the land of the free and home of the brave. Americans by birth and true patriots-you know, the types of people you hear about in all the country music songs that Kansans are such fans of.

Missouri: The Edge of Sanity

"Look to the Lord and his strength; seek his face always." 1 Chronicles 16:11 NIV

When we hit the Missouri border both Brook and I were ready to be done. The constant walking, playgrounds, instability, and sleeping in a different place every night had exhausted us. We had both become conditioned to our lot on the road to the extent that we had lost our focus of the mission. In large part, we had lost our vision and drive for the walk because we were so comfortable in our discomfort. Just as our routine back home before the trip had bogged us down from feeling meaningful and purpose driven, so too did our journey's schedule after a while. This isn't something I am ashamed to write, because I think that when we realized we were just meandering through our days without joy and fulfillment we were able to double our impact, but it was a boring time for us until we reached that point. Though I am not a doctor nor do I pretend to be one, I have an inkling that being bored is what leads to severe loss of reality and can result in insanity. Brook was getting a little cuckoo out there all day on the open road.

"I was talking to myself today for about an hour before I finally realized it. And when it dawned on me that I was doing it, I didn't stop. I just figured it was a part of being alone so much," Brook shared the first day we were in Missouri.

"How often you think you talk to yourself on a given day?"

"Eh, who can tell? Not too much, but enough I guess to puzzle out my thoughts."

"Do you talk to yourself when people drive by?" I asked while I was fearfully thinking "Great, now he's going to get picked up for being a muttering nutter by Missouri police."

"Well it's my road too, I'm not just gonna stop because people are driving by me!" he staunchly proclaimed.

"Wow. You need to call people on the phone or something else, that's kinda messed up."

But when I thought about it, I concluded that it wasn't that messed up. So what if Brook had an ongoing dialogue with himself for weeks on end about Yoo-hoo's plot to be different in their ounce measurements? Who was I to say what is normal for his degree of loneliness? I certainly would have lost my mind out there all day without anyone to talk to, so if he was keeping aligned by sharing his adventure with himself, at least he was witnessing his own journey.

Though I couldn't begrudge Brook the act of talking to himself all day, there were certain discontinuities I couldn't let ignite in his brain as he was getting deeper and deeper into his mind funk. The Numberitis set in at that point of our trip, and it was completely debilitating for the three of us when Brook got a bad case of Numberitis.

"Do you realize that most people go around on about 65 percent less tread than I would deem safe?" Brook started a conversation off this way one night. It turns out that he was calculating the tread on the tires of vehicles that passed him, God only knows how. "No dear, I don't realize that because I don't give a darn about other people's tires."

"Oh. Well I've noticed that trucks especially have a much lower percentage of good tread than do sedans or even vans."

"This has got to stop! It isn't healthy to be out there calculating tire tread on stranger's trucks. You could use that calculation time to pray, or come up with any number of crazy ideas that I would more than willingly listen to than this math lesson on tire tread!" I was genuinely worried about his mental state.

"Well, I did take a picture of a road sign today that was actually two signs right up side by side that said 232. The first sign was for highway 23 and the second was for highway 2. It was orderly. You wanna see the picture?"

"You're telling me you took a picture of a number three sandwich because it was orderly?"

"Yes! The number sequence was just like a sandwich! The 2's were the bread and the 3 was the meat. So cool."

As I beat my husband over his head with a road sign (in my mind of course) I prayed for patience.

"Honey, I understand you get bored out there, and I understand that there isn't a lot to amuse yourself with, but that need to take a picture of those signs was wholly unnecessary and took valuable time away from walking or giving your body a longer break. Honestly, it was useless and I worry that I am going to wake up one day to Russell Crowe lying beside me chatting up his imaginary friends about physics. You've got to stop this."

"At least you didn't say Rain Man this time. I hate it when you call me Rain Man."

I am writing from a small town in Cole Camp, Missouri tonight. We are parked in front of the large and impeding Catholic Church and I am surrounded by cats: small cats, grey cats, orange cats, ugly cats, pretty cats and Brook's beloved "Laundry Cat." Further evidence of my husband's severed normalcy can be displayed in the description of his rapt attention to the "Laundry Cat."

This feline is lovely, orange with a marbled pattern on her fur that would make Cruella consider cats over dogs for once. She smells like clean laundry, which is where Brook got her name. Brook is so factual; everything is named after what his senses can describe. I would have given the cat a name like Michelangelo or some other artist that worked with marble. Anyway, Brook is obsessed with this stupid cat and driving me crazy by sticking it in my face to sniff it and pet it. He was so obnoxious that I finally told him to go to bed so I could get some work done. He even tried to take the cat to bed with him. I am not sure if he succeeded. I hope that he didn't. The last thing I want to deal with is finding some angry cat that just wants to be cozy in its home with its little old lady trying to spray my pillow because my loopy husband has kidnapped it. This cat was clearly loved and well maintained as a family pet, I only hope our cats are ready for some mauling when my husband gets home to them.

These aren't the only animal companions that Brook has been experiencing of late. Missouri is the Chasing Dog capital of Brook's walk. Nearly every day when we catch up together he has a new nip mark on his leg or a story about how he had to shoo a dog away with shouts and commands. My favorite dog story happened as we were nearing the end of Missouri.

Brook was walking along when a sweet young pup ran up to him with a long line of chain dragging behind. The pup had just broken free from its home in order to meet Brook. The dog followed him for about a half mile when a car drove by. The dog ran in front of the car and the driver had to slam his breaks to stop from hitting both the dog and Brook. That was when Brook got concerned. "Get on! Go Home Dog," he hollered, trying to spook the thing but the dog wouldn't go home. Brook walked another half mile figuring the dog would lose interest and when it didn't he got frustrated. "Oh, you silly mutt!"

It was then that Brook took the dog and tied its chain to a grain silo on what appeared to be a busy farm. He continued walking for a few minutes but the dog kept on barking at him, and he said the sound of the barking made him feel guiltier and guiltier. Brook turned around, untied the chain and proceeded to walk the dog all the way back to where he thought it had come from originally. He tied the chain around a tree in the front yard of a house and hoped he had picked the right home, but figured the dog would be better off near his home than on the road walking or on a farm a mile away. Brook was annoyed to have to back track, but he did say that "I'd rather walk an extra mile to share the company of a nice mutt than have to listen to barking or have to whack an aggressive dog from coming at me with its teeth barred."

My parents had been planning on joining us in September since we started our journey way back in June on the coast of Oregon. September had arrived and so did the painful news that weren't going to be able to join us at all on our journey across the country. My dad is a mailman, and works overtime hours like you wouldn't believe. My mom lost her job a few years ago and had been cleaning houses trying to boost their income while still maintaining a home-schooling environment for my baby sister. Just like most middle class families in this country during the Great Recession, they were tight financially and not taking any risks.

However, my dad took a week off from work as soon as he found out about our trip, because he wanted to be there and be a part of the walk. My dad loves Brook, he is his first 'son' and they have always been close. My mom goes through withdrawal-like symptoms the longer she is away from KO and she and I have always been best friends. They were going to bring my baby sister Caeley, who both Brook and I adore so we were all super excited about the week in September when they would be joining us on the road.

Then my mom found out about a job opening in her field and so three weeks before they were supposed to visit, my mom took the job. My mother works with severely handicapped individuals, and her new position was as the primary caregiver of a young man who had previously been neglected and malnourished. This guy was named Johnny, and when he moved into my parents home there were major changes that occurred.

The first few weeks anyone spends with a new house mate is a time of learning limits, adapting schedules and figuring out a comfort zone for everyone involved. This was the same with Johnny, with the added complication of years of neglect he had suffered. He had been nearly starved, had improper equipment for his medical needs, and had been rarely cleaned. My mother called me in tears five times the first two weeks she had him, and my mother *never* cries.

Every day she seemed to find some new form of neglect or abuse, and in the first two weeks they saw fourteen doctors. To see an average of 2 doctors a day is an extreme horror to me; I hate all places that have to be sterilized on a regular basis. She was exhausted and overwhelmed. Then one day, about five days before my family was scheduled to come, I called my parents and my dad picked up the phone. He sounded so tired that I could feel his weariness in my own body. When my dad is overworked and upset, his voice gets this nasal "ehh" sound, almost like a person from Wisconsin. So I was listening to the nasal Wisconsin voice of my father's as he spilled out all that had happened the past two days I hadn't had cell service.

Johnny is 16 and he weighed 52 pounds when he came into the care of my parents, and he was given one more month to live at that weight by one of his doctors. Had my mother not been able to seek proper feeding and increase his intake of calories, he would have starved to death. When I finally got to talk to my mom, I remember saying "Mom, you need a rest. I need to know that you and dad are ok, and that Johnny is not going to have to go through anything else awful. He'd likely be very scared if you mysteriously left for five days right after he'd gotten attached to you and that can't be good for either of you. We'll be there soon and I want you to rest until we get there. I'm not telling you not to come, but I am telling you that you need to rest."

While I was telling my mother this, what I honestly wanted to shout was "I can't believe this is happening! Why can't I ever get some attention?! How does this always happen to *me*?" Because when I am feeling the most selfish, I always think those awful thoughts. My spirit stirred when it realized that I am forcing my son, by association, to suffer in order that those who are in greater need might be blessed. I was ashamed of my selfishness, and as I counted all the ways KO had suffered that summer in order to bring clean water to other children who might not otherwise get it, I found myself asking God for forgiveness for my selfish inner protests. My parents were sacrificing their desires and mine in order that someone else's quality of existence would improve. I sucked it up in the hopes that I could instill the lesson of sacrificial love in my son after experiencing it fully myself.

And that was that, they didn't come. It stunk like Brook's feet after a day of walking because they will never know exactly what it was like for me to live the way I did for nearly half a year of my life, but it was for a good reason. One of the magical parts of the individual was apparent; my parents can't know my life story any more than I can know theirs'. They will have to experience my adventures through my stories, just like I had to meet Johnny through their description of him. I think it's special that we get to live life this way; each individually and then collectively share it as we must. God makes me smile when I realize how important the individual actually is to Him.

We ended our first campaign on September 19th, 2011. It closed with a total of $14, 624. Approximately 730 people will be impacted from the generous donations we were able to garner from individuals throughout the country. As we closed our first campaign, both Brook and I reflected on who had given and what it had meant to us that others were able to look beyond their own desires and donate out of compassion for individuals oceans away. Our greatest triumph was not in the dollar amount, or even in the number of people that would have clean water from the campaign. Rather, our greatest pride came in the inclusion we were able to afford to others, like Brad from Idaho, who had never even donated to a charity in their entire lives. As we opened a second mycharity: water campaign, KO especially got excited. This time around we were partaking in a campaign to raise funds for a drilling rig that would perform the difficult task of drilling for water in Ethiopia. KO loved to log online with his mommy and daddy and see the big green "Brmm Brmms" that we were working so diligently towards funding in our efforts. Every time someone donated we felt our efforts to be worth it, because it meant we were meeting our goal of including others in the walk.

Let's talk about playgrounds. I have decided that any sociologist that wants to study the state of the American family needs to spend as much time as I have at the playground. It is there that one gets to view the dynamics of families, the sad state of children in this nation, and maybe even gain some insight into why we have such troubled youth.

Here is KO in his 'pool'. Let's try and keep our parks
as clean as the water we would like to drink!

For starters, the children and teenagers of America are obviously too young to be using the swear words they think are so cool when they can't even spell them correctly as they write them all over playground equipment. I have never been more disturbed at the unintelligence of humanity as I was when I realized that the majority of cuss words that have vandalized kid's equipment at family parks are spelled wrong! I mean they are almost all four letter words and fairly phonetic!

And it's no wonder that kids are trying to get attention through vandalism; parents at parks are either ignoring their kids, yelling at them or both. I have rarely been more saddened as I was yesterday at the park. We were playing in Eldon, Missouri, where a little girl with a classic case of childhood obesity was climbing and sliding with her baby brother. She was about eight, and he was one. This little boy had two black eyes, was filthy, and his clothes were so big they were actually hindering his movement. He kept falling and hurting himself because his parents wouldn't roll up his pant legs. Neither of the parents were within eyesight of their kids the majority of the time they played. When I looked over at them they were chain smoking.

I am not judging this family, everyone does thing differently, and I am a prime example of a parent that marches to the beat of their own drum. However, this little boy was clearly neglected, whereas KO is not. What made my blood boil was when he finally tripped over his three sizes too big pants and *really* hurt himself his mom came over and yelled at his sister for not watching him. The little girl and I had been chatting and she was clearly in need of help, so I'd been aiding with the little boy as best as I could while playing with my own son. When the mom finished her screaming bit, the little girl pointed at me and said I was trying to help her and that it wasn't all her fault but that *I* had messed up too.

This little girl was willing to blame anyone, even the person helping her, to avoid the cruel and undeserved embarrassment she was receiving. My heart broke for that child because she doesn't get to go home and feel like the helpful big sister she is. She feels at the age of eight, like she is a failure, and her resentment towards authority figures, her brother and herself were already growing by the second. And this wasn't the first time I'd dealt with this at the park. It was becoming a daily occurrence in my life.

What on Earth are people thinking cussing at parks? There was a man at a park last week with his son and his baby's mother. He picked up his cell phone when it rang and had the foulest mouthed conversation I have ever had the displeasure of hearing. You can't ignore it when the conversation is being yelled into the phone. I heard more about this man's sexual partners, alcohol and drug use, and every single derogatory term you could think of, as well as every single profanity I know(and some I don't) in the time it took this man to talk on the phone until we left because I couldn't take it anymore.

How would that man's son grow to be a healthy, responsible and considerate person with that as his example of adulthood? He was going to have one heck of a time being an upstanding citizen with that behavior being displayed by his role model. That little boy was the same age as KO, and I shed tears for him while I drove my own little prince to sleep that afternoon.

It's not just little kids that I see all day struggling to find goodness. Yesterday I saw a group of four teenagers, two boys and two girls that made me cry (again) as I fell asleep thinking about their futures. The kids were definitely high on some sort of drug, and they were not being supervised by anyone or anything. I heard them cussing, laughing and telling dirty jokes, typical of unsupervised teenagers. The time came for the girls to get picked up and the mom that arrived waited 15 minutes for these kids to get off their lazy butts and make their way to the car.

Then one girl got in the car and waited for her friend to offensively kiss not one but both of the boys until I hollered over at them to quit and for her to get in the car and go home. I made sure they knew this was a family park and not a place for that type of activity. These kids were fifteen at the *oldest*.

The mom waiting in the car shouldn't have had to wait fifteen minutes, but it's no wonder that her daughter had no respect for her if she is allowed at such a hormone driven age to be alone with such wild and dangerous opportunities with no supervision. And that little girl that kissed both of those boys so vulgarly in front of the whole world back to back; it is a near certainty that she will get an STD or have an unwanted pregnancy to deal with. How dare parents squander such precious lives?

Maybe I shouldn't have hollered at her to get in the car but I couldn't handle the lip locking for one more second. Beyond the uneducated vandals, abusive parents, and sad children, there are the cigarettes. What are people thinking when they light up their cigarettes at a children's park!? I mean how inconsiderate do you have to be to breathe your toxic fumes in the same air as not only your own child but mine as well!? My son was born nearly five weeks early and had underdeveloped lungs; as soon as someone starts smoking it affects him. He starts to cough and gets short of breath. He isn't the only child in the world that has this issue. Being selfless and not lighting up for the few minutes you're at the park, or just walking away from the playground for a few minutes while smoking would be so appreciated by people all over the country. I am so over people thinking that smoking in family places like parks or restaurants is ok. Yep, this is America, land of the free. It is your right to smoke, but it is my right to whine, complain and ask you to quit when you are endangering the future generations of my society, including my child who is already at risk for asthma. Get a hold of yourselves and stop smoking where kids can inhale your disease filled air.

Finally, throw your trash in the trash can. KO and I made it a daily habit to walk around the park where we were settling down for the day and clean up all the trash within eyesight as soon as we got there. Some days this was easy, others it took a long time. It is really not difficult to walk to a trash can with one's garbage, and if we are able to teach our children how to clean up their messes the rest of the world will truly appreciate it.

To conclude on proper playground etiquette:

Watch your children, love them and cherish their childhoods as precious. If you pay attention to them, they may not end up vandals or burdens to society. Quit smoking in front of my son and leave your teenage hormones at the park gates. Please refrain from cussing on public property, and don't you dare act like I am stuck up for demanding that my son has a healthy childhood, safe from vandalism, uncouth language, public displays of over-affection and toxic carcinogens. Clean up after yourself and encourage your children to respect public property by making them clean up after themselves as well.

I am so saddened by the multitude of familial problems I face every day. When I see kids struggling at such young ages to deal with adult issues it's like a stab to my heart. The wisest man who ever lived has been recorded as saying "Know well the conditions of your flocks, and give attention to your herds; for riches do not last forever, nor a crown for generations," Proverbs 27:23-24, NRSV. People shouldn't judge, and I failed at passing judgment on many individuals as I passed through this great country. I've sought forgiveness for my failures, but I do believe that I was righteous in my anger at the foolish squandering of youth and mistreatment of children that I witnessed. I am certainly not a perfect mother. I took my baby on a possibly dangerous cross country adventure. But I love my son, and I am constantly watching over my little flock, knowing where he is going and what he is doing, and leading him in a way that is filled with compassion for others, love towards all men, and respect. That is a parent's job and one that we must not take lightly.

It was in a little place called Windsor that KO got to pet his first horse. The horse was owned by a Mennonite family and was used for pulling their carriages, riding to town, and for other forms of labor. Windsor had a large Mennonite population and KO and I both stared wide eyed and open mouthed when horse and buggy after horse and buggy clip clopped by. Neither of us had ever seen this before! The entire town was set up to accommodate this population. There were places to tie bridles off and the roads had big diamond signs with pictures of horses pulling buggies that said "Share the Road" just like a bike sign. Horse poop pick-up was actually an issue in these Mennonite filled communities.

I was charmed by the Mennonites because they seem to live a life of simplicity in this ever burdensome world; but then they lost me when I realized some of them would drive cars and others wouldn't. I Googled Mennonite and was surprised to find a broad spectrum of Mennonites. There are Old Order Mennonites who were the ones I was seeing with the horse and buggies on one end of the spectrum and on the other there were apparently Mennonites that are indistinguishable from the masses by dress and even allow the LGTB community to participate in active worship in their church. Yet again, the diversity of this great nation waved its ever changing hand my way.

I thought the Mennonites were cool until we camped at a campground off of a busy by way. It was then that we discovered that these folks were early risers who flew by in their buggies on their mission to do chores at horribly premature hours of the morning while unassuming campers were trying to sleep. It's a whole new world to wake up to a horse drawn carriage clopping by your tent. I was not amused and I learned my lesson. The next night we avoided the before hours wake-up clip clop by camping in a Wal-Mart parking lot, which I thought wouldn't be so awful.

The Wal-Mart in this area actually featured a long metal bar in the parking lot for Mennonites to tie their horses to. Go Wal-Mart for catering to the minority populations! We ended up parking and taking an hour or so to clean our car out while KO slept in his car seat. We had our junk everywhere.

There were piles of trash, clothes, books, gear, and toys. It was only eight o'clock on a Saturday night so the parking lot was hopping. Everyone that walked by us looked at us like we were Martians. If you've ever been to a Wal-Mart on a weekend night, you know that there are usually teenagers that are up to no good shopping for freezer pizzas and weird families that will gather as a large group and take up entire aisles with their crowd. The later you go into a Wal-Mart, the weirder people get. As we sat out in that parking lot working on our car, our own level of strangeness set in. I was one of those weird people at Wal-Mart late at night.

We finally got tired of people looking at us, so we wrapped up our cleaning and got into the bed. After staying up late into the night goofing off and enjoying our Wal-Mart people watching from our bed in the car, we crashed. We were woken up at 5:00 a.m. when the parking lot sweeper showed up. Road sweepers are some of the loudest, most obnoxious vehicles in the world. This particular one was no exception. As it brushed around our car I felt like all the unfairness of the world was seeping into me.

"Here I am in a Wal-Mart parking lot, freezing, tired, uncomfortable and now there is what sounds to be an angry mechanical rhino charging around outside my car. Why me?"

Later that day, after having whined the predominant portion of my time in Missouri I read Acts 5:41 which says "Then they left the presence of the council, rejoicing that they were counted worthy to suffer dishonor for the name." The disciples had just been beaten and put unfairly on trial, yet they were blessed in their hearts because their suffering came from doing the work of the Lord.

That kicked my sorry butt pretty hard and I shaped up fast. I realized that I was suffering and no one could argue with me on that point. However, my suffering was nothing compared to those that I was suffering for. I ought to be, if not joyful, at least content to suffer in order to help others and do God's good work. From that lesson I gained a refreshed sense of purpose for the duration of the trip, and it was a great encouragement in my hard moments of overwhelming frustration and exhaustion. I was constantly reminded of the suffering of others, and it truly was what kept both Brook's and my spirit, mind, and body aligned throughout our time on the road. I needed God's word so many times on the trip for a reality check and encouragement. Whenever anyone asks me how I made it, I always share that it was "With my Bible in hand."

In Miller County, Missouri there is a long road that is mostly gravel and dirt. Down that road there are a good number of cows, some single lane bridges and a few unfriendly farmers. Brook was on this road for an exceptionally long time today. As he was wrapping up his evening, he ran into a pair of brothers who were parked in the road.

"They didn't like me at first. They were both sizing me up, wondering what a hippie boy was doing on their land. They gave me the evil eye," Brook said when he was telling me about meeting them. One of the brothers asked Brook where he was headed, and when Brook said North Carolina, they both dropped their jaws.

After a conversation that Brook says brought him back to the country side of life, Rocky and Rowdy had decided to help our little family out. These are the only people that we met on the road whose real names I have used in this book. Their mother gave them the coolest names on earth and no amount of reason can bring me to change them.

"I've got a place you guys can sleep at tonight. It's got a shower and a kitchen and all. It's nothing much, it's at my hog farm," Rocky offered generously. Rowdy warned Brook "You oughta watch out and not be on roads like this round dark. If I'da been on my porch I might've gotten my gun out not knowing you and all. Everyone knows each other and we don't take kindly to strangers 'round here."

Brook got into the truck with Rocky and as they were leaving Rowdy laughed and said "You'll get to sleep to the sweet squeals of all them pigs."

"Naw, I just sold the whole fleet Thursday, I don't get new ones for a few days," Rocky assured Brook.

We ended up at Rocky's Hog Farm in Missouri, certainly a place I never dreamed I'd be visiting. When I was 12 or 13, my dad got a pig. We named it Pork Chop and it was the smelliest animal I have ever endured, we all hated feeding it. When it finally got big enough my dad had it processed at a local farm and our family ate it. My dad promised never to get a pig again. When we arrived to the hog farm all of my memories of Pork Chop rushed back as the pungent aroma of hog in the air hit my nostrils.

The office Rocky had offered us was a man cave; it had photos of elk and deer that Rocky and his buddies had shot hanging on the walls. The floor hadn't been mopped in KO's lifespan. I found one of those trashy mugs that it is the shape of a lady's body wearing nothing but underwear on display. There were about four guns sitting out on his desk that he grabbed up quickly when we got inside to get out of KO's reach. It wasn't the Ritz Carlton but it certainly beat freezing our dirty selves to sleep in the back of the truck in a parking lot for the umpteenth time.

KO only knew two animal sounds at this point, he could snort like a pig and tweet like a bird. There were little pig figures all over the office, so KO went around pointing at them and snorting for about ten minutes cracking us up. Rowdy had given Brook a bag of cooked bacon and it rivaled the bacon we'd had back in Idaho at John and Naomi's. Rocky stuck around for a bit to tell us some stories. He also took KO for his first ride on a tractor, which KO absolutely loved. When he was leaving he said "I bet this is the only hog farm you'll stay at on your trip."

"I imagine you're right," I replied, secretly hoping his prediction would be right.

Rocky is a real cowboy farmer; and we are so appreciative for the opportunity to sleep in his office out of the 40 degree night and to get clean in the shower. God sure put some interesting blessings in our path.

Not long after we stayed at the hog farm, we found a decent motel and R.V. park that was cheap. We all needed some quality rest. KO had been sick and had puked all over me that day. Brook was exhausted after not having had a real day off in about two weeks. He stopped walking early and met us at the motel where we all just vegged out watching SpongeBob and Dora the Explorer. I was looking at the rules of the motel posted on the back of the door when I came upon a rule that said "NO BOTTLE ROCKETS INSIDE THE PARK." This made me laugh uncontrollably for about five minutes for a number of reasons.

For one, most people who are in R.V. parks are retired and no offense to the over 65 crowd, but I just don't see a whole lot of you playing with bottle rockets. Secondly, I couldn't help imagining what some poor sucker had done with a bottle rocket to get this rule posted on the back of every motel room for the rest of the time the motel existed. Did a guy shoot a rocket off at a person, a pigeon, a dog? What kind of bottle rocket was it? Finally, what killed me was thinking about the lady I had seen going into the room next door, wearing a floor length down jacket in 70 degree heat walking with help from a walker having a bottle rocket go off and set her pace maker into overdrive. The little things that I never get exposed to at home, like motel rules as awesome as "NO BOTTLE ROCKETS ALLOWED" are quickly becoming some of the most meaningful joys of my life.

One night in Missouri we were camping in a church parking lot, and Brook and I were busy setting up the car for sleep while KO played with his fleet of matchbox cars. We were watching him, but had our backs turned for a total of two minutes or less at one point as we made the bed. It was in this two minute interval that he did the unspeakable. He started whining and he came over from where he'd been playing and was pulling us hard. He was obviously trying to show us something as he pulled us by our legs to hurry us along. KO wasn't speaking a language we could decipher; we just followed his "Ehhs" and went to look at what he was trying to show us.

The church had three pipes coming out of the side of the building that were directly at KO's eye level. They were PVC and dipped down and back up, forming a U shape just like the pipe under the sink. Brook is conversant in general construction and he had no idea what the pipes were for. K.O kept pointing at the pipes and muttering exclamations so I bent down and looked inside. Our delightful buffalo boy was trying to show us that he had shoved not one but most all of his cars in the pipes to make a train.

There wasn't a snowball's chance in Kansas in August that we were getting those cars and trains out of that pipe.

"Well, it looks like you're going to be hanging out here tomorrow all day trying to get to the bottom of this with the pastor. This is going to be expensive isn't it?" My poor husband looked so forlorn. I started taking deep breaths, and praying.

How do kids do that? I can't imagine that any parent escapes the overwhelming feeling that they are raising a monster at some point in the process, but it was nearly impossible for Brook and me to remain calm that night. We got into bed and prayed we'd be able to afford to have the toy car fleet removed from the depths of the mysterious pipe in the Middle of Nowhere, Missouri.

Yet again, God saved our sorry bottoms and our wallets. At eight o'clock, much later than any normal church gathering, a small parade of cars pulled into the parking lot. After explaining that we weren't maniacs and obtaining permission to stay there overnight, we broke the news about the cars to the pastor who had come to officiate the gathering. We expected the worse.

The pastor busted out laughing and said, "Well, as long as he isn't going to need those cars we are ok on our side. Those are just intake and outtake air vents for our furnace. No harm done." Thanks to God's wonderful answer to our prayer, we didn't have to shell out 800 bucks for someone to come saw off the cemented pipe and remove the five dollars worth of toy cars. The pastor was impressed by our immense appreciation at his understanding. As he was leaving he gave us a bewildered look, we had thanked him about a hundred times, and said, "You know this meeting I'm about to go to isn't a regular event. We even had it rescheduled to happen right here and now. God's funny that way isn't he?" Then he gave us access to the bathrooms and the kitchen for the next morning and that night. God is so good sometimes I can't bear it.

Brook and I were overjoyed to see the lush green world again after desolate Kansas. Missouri's landscape gave subtle hints that we were almost there, back east in the decadent humidity and fragrant, fresh air. We nearly lost our minds halfway through, but we were blessed enough to be handed them back. Brook struggled his entire time in Missouri. He fought off mangy dogs nearly every day, experienced extremely inconsiderate drivers, and was not a huge fan of Missouri's road systems. Add to the tougher obstacles he was facing each day the fact that he had nearly gone wacko out there; it was a miracle that we made it through another state. God saw us through another hurdle, and we could feel the end of our journey coming ever nearer as we exited "The Show Me State" and entered into Illinois.

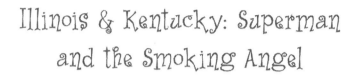

Illinois & Kentucky: Superman and the Smoking Angel

"Unless you people see signs and wonders," Jesus said to him, "you will never believe." John 4:48 NIV

Our first night in Illinois was as action packed as a super hero comic book. We found a church set high on a hill in a town called Wetaug. We parked behind the church and assumed no one would feel the need to bother us. We were fairly secluded so we let loose, sprawled out in the little parking space and relaxed. There was an old cemetery there and KO was fascinated with all the gravestones.

I had to go use the bathroom when we arrived so I trekked through the cemetery to the trees on the other side. While I was walking, I noticed a fresh grave. It had just been created within a few weeks of us being there. There wasn't any grass growing on it yet and the flowers that had been laid on it during the ceremony were still fresh. Never had I taken a bathroom break while a fresh grave stared me in the face. To say I was unnerved is to make a gross understatement.

To top off the fresh grave being so close to our car, there was also some weird animal nearby that kept moaning like it was dying. Every few minutes we'd hear a pain stricken voice let out a long "eeeehahaaaaaaaaawwww." I foresaw a poor night's sleep in the making long before we climbed into the truck. It was getting further and further into autumn and our evenings were getting increasingly shorter. We would have to get into the truck and have everything packed up for the night by seven unless we wanted to be struggling in the dark to get our work done. We'd all pile in the backseat in our varying degrees of filth and exhaustion. KO wouldn't be tired at all so we'd have to turn on the flash light and play games and read stories until he succumbed to sleep. These were the evenings when we realized how much we missed regular access to electricity and what gloriousness a lamp can be. We did our nightly routine that evening in Illinois and tried to ignore the moaning critter outside. Not long after I'd finally gotten into a deep sleep, I was woken up by yet another flashlight being shined in my eye and a rapping on the window, "You guys ok in there?!"

Deputy Dean introduced himself and told us his tale. Apparently he had done a security drive earlier in the night, and we had "Scared the pants off of 'im" when he saw our car parked behind the church. He ran our license plate through his system then called us in to dispatch, letting all the other officers know where we were. He drove off at first, but said he kept having this awful feeling, worried he'd get a call that there were dead people found in our car from suffocating while sleeping or something else sinister. He had returned to check on us, he shared, in a voice that was louder than need be from excitement and adrenaline.

When I opened the door and he flashed the light on my face I was momentarily blinded. Once I got accustomed to the light I began to tell him our story and the reason we were here in this spot behind an old church next to a cemetery. I could tell he was so exhilarated to have something as exciting as a couple of crazy nuts sleeping in a graveyard on his turf that I didn't worry that he might feel the need to arrest us for trespassing. He was in his late fifties or early sixties, had intense blue eyes, and his shirt had a little star badge just like deputies in old western movies. He saw KO and begged us to keep a window rolled down. We assured him we would, said our goodbyes and as I tried to get back to sleep yet again, I felt secure.

It's invigorating to feel so watched over and protected. When strangers want to make sure you are safe and healthy, and they actually double check on you just because they can't help themselves, you are a truly blessed person. I love America, its' small town law enforcement, and the kindness of strangers found within these 50 states. My love for my country fills me up with a pride that I never had before this adventure. I am forever grateful for the opportunity to fall in love with my land and the people in it every time I consider these days on the road.

We were only in Illinois for a few days, but while we were there we happened upon Metropolis, a city that shares the name with Superman's heroic hometown. Brook and I love the TV show Smallville, so we were stoked to find a giant statue of Superman and a museum that boasted more Superman memorabilia than anyone could imagine. Brook took his first day off after his longest walking streak yet of eighteen days and we had a blast spending time together.

We stayed the night in a Super 8, so when we woke up the next morning we went for a family swim in the hotel pool. Then we went to Fort Massac State Park and found a trail named after one of my ancestors, George Drouillard, who helped lead Lewis and Clark on their famed expedition. After our hike at the park, we toured the cheesy Superman museum and laughed as we found the original telephone booth and the costumes worn by the first cast in the 40's. Metropolis also happened to be having a bar-b-queue festival while we were there and Brook was as close to heaven as he could be by the evening when we walked through the celebration.

If you have never been to a bar-b-queue festival you haven't lived. The scents alone seduce your mind, tongue, and stomach in the first whiff. Once you're lured in, you get the joy of watching some of the most subtle entertainers in the world. If you give a beefy guy a giant smoker grill and a few hundred pounds of pork, the challenge of beating another beefy guy with the same supplies at making the best meat ever, you're in for the spectacle of your life. Besides the bar-b-queue, there were the funnel cakes, giant turkey legs, and other fatty delicacies that we American's cherish just calling out to be eaten. We were so mesmerized by the grub that we nearly jumped out of our skin when a big black guy behind the largest bar-b-queue tent said "Y'all were at the Super 8 right?!"

We had been, so we went over and talked to him. He was the leader of his grill outfit; his team went all over the country doing bar-b-queue competitions. They had a huge trophy display out front and if his big belly was any indication, the food had to be good. He was astonished by Brook's walk, and his friend who came over to chat with us was too. They both told Brook he was "too darn skinny" and then he made one of Brook's dreams come true. He bestowed the gift of free ribs upon my husband. Nothing makes my Billy happier than the word free and food in the same sentence, so he was ecstatic. Those were some mean ribs. I mean lick the bone dry and still wish there was more, good.

After we feasted on ribs and got an ice cream cone for KO, we walked down to the Harrah's Casino that was built in Metropolis. It was huge and everyone going into the building looked old enough to be members of AARP. We were stunned when we went inside, it was palatial! Casinos are always so aesthetically pleasing in movies but this was the first one I'd ever been in. We laughed and joked about getting a room in the resort, but after I asked what a room cost on a Friday night we joked our way right on out of the building. That day off was one of my favorite on our journey because it was what a rest day should be; refreshing, fun, and filled with a lot of laughter and family togetherness.

The day after our Metropolis adventure, Brook had to cross a narrow, rickety metal bridge that spanned across the Ohio River. He didn't want to walk across and I didn't blame him. It was sketchy and the traffic seemed steady when we scouted it out. After some brilliant deducing, we came up with the idea to have him charge across running full speed while I followed with my hazard lights flashing, in order to keep him safe from following traffic.

We tried it. He was running and I was laughing and recording the whole shenanigan. He ran so fast and so hard that he crossed that bridge in about six minutes, and it was just over a mile long! One woman passed us, a few people honked, but Brook made it across safely. I wish I could say the same for the car. While I was filming the incident, I lost my focus of the bridge and got too close to the rail. The result was a pale blue streak of paint from the impact of the car crunching into the blue bridge. I am a horrible driver.

Frank and Wendy have two sons and I figure as I am the first daughter they ever get the pleasure of experiencing I am teaching them new and wonderful things about young women, such as how expensive they are and why you carry good insurance on your vehicle if you have a daughter. I hoped that would be the absolute last thing that happened while I was behind the wheel of that Yukon. I was so embarrassed, and the worst part is that I caught the whole ordeal on film. Everyone in our family loves to watch that one; I only hope I can destroy the evidence before KO is old enough to begin driving.

Last night we slept in the Wal-Mart parking lot in Paducah, Kentucky. While I was falling asleep with Brook's feet in my face and KO hogging all of my limited space, I realized that our adventure was wrapping up. We only had a few more weeks until our way of life was going to end. I was shocked to realize that I'd miss the closeness we'd had on the trip, a togetherness that most families can't even imagine. We depended on each other so tremendously for everything which made us much more understanding and reliant on each other. I prayed falling asleep in that parking lot that God would help keep us close enough to be a blessing to each other as long as He could. I know KO is going to grow up and leave, like all kids should. I only hope that our time with him could be spent in such loving proximity.

This morning I woke up before KO and Brook and prayed for about an hour for the walk. I desperately want to help as many people as I can and felt like I hadn't been doing enough the past few weeks so I prayed that I would be given the stamina to do more.

Later, while I was rearranging the car and getting ready to get Brook back on the road, a man walked up with a cigarette in his mouth and started asking if I needed help. I guess since the hood of the car was up and there were suitcases and bags all around the truck, he figured I was broken down. When I explained that we had slept in the parking lot and that we were on a journey to help those needing clean water his entire demeanor transformed.

Mick was his name, he was about 5' 8", and very friendly looking, but could easily blend into a crowd. He was the picture of an average guy. He spoke at first with a thick southern accent, but either it lightened up after we got to talking or my ears had grown rusty to understanding my native language and eventually just realized what they were hearing. Mick insisted that he wanted us to come to his church that morning and promised us we'd be blessed. He kept smoking and took a brief trip into the store to buy an energy drink and a National Enquirer between our initial meeting and our final farewell.

We went to get breakfast from a drive-thru but promised we'd be right back and to go to church with him. It ended up taking a million years for our food to be finished because I ordered off the lunch menu for breakfast and that is a stupid thing to do. When we finally got back he was gone. Mick had mentioned the name of his church so we went anyway. We were lucky to find there him because it was a huge place. He shyly introduced us to a few people. I could tell he was excited to help but thought that he was nervously wondering if he was crazy for what he was doing.

When I was about ten my parents took a guy who had come to our church out to lunch with us, then they gave him a ride home. He smelled awful, I mean absolutely awful. I remember thinking, "I can't believe this guy doesn't take showers. Why on earth would anyone stink by choice?" My parents gave that man his first real meal in what appeared to be a year because he ate everything so voraciously I was nervous he'd eat me. They offered him a shower but he turned it down and was just happy to go on his way. People in the restaurant looked at us funny for having him at our table, and it bothered me, even at that young age, "Couldn't these people see that this man was hungry?"

Mick, like my parents, took two people who hadn't showered in a few days, one of which smelled atrocious, into his church with him. He had reason to look nervous when he introduced us. He was probably wondering if he'd be looked at funny for being the guy who brought stinky, homeless people into such a clean place of worship. He did it lovingly, and for that I hope he is eternally blessed.

After Mick introduced us to his pastor, he literally disappeared. He just kind of faded away and Brook and I couldn't find him anywhere, though we looked all over in order to thank him. We ended up going to a Sunday school class for young married people and had a great time. Everyone in the class wanted to help and was greatly interested in our walk and our work. After Sunday school we went into the service where we heard a sermon about the grace of God.

Now this was a southern Baptist church in Kentucky, which means everyone was dressed in their best clothes and looked fantastic. I have never seen such a large group of well dressed people in one building in my life. They were all so friendly; Brook and I melted at the re-introduction to southern hospitality. Everyone called each other brother or sister, like if I were to attend I'd be called Sister Angel and Brook would be Brother Brook; I love that. The Baptist ministers are also known to be pretty passionate, and Brother Louie didn't let us down. He was preaching it at the top of his lungs and there were a lot of "Amen's!" in the congregation that day. Brother Louie, when he was describing the faith he had in the grace of God said that he was so confident in God's grace "that I could swing out over Hell on a rotten corn stalk and spit in the devil's eye right here and now!" Now that's some faith.

We felt blessed and restored after our visit to church, as Mick had promised. KO, who had been in the nursery the entire time, had more fun than I can imagine and was a changed toddler when we left. That boy loves to be with other kids! Brook and I were both bummed that we didn't get to say goodbye or even thank Mick, when it dawned on me that Mick may have been an angel. A cigarette smoking, Red Bull drinking, trashy tabloid reading angel that we met in the parking lot of a Wal-Mart. If that doesn't change your life I don't know what will.

Before Mick left us he had asked about our route for the next few days. When we told him where we were going he told us about a campground we'd be coming across, and that we *had* to stay there for the night. Brook and I just rolled our eyes a bit originally, mostly because campgrounds could run us close to forty bucks a night and we were on a tight budget. But I didn't forget the name of the campground, and later that same day I came across Mick's recommendation.

I went up to the office to find two older gentlemen sitting in white rockers just outside. They were letting the time roll on by, blabbering on about whatever crossed their minds. They greeted me when I walked up and then they asked me what I was up to. I handed them each a business card, gave them the brief diatribe about the walk I had memorized, and left once I got a quote for the camp site.

I was driving away, with the intention of meeting Brook and asking what he thought about staying at the site, when my phone rang. One of the older gentlemen I had just spoken to was on the phone and he simply said, "Little Lady, you turn your fanny around and come back on in here. I took care of your site for the night, and I want to see you and your husband get some get old fashioned rest." Naturally, I turned my fanny around and did just as he instructed. I thanked him profusely, as did Brook when he returned and all he'd say was "No need for thanks, Little Lady. Just keep doing what you're doing, it's a good thing."

The people at this campground were possibly the nicest people in the entire world. Everyone wanted to make sure we had enough blankets since we were the only weirdoes camping in a tent that late in the year. We were only in Kentucky for one day when I realized how gloriously close we were to home and that we had made it back to the south. I heard real southern accents everywhere and when I looked at the map I read the names of towns like Possum Trot. These fellow campers were true southerners and we loved them all.

After hearing our story, one kind gentleman brought us a bag that he said had some left over steaks in it for us. When Brook and I opened that bag our jaws dropped to the ground and about enough saliva to fill up a gallon jug started leaking out! These were the juiciest, biggest, most tantalizing, Angus T-bone, farm raised beef steaks I had ever seen. Excepting the bison steaks I'd eaten a few years back, they were also the best steaks I've ever had the pleasure of consuming. I called my mom that night and she asked how we were. I told her we'd just had the best day of our entire journey. I told her about my smoking angel, my new friends in Kentucky and the delicious steak. She said "Nothing is better for a mother to hear than her kids are being well taken care of in this world!"

When she said that, I felt God smile. He agreed with her, and as Brook and I were His beloved children, He, like my mom, was so pleased when people who had no obligation to help us decided to anyway. As I realized this, I thought about the children and adults in Africa that I was suffering for. I said a prayer asking God that they too might be well taken care of in this world. When people rained blessings down on us, it was so easy to keep on going. Encouragement, especially from strangers, is one of the greatest miracles in the world today.

In the intimate moments before we fell asleep that night, I told Brook all the things I'd learned so far on our journey.

The Importance of Touch

When I touch people, like shaking the hands of stranger or helping little children at the park by holding their foot when they need a boost, I feel a special bond formed. I am not a touchy person, and touch isn't super important to me, but I realized how crucial it is to human togetherness that summer. I have met so many people who just don't get touched enough. Their hug quota is severely lacking. This trip has helped me to realize that the guys sitting on street corners asking for a dollar, the old people in parks, and the children being ignored by their parents at playgrounds could all use a special touch. Just a handshake to say that you acknowledge their humanity or a hug to say you are real and so are they can be a life changing way to bless a person.

Family Togetherness

I told Brook that night, as we felt the cool October breeze creep into our tent that I never want our kids to feel like they are baggage. After all the time I'd spent with KO that year, I realized the incredible bond that families can have. I need for one of us to always be available to KO, and any other children we might one day have in order that they see the realization of God's will in our family. Our kids needed to receive constant love, attention and guidance, and that was more important to me than almost everything else.

KO was always so excited to see his daddy when he got back from walking.
Photo Credit: Wendy Hinman.

Faith without Works is Dead

As Brook walked across America, and as I made phone call after phone call requesting donations, I realized that our work wasn't being done in order to bring clean water to those without it. Certainly, the clean water was a worthy side effect of our efforts, but the real reason we were performing these tasks was to follow our God in faith. James 2:17 says that "So faith by itself, if it has no works, is dead." We believed God's promise to us that He would care for us throughout this adventure even though we didn't always see how He could provide exactly what we needed when we needed it. Our faith was far from dead as we neared the end of the walk, and we were blessed each time we refused to *look* for an answer but rather chose to stand strong in faith.

Avoid the Bad Apples

Before this journey I had positive people in my life overall, but there were still a lot of negative influences that spurned me into a constant state of distraction. I hate that I allowed small things to ruin my day and rob me of time. After this summer of true survival I have learned that one of the most important things I can do in life is to weed out the bad apples from my barrel of life and only let positive people and things in. When I am around people whose hearts are in the right place and are uplifting to my own weary heart, I notice all my stress fading and my ability to enjoy life increase. I also see my ability to encourage others heightened. My hope is that as I grow older, I can become a pillar of optimism and love for those I come into contact with. As cliché as it is, life is too short to waste, especially being grouchy, frustrated, sad, or stressed. I am going to keep the bad apples out and only let the good ones in, for the rest of my life.

There are countless things I've learned on this trip, but to save this from sounding too preachy, I'm going to wrap up this sleepy time conversation I had with my husband by sharing my lifelong motto; "You only live life once, so get it right the first time."

We stayed in a cheap motel in Hopkinsville, Kentucky last night. There were a few vans that look like they could be used for running drugs, some beat up looking cars and our own SUV. The chair to the desk in our room had holes in it from cigarette burns and was eerily stained by who knows what; it was quite a room. It had two comfy beds and we all fell asleep before nine o'clock out of exhaustion. Even though Brook was tempted to hyperventilate when he saw the desk chair, and I was not reassured by the thumping bass of the cars that pulled in and out of the parking lot all evening, we worked hard to not judge others. Especially bass thumping, possible drug dealing, scary men. It's hard to remember not to judge the lady who brings illicit gentlemen to her room at night, but after this summer and all the people that have had the opportunity to judge me for being a spacey hippie and an awful mom for bringing my son into such a trying lifestyle, I have worked hard at being judgment free.

Today, I took KO to the city park and it was conveniently located beside the fire and police stations. I love when towns put the emergency and law enforcement agencies in the same complex, but today I was not so thrilled to have them in such proximity to each other. That is because, when reversing out of the parking lot, I sideswiped a handicapped sign and scratched the side of the truck royally. Not only did I mess up the truck, but I bent the sign a bit and it now stands at a slight angle. Walking my sorry butt into the fire station (I didn't dare try the police) was not a proud moment for me.

Fortunately enough, just before I hit the sign, KO had charmed the firemen by soliciting a tour of a fire truck. He had gotten to sit in the driver's seat and investigate the compartments at the rear of the truck. When I walked over to explain what had happened, the firemen laughed, made sure that the sign was fine, and sent me on my way. I was thanking the Lord for my charming child and I felt a little better so I got on my phone. I texted Brook to tell him what had happened and he promptly replied, "All said and done you have done about 6k in damages to that truck." I called him later to talk about it and he said, "Honey, you are never getting a car bigger than a minivan, and even that might be too big for you." I prayed, yet again, that this would be the last act of cruelty I would put the truck through.

Kentucky, though we were only there for three days, was one of our favorite states on the journey. Everything was in the transition from summer to autumn, the yellowing and orange leaves stunned us. We'd been gone so long! We were ecstatic to hear the southern accent after what felt like a lifetime, and nothing got us excited like the southern hospitality we were given. Only one more state to go before we were home!

Tennessee: The End is Near

"However, I consider my life worth nothing to me,
if only I may finish the race and complete the task
the Lord Jesus has given me..." Acts 20:24 NIV

I don't look at the map if I can avoid it. I desire to see the entire U.S. map when we are done with the journey. I want to see everywhere we've been as one big collective image. I'll feel so much more accomplished looking at the atlas and seeing all the little towns, communities, forests, cornfields, and miles and miles all lined up in one big picture. This has worked for me the majority of the trip but it drives Brook crazy. I didn't realize how close we were to Nashville when Wendy called and asked when we'd be staying with Brook's cousin who lives there. When I found out that Brook's route was only twenty five miles or so north of the country music hometown, I figured we couldn't afford not to do the extra driving to her house.

I love Nashville. It has a great vibe; all the music, food and entertainment that you can imagine as well as excellent universities. Their parks system is well maintained and KO and I had a blast playing there. It's also one of the most well manicured cities I've visited. There is green everywhere, even the medians on busy roads had fantastic landscaping. It is breathtaking in the fall when all of the leaves are changing colors. Frank and Wendy joined us for the weekend while we in the Nashville area to walk with Brook and spend some time with KO and me. While we were there, Wendy and I had the joy of visiting what is in my opinion the best toy store in the world.

Toy stores around the globe should take a lesson from Phillips Toy store in Nashville, Tennessee. It was the most inviting, fun and enjoyable toy store I have ever had the pleasure to shop in. I don't like going to mega toy stores or even Wal-Mart or Target, because they often seem over-done and sterile. I tend to gravitate towards outfits like Phillips anyway, but this was a unique place. For one, it had a friendly, well informed staff that was delighted to talk about the toys they were selling. Every single staff member could describe the toys and provide anecdotes about how their own children and grandchildren enjoyed the product. Most places that sell toys have a bubble gum blowing, way too much makeup wearing, attitude problem wielding teenager on staff that is only too grouchy to assist you with finding the aisle you are looking for. It was refreshing to be in a place that was not the norm.

Beyond the staff, there were actually toys that kids were not only allowed to play with, but encouraged to try out. I felt like KO could have played with just about anything in the store and no one would have been upset. There is a fantastic electric train set on display that he laughingly watched from an observation tower built in the store. I doubt that any parent with a positive balance in their bank account could walk out of there without having bought something. It was a fun place to shop!

Dismembering a one handed person's remaining hand from their body with a rusty saw without providing them with anesthesia would probably be easier than it was to get KO to leave Phillips'. For once I understood his disillusionment. What kid in their right mind would want to leave Phillips' Toy Store? Wendy tempted him with a train whistle and he calmed down pretty quickly trying to figure out how to make the thing work. Sometimes I wonder if, at times, life would be incredibly easier if it was as simple to calm down adults as it can be kids.

Brook and I wanted our North Carolina leg of the walk to be the biggest and best that it could be, so it was long agreed that when we got to Tennessee, I would leave Brook for a few days and head back home to do some campaigning work. The time had finally come, we were almost there and I needed to get North Carolina ready for us. Frank and Wendy planned to stay with Brook one more day after I'd left, leaving him alone for three days. These would be his first days alone on the entire journey. He was excited to have the freedom he thought would come with carrying his gear on his back and the ability he'd have to walk for endless hours, since he figured he wouldn't have to be back to a camp to see us. He waved us goodbye eagerly anticipating his lonely three day trek.

Brook walked with both of his parents on the last day they were with him. Now is a fitting moment to award Wendy with a blue ribbon for enduring the most severe injury incited on the Water Walk America trail. She was walking with Brook outside of Nashville, when she took a step that she said sent shooting pain up her foot that didn't dissipate over time. When she arrived back home, she went and had her foot looked over by her doctor; turns out that she had fractured a small bone within. It's a wonder it didn't happen to Brook but also a blessing. We only wish the walk had been fracture free!

While poor Wendy was breaking her foot, I drove all the way back to N.C. in one day with KO, and he was as perfect as an almost two year old can be. It was both shocking and refreshing to roll into my parent's driveway after having driven with a delightful companion for nearly eight hours.

North Carolina is my home. I grew up there, have traveled all over it, went to college at it's (in my opinion) best university, and I bleed Carolina blue. No matter how much I love it though, arriving there after such a long stint away was beyond bizarre for me. When I entered the brick rancher I grew up in, the familiar smells of my childhood greeted me. My pictures were still on the walls in the exact spot they'd always been, and though one of my younger sisters had moved out while I was on the road, everything still seemed the same.

It was awful being there without Brook after all we'd been through. I felt guilty that first night when I lied down to sleep in our glorious bed with our glorious sheets and blankets that my parents had gotten out of storage for us. I was foreign in the very place I grew up. I called Brook that night to wish him good dreams and I said "This is too weird. I wish you were here. I hope this won't feel so awful when you are with me. Then I'll have to think something is wrong with me."

I continued to feel an overwhelming sense of obscurity as I drove around the town I grew up in the following day. I went from business to business asking for sponsorship for our campaign. I nearly imploded with anxiety as I grabbed lunch at a restaurant I haunted as a teenager. I felt like the whole world had just warped from a land of continuous discovery into an overwhelming memory of what I once knew. I struggled to focus on my campaign work as I realized that places barely change. It is us, humanity, that transforms and progresses. We might update our land to keep up with our ever growing knowledge, but we are the change that happens in the world. I prayed that day that God would influence all the change that happened in me as I aged. If it isn't Him, it won't be change for the better.

While I was campaigning and relearning my hometown's streets, KO loved the time he got with all four of his grandparents. I was delighted to find that he would be adapting well into a life of consistency if this brief sabbatical from our trip was any indication. He was the happiest I'd seen him in a while those few days. Brook, on the other hand was far from being happy. The day his parents left him to fend for himself, my phone didn't stop ringing.

The first call I got I could tell that Brook was lonely and frustrated. "It's freezing, this pack weighs a bloody ton and I am bored out of my mind!" Then it started to rain on him, which wouldn't have been a problem if Brook had packed *his* rain gear. This is what happened. Way back in Oregon, laundry detergent had spilled on Brook's poncho. No matter how many times we rinsed and dried it, the detergent wouldn't come off. Every time he wore it during a rain storm, he'd be a sudsy, soapy mess. His dad had left him with a new poncho as I had taken his rain suit with me back to NC. Unfortunately, Brook figured that a poncho is a poncho, and not likely to have different sizes, lengths, etc. which is why he failed to try it on before he was completely alone without transportation besides his own two feet. Being that Brook is a short man, and the poncho was a full length size large, it ate him alive. He called and I tried not to laugh when he exclaimed "I can't even walk because it's so long I am tripping over it!" His luck never seems to be high when it comes down to having the proper rain gear.

Brook's first night alone he called the local authorities to ask if there was anywhere they could recommend him sleeping. They didn't have any suggestions, but they did send out the sheriff to talk to him about an hour later. When the sheriff showed up, it was nine thirty at night and Brook was freezing from sitting out on a church stoop after having been rained on all day in the fall chill. The sheriff asked Brook where his route was taking him the following day. When Brook told him he said "I wouldn't go up there if I was you boy. There are some wicked folks up there that don't like strangers. You gotta gun?" When Brook informed him that he had a knife but no gun, the officer was neither reassuring nor comforting when he laughed and said "I'd look at that map and see if there was any other way you can walk, son." That night, the temperature got down to the mid thirties, and Brook slept on his sleeping pad under a tarp at a church in a tiny town called Monterey. The next morning the rain still hadn't let up.

"Just go get a hotel room honey, there is no point in you walking until you figure out a new route anyway. Because you sure aren't going where there are psycho hillbillies that'll kidnap you and eat you for dinner," I urged the next morning on the phone when I had been filled in on the sheriff's warning. Thankfully Brook listened.

He got a room at the only hotel in town, and relaxed all alone while cold rain poured down outside. When I asked him how it felt he said, "Stranger than I thought it would. Lonely, and boring. It was great to have the king size bed to myself though." Because his pack weighed about 45 pounds, and he didn't have the correct rain gear to press on this way for two more days, when he checked out of the hotel room the next day, we decided it was best for KO and me to return to him earlier than planned. We couldn't afford for him to lose one more day of mileage because it was getting colder each day that went by, so I cut short my campaigning and drove back to him. During my drive Wendy called and asked me how the four day break had felt.

"I never thought I'd get to this point, and I am surprised to be saying this right now, but home is where your family is, not a place. I didn't feel like I was at home because Brook wasn't there, and I don't think anything will ever feel normal for me without him there to partake in it with me."

That's an absolute truth for me now after being on the road for about six months and living the Spartan life. Home isn't a place; it's just the way you live with the people you love. I am happy I've arrived at this realization of home because it means that I will feel all the comforts of home that are so important like peace, laughter, joy, coziness, fun and rest wherever I am with my husband and child. It is life changing when you understand that you don't have to depend on a place or a building for those things. Life isn't about where you are, but who you are with. That's something I thank Jesus for everyday.

When I got back to Brook it was a challenge to snap back into using the one propane burner stove after using the five burner range my parents have. I didn't get a shower for three days when I returned, which was exponentially harder on me than it normally would be because I'd just had unlimited access to bathing for a few days. I was not a fan of sleeping in the car on the air mattress in the freezing temperatures either. We were both miserable by the time we were connected with a couple that lived in Knoxville that had agreed to host us. We gave them a day's notice of our arrival, and I hoped it wouldn't be too last minute to stay, because we were desperate for warmth and a shower. Sure enough, the woman who answered the phone was so excited to have us that she couldn't wait for us to arrive. I cried tears of joy that day when I was told my family wouldn't be sleeping in the cold after a crummy dinner and no shower yet again. God was good to us.

When we arrived at 7:30 that night, it was already forty degrees and pitch black outside. Fall had crept into our world with such subtlety that I was stunned by its presence. No longer could we even say that we were doing this over the summer, now we had to say this was a half year journey. Linda and Lee welcomed us into their home like you wouldn't believe. Lee is a loud talking, Larry the Cable Guy sounding, hard working, orange bleeding Tennessean. Linda has a drawl, happy eyes, and she looks southern in that tanned skin way that you only get here in the south, but she kept Lee in line the whole time we were there much to my laughter and amusement.

Their home is incredible. Every inch of it was stunning, each detail was carefully considered down to the light switches. KO was allowed to touch all that was within which was pretty darn relaxing to a stressed out parent like myself. There was wine and more food than we'd seen together in a long time. It was like Thanksgiving for us! Linda had made chicken casserole, pot roast, salad, potatoes and carrots and she'd even had appetizers set out for Lee and Brook while they watched, get this, a football game!!!

There isn't much in this country as quintessentially American as a football game. Tennessee was playing Alabama, and even though they were being slaughtered, Lee was still cheering, hooting and hollering like any good fan does from the sofa in their living room. What I love about fans is that even at a game you watch in your home, people will put on their teams colors and drink beer set in cozies that bear their teams' logo. Linda and Lee even had their appetizers on Tennessee Orange trays! I love that about America.

They set us up with two bedrooms, one with a queen bed for Brook and I and one with a queen bed and a crib for KO. I shared the queen bed in the nursery with KO and Brook got the other bed to himself. The first night we were there, when I took KO to lie in bed after he'd had a bath, and eaten a wholesome, home cooked meal, he looked up at me and gave me a look of incandescent bliss. He was comfy and grateful. My heart nearly exploded in my chest when he gave me that look. I got tears in my eyes as I snuggled him to sleep and I whispered in his little ear "We are almost there baby! And when we finish, I promise you will feel this comfy every night."

As I lied there teary with my heart full of the intense gratitude that comes from having one's needs met by unfathomable circumstances, I thanked God. I thanked him for every host family up to that point, and I prayed blessing over each one of them again and again. I recited Proverbs 11:25 NIV, "A generous man will prosper; he who refreshes others will himself be refreshed." I charged God with this promise and let Him know that I expected to hear good reports of times when all of the people who'd hosted us had been helped by complete strangers when they needed it the most.

Though I couldn't wait to give my son that same smile every night of his life in his own little bed, I was at peace remembering that in return for the suffering of my family, God was showering the gifts of kind stranger's hospitality over us like the clean water we were trying to shower over others far away. That night I begged God for there to be another mom that would see that same satisfied smile on their child's face after they got a drink of clean water, possibly for the first time in their life.

The next morning, Linda and Lee made us turkey and pork bacon, sausage gravy, biscuits, and eggs that came from their own chickens. Thank God for Southern Hospitality! Brook was exceptionally slow getting out of their house and back on the road after that meal.

Lee drove Brook to his starting point while I got to play and rest with KO, a welcome reprieve from our typical morning. With Lee's return came the excitement of "chicken time." "Chicken time" consisted of letting about twenty trained hens out of their coop to play, roam, and eat. KO got to feed the chickens and was highly interested in this new experience. He kept walking around and poking the chickens in the side which would of course make them hop away disgruntled. He laughed hysterically when he threw bread to them and they ran up all squawking and pecking to get the scrap. After all the birds we've fed throughout the journey, surely the blasted things will stop pooping on my head and my car.

Then Linda and Lee let their iconic American lab come out to play fetch. You would have thought that Mickey Mouse or Santa Claus had arrived as excited as KO was to play with this dog. He let him lick all over his face and laughed uncontrollably when the lab knocked him over in excitement. As a first time mom to a boy, especially after such little exposure to boys growing up, I realize why so many people write and talk about a boy and his dog. It's weirdly adorable to me now, though I used to think it was a cheesy greeting card concept.

After all that fetching and chicken feeding, KO was ready for a rest. He fell asleep as soon as his head was lied down, and I realized that he is doing that more and more lately. I never thought my son would go to sleep without an hour long battle of epic proportions, but just as I was growing in my maturity, he was too.

Lee left for work while KO napped. He worked in Virginia and it was a five hour drive. He wouldn't return until Friday evening. Every week, he is gone from Sunday night until Friday night, and Linda is all alone in that great big house when she gets home from work at night. I'd be lonely and bored with all that peace and quiet, and since I tend to get carried away with online shopping without any supervision, I'd be in a world of trouble with all that solitude. I casually asked Linda how she managed to be alone for so long, when *it* happened again.

Linda opened up to me about her loneliness, which led her to share about her intense battle with cervical cancer that she'd beaten just a few years earlier. The cancer wasn't the worse of it; it was only the little red caboose to her freight train of woe. She shared her marital issues and what it felt like to be in such a strange place of life, "I never thought this is where I would be when I was younger." Her story was one of the most pitiful I have ever heard. She fought cancer and went through chemo and radiation with an allergy to every pain and nausea medicine excepting morphine which she refused to take because she didn't want to gain dependence to it.

While she was going through all this physical pain, her beloved mother passed away from Alzheimer's. She had built her house planning for her mom to move in and to care for her, and when her cancer hit, her mother was admitted to an assisted living facility which absolutely crushed her. Then she had to deal with pain from family and her beloved spouse of twenty five years who she told me that "still gave me butterflies in my stomach every day until that year." The things she unloaded were shocking, ghastly and deeply private. She finished her remorseful tale by detailing the birth and death of her first granddaughter who passed away, after only six weeks, from an extremely rare genetic disorder.

Trying to imagine enduring that extensive pain was pointless, because no one can capture that suffering in a thought. As the untrained and unpaid therapist that I am, I engulfed her in a hug that I hoped was as comforting as a mother's goodnight kiss. I listened and made careful observations when I felt the conversation allowed them and I offered as much pity as I could. I prayed for her. Even though I felt that she needed me there that day to listen to her, I realized later that I needed her to share with me, because even through all that she survived, she loved the Lord. She gave Him all the credit for her recovery and healing, and she swore to me that without God carrying her through those miserable months, she wouldn't have been alive to share her tale with me.

I needed to be reminded of God's unfathomable power one more time; her story of survival and reliance on God was like a drink of cool water to my weary soul. I called my mother that day and told her jokingly, that I was enrolling in grad school as soon as I got home. I said, "Mom, would you ever share deep, painful secrets with someone that is basically a stranger? I just can't imagine sharing those types of private emotions and experiences with almost anyone, let alone someone I barely knew."

"Well honey, I think there are a lot of people out there with no one to listen to their woes and no one to care. Those are the types of people that will seek you out; lonely, hurting folks who need either a reality check or a little prayer and pity."

I don't mind in the least saying some prayers for people I barely know, or don't know at all for that matter. I definitely am getting used to hearing all the hardships of life from everyone that zeroes in on my invisible to me "Good-Listener" neon sign. I do wonder if God places these people in my path because there is no one else in the whole world to pray for them. I think if everyone that believed in prayer would pray for someone else regularly this world wouldn't be half so ugly.

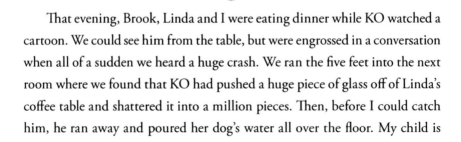

That evening, Brook, Linda and I were eating dinner while KO watched a cartoon. We could see him from the table, but were engrossed in a conversation when all of a sudden we heard a huge crash. We ran the five feet into the next room where we found that KO had pushed a huge piece of glass off of Linda's coffee table and shattered it into a million pieces. Then, before I could catch him, he ran away and poured her dog's water all over the floor. My child is impossible. Linda refused to let us replace the table and was just glad KO wasn't hurt. Brook wasn't very happy, and I was so frustrated. I knew that children existed in this world that are absolutely not safe when left to their own devices, but I never figured I'd have one of those kids. I couldn't wait to have my own fully bubble wrapped home in which my child could run headfirst into walls and not have a single consequence excepting a sore noggin.

We left the home of Linda and Lee clean, stuffed with delicious food, and rejuvenated. We headed back out into Hillbilly territory east of Knoxville, ever nearing our home state. KO and I went hiking in the mountains of Tennessee around this time. I had him in the backpack carrier and was looking over a cliff at a waterfall that was pouring down it into a bubbling pool below. I was trying to figure out how to climb down from the cliff to see the pool close up. I turned around to continue hiking and somehow got tangled up in a branch that was pulling us backwards *over the cliff.* I was fighting that branch with all the stamina and power I possessed but I couldn't see what was happening and I didn't understand how I was being pulled because I couldn't see the branch. I was yelling at KO because I figured he was holding onto something with Herculean strength, when all of a sudden he let out a pain stricken cry. I panicked. I craned my head around as far as I could, while pushing forward with all my might and finally saw the branch lodged in his carrier scraping his poor cheek and trapping us. I turned at an impossible angle and thankfully got loose from the tree.

We were safe but I had used every ounce of my strength to fight that branch and have never been so scared in my life. I decided that hiking alone might be a thing of the past. I had messed my back up in the tree fight, to the point where if I tried to turn my body, my breath was taken away. It stayed that way for a very long time. KO also bore an unsightly cheek scratch where the branch had accosted him.

I called my mom and told her about what had happened on the side of the cliff and she said, I am not even kidding, "I'm glad you're o.k., but man, if you guys had died I bet your book would have sold a bunch of copies. People eat that stuff up."

"Wow, Mom. If I was dead and gone I sincerely doubt book sales would matter that much to me." I was so glad that my own mother could take my near death experience so cavalier. I was reminded, yet again, that when I need a pity party, my mother is not the person to call. Why I forget this, after growing up and hearing "Do you want me to cut it off?" every time I whined about something being hurt, will never make sense to me. Perhaps she wasn't the most doting mother, but I guess all her threats to "cut it off" gave me the strength to fight that branch and everything else this adventure threw my way. I guess I should thank the woman for my thick skin next time I see a montage of my life flash before my eyes because I am about to pass into forever land only to somehow get pulled out of it.

Last night we slept in another hotel parking lot and froze our butts off. It was so cold that I had to do the old cover my head and inhale my own stale morning breath trick for hours on end. We woke up miserable, in pain and wet because KO had yet again wet through his diaper at the most inconvenient time(not that there is a convenient time for that but I would prefer it not in my only linens when I have nowhere to wash laundry and I am already miserable). We packed up and got the day started.

KO and I had picked up going into libraries about a month before when the weather started getting cold. That day, when we went into another library and I was confronted with yet another place that didn't have a child's changing station, I nearly blew a fuse. This is a problem I've encountered countless times throughout the country the past five months. I have been in more libraries, public parks, restaurants and shopping places than most people, which is why I can honestly ask why changing stations in public restrooms are so hard to find.

No public library should ever be without a changing station, *ever*, especially if there is a kids program at the library. It is absolutely ridiculous to assume that parents don't mind walking out to their cars to change their kid's diapers. And come on McDonalds, get with the program! I have been in more McDonalds that are without facilities for the diaper wearing crowd than I could ever imagine possible. City parks, places that are meant to be family friendly, are the worst culprits in this debacle. I cannot fathom the lack of consideration for others that goes into forgetting to place a changing station in a family friendly location. It infuriates me, complicates my life and makes me question the intelligence of others. Get with the program people, and put one of those fold out changing stations in every public bathroom that kids visit with their parents.

After we had two poopy diapers back to back at the library, both of which I had to leave our cozy warm reading station to go into the freezing cold car to change, I was struggling to be positive until I got a flood of good news. First, a woman called to host us for two nights in Johnson City, Tennessee, which would mean we'd be warm and comfy for the remainder of our time in The Volunteer State. I got an email from a massive church that had posted our story on their blog so we had gotten the word out about the clean water crisis that day. We also started getting offers for interviews in North Carolina that day. I perked up after God blessed me with so much encouraging news and had a great afternoon playing with KO in Tusculum, Tennessee.

In Tusculum, there is a quaint college tucked away. At this time of year, with all of the different colored leaves peacefully floating to the ground and dancing together in the wind, you can't ask for a prettier setting. I attended a large university which had a great landscaping team and is gorgeous in its own highly organized, well planned way, but Tusculum could boast an understated, cozy attractiveness that I hadn't yet seen from a campus. It just made me want to go "Ahhh." I will miss finding little spots like this after this journey is completed. When you get into a routine it can be hard to discover the "Ahhh" spots of life, but I am going to try hard to always look for places, people and things to move me. One of my most favorite things that KO does is insist on smelling every single flower we pass by. If we pass a pot of mums, which are everywhere this time of year, we do a whole lot of sniffing. I hope that after Brook's walk, KO won't forget to stop and smell as many flowers as he can.

As we enjoy our last host family in Tennessee, I've spent some time looking back over who we've stayed with, what we've experienced. I've compiled a large list of things I'll genuinely miss as we leave the life on the road:

◆When I use the bathroom in a host's house, I get to read all different types of literature that I wouldn't have at my own house. The past five months I've enjoyed medical journals, science magazines, architectural digests, Catholic subscriptions, the latest in massage therapy techniques, and a myriad of other toilet reads you will never find in my home. These little pages of foreign information have enriched my days and I daresay I will long for them when this is finished.

◆Meeting new people in such an intimate setting is not unlike being a scientist peering down through a microscope into a Petri dish. There's nothing like stripping away all the social expectations of meeting others in public and entering their safe haven as a stranger, observing them at the closest range imaginable. Getting to see all different types of people living life in varied and meaningful ways forces you to appreciate humanity's uniqueness and praise God for His love of individuality.

◆I will miss taking my sweater out of my bag and wondering where the hair that is stuck to it came from. Was is the Great Dane at the family in Boise's or was it the Laundry cat in Kansas? Having a piece of each place with you that you keep on finding is magical.

◆People in this country can cook! Both my palate and my stomach are going to yearn for all the new recipes we got to try coast to coast.

◆It's exciting to step into a house and know that you are about to be served. Every single person that hosted us around this nation was hospitable and welcoming, and though I have missed having my own home, it will be hard to leave the life of being served by others because it makes me so grateful to God for His own servant Jesus.

More than anything, I will miss meeting new people and hearing their stories. The tales we've been told from our hosts are enchanting and have kept me going through some of my darkest moments on this journey, and beyond.

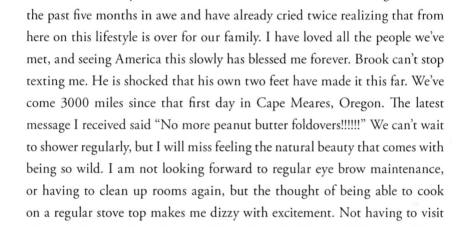

It is our last day before we enter North Carolina. I am looking back over the past five months in awe and have already cried twice realizing that from here on this lifestyle is over for our family. I have loved all the people we've met, and seeing America this slowly has blessed me forever. Brook can't stop texting me. He is shocked that his own two feet have made it this far. We've come 3000 miles since that first day in Cape Meares, Oregon. The latest message I received said "No more peanut butter foldovers!!!!!!" We can't wait to shower regularly, but I will miss feeling the natural beauty that comes with being so wild. I am not looking forward to regular eye brow maintenance, or having to clean up rooms again, but the thought of being able to cook on a regular stove top makes me dizzy with excitement. Not having to visit playgrounds every day, all day, will be such a relief. Having KO potty trained and tamed to a more normal standard of wild will be fantastic. Getting my husband back safe from the mercy of crazy drivers and psycho hillbillies will mean so much for my nerves. There is a trade off in my mind, as there always is with us fickle humans. We are leaving a lot of special things for a different set of blessings as we close this misadventure story.

Of all the things I'll miss, I'll long for my time alone in the wild with my family and God the most. When you are out there struggling for everything it makes you rely on whoever is with you so much more than you do in a comfortable environment, and I am afraid I will not rely on God and Brook in a way that has been so great for my growth after this is over. I also will miss the tranquility that comes when one suffers for the good of another. I have kept little Isaac in my heart these long five months and dreaming about seeing the wells we suffered for in a village in Africa has kept me from losing my patience, endurance and mind many days out here. I only hope that as we transition back into the mainstream, we can find a way of life that will continue to provide useful blessings for others.

Thinking about where I've been makes me wonder about where I am going. Will we be able to revert back to using a flushing toilet instead of the woods? How will I cope with regular interaction with neighbors after not having any for so long? Will I be able to remember to feed my cat after trying to keep food away from animals for five months? And how will Brook handle his life without walking for eight hours a day? Will KO and Brook be able to mesh together again with more time to play and enjoy each other? The thought of looking for new jobs and a place to live makes me queasy. I've prayed a lot today for God to take my next few weeks as we wrap this up and organize it so that as we complete our journey we can be brought into something new peacefully.

I woke up in Johnson City, Tennessee on October 28th excited because I had booked my first live television interview the day before. I had gone shopping and bought a new pair of shoes and a sweater to wear in the piece. I arrived at the TV station feeling glamorous and excited to share our story with the viewers in the area. They gave me a microphone to wear, and I prayed to God that I wouldn't have something mega embarrassing happen like passing gas or falling backward in my chair. I wore my new shoes, leggings, and a white blouse with a belt around my waist and the black sweater. I spoke about the clean water crisis and did my best to share our story in the four minute segment. KO was there with me, the station's receptionist played with him while I went on. As soon as I returned to him, he stood up, packed up his diaper bag and said "Bye-Bye."

"He's got it right," I thought, "it is about time to pack up and say bye-bye."

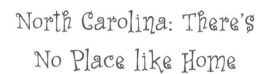

North Carolina: There's No Place like Home

"So we make it our goal to please Him, whether we are at home in the body or away from it." 2 Corinthians 5:9 NIV

A few hours later, Wendy and Frank had joined us and my parents were on their way to our meeting spot. We gathered together and joined as a large band of walkers to cheer our last few miles from Tennessee into North Carolina. On Friday, October 28th, 2011 in the freezing rain, my husband, alongside his parents, my parents, my sister Caeley and me and KO, marched in a line down a busy trucking route that was horribly loud. We got a whole lot of looks as we paraded on our way to the "Welcome to North Carolina" sign. I bawled as we took pictures on that cold, rainy day. My tears were of joy for finally making it, sadness for leaving behind our adventure, and overwhelming emotional excitement at the prospects to come. I was so proud of Brook; we all were just amazed that he had finally made it home.

I asked Brook how he felt, and of course he said he didn't feel much different, he didn't think he would until he hit the Atlantic Ocean; but I could tell he was excited when he grabbed KO and ran to the sign with him in his arms. As we faced the last three weeks of our journey, with only about 350 miles more, we felt so relieved. It was one of the most special moments I have ever lived, crossing over that border, and I will always cherish that feeling of accomplishment in doing God's will.

The next morning we woke up in Banner Elk, NC, to snow falling rapidly from the sky. This was an early snow storm for N.C. We were excited to play in it with KO, but irritated when we realized that we couldn't walk that day and were going to get behind. We had a blast throwing snowballs, playing with our son, Wendy and Frank in the white winter fluff. We headed back to Advance, NC where we had grown up and where we had a speaking engagement the next day after our fun as we were unable to walk in the poor road conditions.

One of my best friends was throwing a party that evening and we went. When we arrived at the party it was every level of strange for us. Being with a group our age, letting loose, playing music and video games; the whole arena of socialization was foreign to our senses. We had a great time and enjoyed sharing our stories, which most everyone was interested to hear. You know when you go to a party and you don't feel like you have a lot to talk about besides the weather or a sports team, the topics we always revert to that can bore the heck out the best of us? I realized that never again would I be at a party with nothing to talk about. I had enough stories in my arsenal for every party that I attended for the rest of my life, and I was only twenty two!

As we drove home Brook and I talked about how weird we felt with everyone. "I'm not sure we are cut out for this anymore baby," Brook said to me, and I understood what he meant. We had changed in every way the past five months. I thought that perhaps when soldiers return home after war they probably go through a much more intense version of what we were experiencing.

The next morning, we woke up and prepared to speak to the congregation at Cornerstone Christian Church in Advance, NC. We went up on stage in front of everyone that day excited to share our story of God's amazing provision. It was His provision for us to have food, lodging and fun through the generosity of others and His provision for clean water through our sacrifice of time and efforts. We shared about Mick, the possible (cigarette smoking) angel, and how rewarding it feels to be so near to finishing a job like this. Afterward, we were prayed for by the pastor, and then we enjoyed a church service. It was a fantastic feeling. When the service was over, we waited in the lobby at a table with information about where people could donate and how they could help the clean water crisis. We were handed twenty dollar bill after twenty dollar bill. People didn't care about the tax deduction, they just wanted to help. So many stopped just to say thanks to Brook for his walk and congratulate us. It was kind of like our wedding day, with tons of people we barely knew or didn't know at all coming up and cheering us on. Afterwards, I was so exhausted I could barely think straight.

It may have been the party the night before, but I am fairly certain my exhaustion was the result of realizing how many people I was going to meet the next few weeks, months, and years. People that would need something from me, a story, perhaps a swift kick in the butt like the tow truck driver, or maybe just a handshake and an assurance that there is something bigger out there worth working for, living for, even dying for. I told Brook that I understood how presidents aged so much in their short four year terms. They had so many people taking from them that there was no way it couldn't wear them out.

Caeley, my baby sister, turned eleven a few weeks earlier and had waited for us to return to N.C. to be baptized. She wanted to be baptized in a pond or a river, like Jesus, and not a baptismal. She was baptized on October 30th in a cold pond; and as she came out of that cold water, with pond scum in her hair and smelling funky, I was reminded that my exhaustion was well worth keeping other 11 year old girls from having to wash their bodies in ponds around the world as a regular practice. Getting baptized in a pond when you can rush home and take a shower is one thing, but having to bathe amidst algae and pond scum is another. I was tired from all of the public speaking, storytelling, traveling and change. I was tired for an incredible cause, and it was well worth it.

The next day we had a radio interview which was a lot of fun. Radio is a great medium and I often wish my generation could enjoy it like they did in the olden days when families would gather around to listen to programs together. Listening is such a lost art, just to be able to sit and let words and sounds consume me is an act I wish I was better at. After the radio interview, we had to go to our storage unit to get a few things for our remaining weeks of walking. I had been in the storage unit when I returned two weeks before and it was shocking to me to see how much stuff we owned. I tried to prepare Brook for the sheer volume of possessions we had accumulated over the four years we'd been married. When he opened the door and flipped on the light he became very quiet.

"Well, I guess we know where we'll be and what we'll be doing when I finish walking," Brook said after a minute pause as he took everything in. We both were so overwhelmed after having and needing so little that we agreed we just didn't see the point in owning half of what was in the storage unit. The sheer excess of my wardrobe alone bothered me so much I started giving away as many things as I could to friends and my three sisters.

The following day, Brook and I were the guest lecturers at a community college for an extra credit assignment. My sister LeiLani created these water droplets out of paper and had recruited her entire student body to buy these droplets for $1 in order to fundraise for our walk. Altogether, they had raised about $550 towards our cause. We were asked to come speak to the group because of their efforts and we were thrilled for the opportunity to share with them as they had all committed to the walk and helped make a difference. We arrived and had set up our presentation, when all of these early college students filed in looking like they could care less about the clean water crisis or a nutso guy who walked across the country. They surprised me the longer we were with them. They asked great questions, and were visually bothered by our presentation of what was happening to women and children in developing countries on their trek to get water.

They laughed at us when we told them about our adventures, and most of them paid close attention to what we were saying. The class surprised us both by wanting to hear more about our relationship than the walk. They wanted to know how long we'd been together, where we'd met and how we'd gotten married so early. I keep looking younger and younger according to my sisters and closest friends, Brook does as well, so maybe it's because we both look like we are about 15 or maybe it's because they were so hopeful to hear about a young relationship that thrived on past high-school, college and now into the twenties. For whatever reason, it touched me. I think I was so moved by their desire to hear about our relationship because it reminded me of what it felt like to be 17, to wonder what was going to happen to my newfound love of another person. I was trying to get these kids to understand that they could make a difference for others by volunteering, donating, and raising awareness and they were opening my eyes to how far I've come since I was their age. It was a wild revelation. That was a fun hour for Brook and me. We both left reminded of the special relationship we'd been gifted seven years ago. It seems that every time I go into something to teach others, I end up learning something new myself. I like that about humanity; that we are always teaching each other. As long as we wake up every day eager to learn, I figure we'll get out to the other side pretty decently.

I am writing right now, from a public library in the high country of North Carolina. I am surrounded by magazines, books, and newspapers. As they peer out at me from their shelves I am wondering where they were written, what the person who wrote them did to prepare their words, and how the authors must feel being published and successful in the completion of a project. My book has been written across America, on a beat up old laptop that has to be plugged in or it loses its charge in 30 minutes. I have typed these words at parks, in the woods, in houses of kind strangers, at hotels and motels, on mountains, in valleys, and in Wal-Mart parking lots. I have stayed up late to get a few hundred words out, and I have woken up early to do the same. My stories are written because I've lived them. All I had to do to prepare was show up in this big thing we call life and be open to whatever came my way. I don't know if I'll ever be published, or if I will ever get to see a book written by me sitting on a shelf in a library, but I do know that if I've learned anything this summer and fall, it's that our stories must be told.

We were interviewed today by a local newspaper in Boone and the man interviewing us was very direct, had thoughtful questions, and was masterful at capturing our story through his probing. I wanted to know how he had grown so skilled at interviewing. Was he born that way or did he learn through practice? Maybe I'm too curious, but this journey has helped me to hyper focus on the paragraphs of life that we live with others. I lived a paragraph with that reporter, and he and I will have so many more pages filled with other stories; life is one page turner of a book.

The reporter asked two questions that I thought were fantastic. He asked me if Brook was a changed man after this experience. I replied that he was a "new and improved version." Though Brook will always suffer from Numberitis, and though I will always be married to a little old man, he has learned to adapt to small things that go wrong. He is letting life's unimportant blunders roll off his shoulders in a way I could never have imagined possible. He is also more outgoing. He used to be so quiet and brooding; now, he's talkative and brooding, which I find more interesting and a lot more fun. He will hold captivating conversations with strangers and he doesn't rely on me to carry him through a discussion with new people as he would have before. He has also gotten a lot of that adventure bug out over the past five months in a necessary and productive way. His walk was exactly the escapade he needed, and it is doing great things in the lives of others, which is why I am excited that he was able to do it at this time in our lives. And lastly, he is going to be so much cooler with who KO is shaping up to be after this summer, which I think is one of the best changes that could have happened. Our son is a wild, free spirited, adventurous conqueror and now that Brook has walked across the country, I think he'll be a little more receptive to handle all that is KO.

The second question that I appreciated, the question that we get asked tirelessly is, "What's next?" I was refreshed to find that when we told him we had absolutely no idea as to who, what, when, where, why or how we are going to live after this, instead of being a tad awkward about it, I was just plain excited. We have no home, no jobs, just about no money, and I am excited.

I figure that if God is going to bring us down to such a level of unknowns, there's something coming that is worth getting butterflies over. And so we wait to see where all this will go.

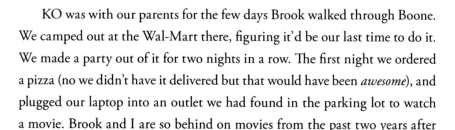

KO was with our parents for the few days Brook walked through Boone. We camped out at the Wal-Mart there, figuring it'd be our last time to do it. We made a party out of it for two nights in a row. The first night we ordered a pizza (no we didn't have it delivered but that would have been *awesome*), and plugged our laptop into an outlet we had found in the parking lot to watch a movie. Brook and I are so behind on movies from the past two years after becoming parents and then living on the road that we have a lot of catching up to do. We were shocked that Redbox had raised their price 20 cents, and Brook immediately started calculating how much this increase could cost our family in a year long stretch.

When we went in Wal-Mart to use the bathroom in the mornings, I felt my excessive weirdness acutely. We were a mere 90 miles from where we had grown up and our parents lived, we knew people that could host us in the area, but we had *wanted* to freeze our butts off in the back of the truck together one last time. I told my mother on the phone that I hadn't realized how strange I'd become until it dawned on me that I wanted to sleep in a Wal-Mart parking lot in 30 degree frosts with my stinky husband. She said we'd grow out of it, like it was a phase we were going through. I'm not sure she was right about that, only time will tell, but she also said "If I were you guys, I'd sleep in Wal-Mart parking lots at least once a year for old time's sake. Since you seem to like it so much."

I could just picture Brook and I having an annual Wal-Mart parking lot campout together. It would become a family holiday, for sure. We'd drop off KO and any other kids we may have at grandparents houses until they were old enough or crazy enough to want to participate, drive to a Wal-Mart in the next town over (so people we knew wouldn't recognize our car chilling in the lot and come over to say hi), go inside and buy a six pack, blow up the air mattress and settle in for the night to laugh at having to sleep under a ridiculously bright street lamp while the cart guys made as much noise as an elephant stampede collecting the grocery buggies from the islands around us. I'd even pull out my pigeon lady sweater and Brook's old, beat up hoodie so we could wear the same clothes we wore this year. Some couples go on spa retreats, some go on wine country tours, but me and my man; we camp out in Wal-Mart parking lots in homeless attire. Our kids are going to need a lot of therapy one day.

Once Brook made his way down from Boone and on through Wilkesboro we were close enough to stay with our folks again for a few days. Having my body enveloped in the feathery perfection that is my bed after five months of dreaming about it was wonderful in ways words will never capture. Leaving my bed for the last two weeks of the journey was not distant from torture. We were at Frank and Wendy's on the last night before we headed off into Greensboro and the rest of N.C., when Brook pulled me aside and showed me our donation website. He revealed that there had been a five thousand dollar donation made by his parents that day. They had donated enough to buy an entire well, a well that would help 250 people for years to come.

Though I wasn't entirely surprised, I was wholly grateful. I think the appreciation I felt for my in-laws was so deep after this adventure because they had pushed themselves beyond every level of comfort in order that they might support us. To have someone do that for you is something that you had better be grateful for! I tried to formulate words to thank them. I practiced in my mind things like "Wow! That was quite a donation you guys made!" and "Thank you thank you thank you!" I couldn't muster up enough words to express my gratitude in the feeble grey cells I had left. Eventually I settled for the simple, honest "That was an incredible gift, thank you both forever." It wasn't Shakespearian, or even poetic. I hate that about myself! I never feel like I express my gratefulness adequately. But I wonder if it is possible to express thankfulness fully to anyone in this world especially after such an incredible act of love.

During my college years, I babysat for an awesome family. The parents were young, cool, and ultra understanding. Their kids were fun and I adored being with their two year old daughter for about twenty hours a week. I've kept in touch and we've gotten our little monkey together with their little monkeys to play. When Brook got close enough to their area with his trek, I called and asked if we could crash at their home. Only the dad, Michael, would be in town but he said he'd welcome the company, and so the three of us invaded Michael's solitude.

I already dream of time away from my boys. A weekend without Brook and KO to drive me insane is something of a mythical fantasy. I wish for it at particularly difficult moments such as when Brook is exhibiting classic Numberitis or KO is throwing mash potatoes in my clean hair. Here was this dad of three awesome but rambunctious kids in his house alone for a few days. With one day's notice we were the invaders, taking over his peace. Michael took our company like a trooper. He nicknamed Brook the "Dawn Treader," which was a welcome change from Forest Gump for all of us. He fed us the first night and we had a good time catching up. We slept in his son's Superman bed under the world's most famous crest, that golden 'S'. We were warm, well fed and blessed. The next day, KO and I played at his house all day. It was funny to me because I'd spent so much time playing with Michael's own children there and now I was playing with my son on the same equipment and with the same toys. This trip had certainly refreshed my memory of every inch I'd ever lived.

Graduating from UNC requires you to have some sort of team spirit. Seriously, you can't make it through the rigorous sea of blue without a little love for the Tar Heels. When Veterans Day rolled around and we heard about UNC playing a basketball game on the USS Carl Vinson against Michigan State, we were pretty stoked that we got to watch the game at Michael's. The game was a spectacle for the eyes. The president was there, and while we watched, we commented on the political state with Michael, especially on Obama's promise to pull troops out of Iraq by Christmas this year. Michael, who served in the navy when he was about our age had a lot to say, and we had a lot to listen to. The halftime show rolled on and we laughed when Brooklyn Decker didn't make a single free throw shot during the half time show.

The game progressed and Michael started to talk about watching the Chicago Bulls "back in the day" and we laughed with him as he realized how old he was sounding. When he stood up to go to bed his entire body creaked. Every single joint popped that awful pop that makes so many of us cringe. Michael started to laugh and said, "Just wait. Another ten years and that's what you're going to sound like!" For whatever reason, Brook and I died laughing. Probably because it was so true and terrifying that the only way we could face it was with laughter. Everyone ages, and so long as we are still having fun like Michael and his wife Victoria, I am ok with some creaky joints and the ability to tell "back in my day" stories. Our time in Cary at Michael's home was a much needed dose of fun and good company. We could feel our desire to finish growing ever stronger as we departed from yet another friend's home.

Brook's parents met us again as we left Cary in order that I might walk with Brook for a few days. They took KO, and I set off for my first ever full day walking with Brook. I'd walked mostly 14 mile days with him so far. I had done it without major discomforts, besides the bathroom emergencies I've told you about, and I desperately wanted to get at least one 20 mile day in before he finished the walk.

It was important to me to get a twenty mile day in because Brook walked an average of twenty miles a day during his trek. He took a lot of days off, and usually he walked closer to 25-30 miles a day when he was walking, but I felt like 20 would cut it for my personal satisfaction. We had been walking for about two hours when we ran into a lady picking up trash at a small, private airport. She was so excited to hear our story that she sent us on over to meet all the other pilots at the Kennebunk Flight Club in the Angier, NC area. These were some daring folks, all pilots of small planes looking for the latest in adventure. They were all over the age of sixty as well. I hope to God that when I am older than 60 I can still be wild and free, flying planes or whatever else they have when that time comes!

As our walk stretched on, I was doing fine. There were a lot of bathrooms because it was a populated area, so I wasn't too hard off. Then we hit 15 miles. Once we hit that magic number 15, my body began to protest, and by 17 I was in agony. My joints were whining under the pressure, and my poor slob of a knee was rigorously complaining. We had been talking cheerfully and happily for hours but I grew quiet. I had to draw up on my mental strength to diffuse the discomfort and mechanically put one leg in front of the other for that last hour and three miles. "So this is what it feels like huh?" I asked while sweat beads formed a lovely crown on my forehead.

"What'd'ya mean? Oh! You're feeling it now huh? It'll be over soon baby. Just focus on whatever else you can or you'll get grouchy like I always do."

My husband, always the wise sage instructed me. His instruction fell on sun burnt ears that were tired of listening to cars and tractor trailers pass by noisily. "No wonder you wear earplugs!" I fussed at one point during that miserable hour. What was so overwhelming wasn't the physical discomfort, but it was the realization that if I was in one of the cars that was whizzing by me obnoxiously I'd be to my destination 10 times faster. I asked Brook if he thought that thought often and he replied, "I did at first, when I was getting the mental training that I needed. It took me through Oregon to realize that to keep my mind on the task at hand I needed to pretend that cars weren't an option for me. I just told myself that they weren't a tool I was capable of using and focused on the two tools I had: my legs."

Wendy and Frank set us up in a hotel room that night. I have never been so relieved to get off my feet. My body was exhausted and I was extremely hungry. I ate a bazillion calories that night. The next day I could barely bend my bad knee. Don't get me started on the rest of my body. I am telling you all of this whiny sob story because it was my first real glimpse at what my husband had been doing day in and day out for over five months. I was beyond impressed because I would have given up ages ago had I been the walker. I would have woken up one day and said "There is no way in heck that I am going to put myself through one more second of this kind of pain, boredom or monotony. No way, no how."

219

But Brook didn't give up. He kept on going, for five months, for thousands of miles in all variations of extreme and awful weather on his lone two feet. He didn't always do it cheerfully, and he didn't always do it without some cussing and fussing, but he had done it. We were so close and I was just beginning to fully appreciate the gravity of what we had accomplished.

One of my best friends has a very cool mom. Her name is Caroline and we have been visiting her for years. She lives in Burgaw which is about 30 miles west of Wilmington off of I-40, so we were excited to have a place to stay for the few days leading up to our grand finale. Caroline has three daughters, all of which she raised on her own and all of which are incredible. Caroline was recently laid off from her very well paying job due to the economic fiasco of our nation and has been searching far and wide for employment. With a mortgage, three college tuitions to take care of and all the other pressures of single parenthood; I have always been enamored by her positive outlook in the face of so much work. I fully understood the need for resolve in our country while I watched Caroline actively pursuing the answer to her problem. There were books piled all over her home with interviewing tips, resume examples, and pointers on how to make it ahead of the other 13 million or so unemployed people in this country.

Our first night at her home, we sat down to relax after getting KO to sleep. We watched Caroline's favorite reality TV show which featured a lot of singing groups fighting for a record deal. It was a typical night at Caroline's; we were well fed, and relaxed. I wondered why we were always so peaceful there, when I came to these simple conclusions. For starters, her home is so peaceful because it is in the middle of the boonies. Her home is this darling country farmhouse plopped down on acreage where umpteen cats and her sweet old pooch Logan play. Logan is getting gray hair. I didn't know dogs could get gray hair. Magical things like graying dogs and umpteen farm cats increase one's chances of being relaxed. The second reason we were chilled out was because Caroline is that way. Her peace transfers to you. I've been at Caroline's when there were baby showers and the big preparations of a wedding day going on, and somehow, amidst all of that hustle, bustle and excitement her home remained peaceful. She is a transcendent chillaxer.

Caroline has these little signs all over. You know the types, they say encouraging or funny sayings like "Home is where my dog is," "Live, Love, Laugh," "Smile, Jesus loves you" or my personal favorite that she has hanging in her bathroom which reads "Changing the toilet roll will not cause any brain damage." Caroline has signs everywhere, and though I didn't think it could be possible, they caused me to slow down, chill out, laugh, and dust all the little irritations of life off my shoulders while we spent two days at her home. If I ever live in something besides my car I am going to have signs up like Caroline's all over the place.

KO loves being in the country. He'd picked up this habit of howling at the moon every night while we were in Colorado, so we went outside and howled at the night sky before bed even though the moon was nowhere to be seen. It was refreshing to know that our howling wasn't going to bother any neighbors, because it certainly had done so at some of our motel stays. They were harvesting crops down the road from Caroline's house and scads of "bub-bubs" (KO's word for tractors) drove by during the day which tickled KO to the brink. This boy loved space to roam and to howl at the moon. We left Caroline's well rested and filled with the peace that come's from quality time with good friends and the quiet of farm country.

Two days before the end of the walk, we were waiting for Frank and Wendy to arrive in Carolina Beach where we'd rented a beach house to stay for the last few days of the journey. I picked Brook up from his last 20+ mile day and was so cheerful I couldn't stand it. Brook didn't share my sentiments. "I just don't feel right seeing the ocean before I finish. It seems cheap, like I'm not earning the grand finale I have been waiting for the past five months."

Brook is so black and white and some days it can drive me so crazy I can't stand it, but for once, this need to be an absolutist made sense. I offered up what seemed to be a compromise in my mind. "Why don't we, just the three of us, go see the beach before anyone gets here and before this circus act begins? It'll be our own little celebration of making it, and we can do it, our little family all alone."

He bought my idea, and so we parked the car and walked down to the same beach access point we'd entered a hundred times before when we'd lived a few blocks away.

It was dusk as we headed to our sandy shore. The aromatic air, which hinted at salt, dive bars and oysters, greeted us like old friends. The wind was whipping my hair and little KO's golden locks all over. KO bolted ahead, but we grabbed his hands and the three of us, linked arm in arm, ran out onto the sand as a little unit locked into that most glorious moment. It was everything cheesy, emotional and theatrical that you expect in feel good movie endings. We ran around laughing, crying, cheering, and just breathing the completion of our task. Brook had about 17 miles left to walk, but for all intensive purposes we had made it. That moment on the beach goes down in my life as the best moment I've ever had on a shore. I felt God there, in the sand, in the sea air, and in my heart. God was overflowing from my innermost depths in the abundant tears that fell from my eyes. I reached out and grabbed a little part of God's joy as I ran out onto that beach with my boys, it was as near to perfect as I could ask. I asked Brook how he felt after our time on the beach and he just smiled. That was enough for me.

Later that night, we picked up the keys to the house we had rented and Brook's parents and grandmother arrived. We nestled in snug and happy that night, and I was so pleased to be falling asleep with sand between my toes that I cried a few more joyful tears as I dozed off.

I woke up this morning with a weighty heart. I slept three hours last night because all I could think about was the end. I just couldn't wrap my feeble mind around the completion of our task. I'd dreamed of it for so long, but I guess I didn't think it'd ever happen. That's probably how most people feel when their greatest project is coming to a close.

We got ready, and I dropped Brook and Frank off for the very last time. Tomorrow would be the last day of our journey, but today was the last 'long' day at 15 miles. When I left them there at that grocery store I began to cry again. Every tear that fell from my eyes was a memory of the moments of the trip where I'd felt God's impact in our travels. One tear was the laughter at the bear break in, one tear was the smell of hog farm and warm sleep, another was time spent with my beloved son at yet another city park. As I gathered my memories in a McDonald's napkin and cleared my eyes, I felt that nauseating, overwhelming joy that can only be felt; no words or explanations will ever capture it. I am stunned when I reflect on my life so far. I have wonderful parents and in-laws who love and bless me. I am the big sister to three amazing gals and a younger brother in law. I have just about the most incredible husband in the world. My friends are the best that exist and I couldn't ask for a child more perfectly suited to me than my KO. Best of all, I have a God that can see me through even the most outrageous of misadventures and obstacles. That inescapable mirth that was making me cry in our victory was a happiness I never thought was possible.

I got a tad neurotic that last 'long' day. I went to run some errands and every person I came across I insisted on telling about our journey. "My husband just walked across the country for charity," I said to the lady in line for the ATM in front of me. "Congratulations," she said warily and tried to take a step back without me noticing. I was apparently too joyous for her personal space. Six months ago I'd have reacted the same way to a stranger telling me such an outlandish tale while I was withdrawing money from my account. But the joy! Oh what a treasure to be imprinted on my mind and cherished for the rest of my life. I couldn't hoard it; it was a thing that must be shared.

Later that night, I sat around the dinner table with my father and mother in-law and Brook's sweet Nanny. They were glowing with pride. They looked like something that Botticelli would paint with brightness exuding from their faces and a mysterious joy emanating from their bespectacled eyes. Wendy and Nan have the same fair hair and blue-green eyes that Brook does, but otherwise Brook looks like his father. Watching the generations around the table, I could catch glimpses of each person in every other person. No one individual was complete without the parts of the other. As I viewed these connections between the old and young, with the glowing pride and joy spilling out from the people in the room with me, I thanked God. I thanked him deeply, lovingly, honestly and wholly. When I am old and dying, I hope to remember that meal around the table the night before we finished our 3300 mile cross country walk, watching my husband's grandmother and parents smile down on their son and grandson with a love and pride that evades description.

My parents arrived just after that dinner, along with my baby sister Caeley and little Johnny. I was deeply glad that they were there to be a part of our victory.

It was November 18th. The day had arrived. I woke up after another sleepless night with butterflies in my stomach. I rolled over and told Brook that the day had finally come. He told me it was too early and to leave him alone. I got up with KO and started making breakfast.

"This is the last day that I will make breakfast for my son on our journey across America. This is the last day my son will be 1! This is the last day I will have to wrestle Brook into the car for drop off. This is the last day my husband will walk. This is the last day!"

Three little words kept creeping into my thoughts, and they weren't eloquent or profound, but they were just right. "We did it!" All those painfully hot days, freezing cold nights, cans of beans, instant noodles, and miles and miles and miles were about to be completed. We had made it. We gathered together, Brook, myself, KO (on my back in his back pack carrier), our four parents, Nanny, Caeley, Jonny, and our friend Justin. Wendy, Nan, Caeley and I had made posters that we carried, and a friend of Frank's had designed, printed and donated a bunch of matching t-shirts that we all wore. Brook filled a Jerry can full, it weighed forty pounds. He wrapped straps around it, similarly to how the small women and children do around the world every day as they prepare to lug their own forty pound jugs home from their water sources. He heaved it up onto his back with the help of Frank and prepared to carry it the final two and a half miles of his 3,300 mile walk. I asked him how he felt, as we embarked on our little march, and he just said "It feels good to be finishing."

We said a group prayer and thanked God for the past five and a half months of safety, provision, and growth. We prayed that clean water would become a reality for those who don't have it, and that our final steps would mean the end of other dangerous walks for water around the world. Then we set off. I was laughing, crying, cheering, praying, and walking. Brook heaved that Jerry can and kept telling us all how it was tearing into his shoulders. I'm not sure whether it was the literal can that was such a burden, or the figurative journey he was about to unload on Carolina Beach that cold November day, but he was certainly feeling the pain of women and children from around the world in every one of those forty pounds of water.

Local news showed up, and they photographed and film our family as we walked down the main strip into Carolina Beach. People passing by stopped and asked what we were doing; many thought we were protesting Wall Street. When they heard our story, they smiled, congratulated us, and some of them even joined us at the beach to celebrate. When I saw the boardwalk that we'd walked on just a few nights before, tears saturated my cheeks. My heart beat faster and faster as we charged onto the sand. Brook dropped the Jerry can.

I grabbed KO out of his pack, and with our son in our arms we ran into the ocean. That was it, we had finished!

"We did it!" Photo Credit: Wendy Hinman

Our family joined us in the water; we danced around the beach laughing, hugging, cheering, and merry making. We were interviewed briefly by the local news but not invasively, and we were showered with congratulations. The last day of the walk was exactly what I had hoped it would be: a storybook crisp autumn day, filled with loved ones and overflowing joy. There were strangers and media speckling the horizon like seagulls and adding to the ambiance but not invading the moment. God was there again. My spirit soared on that blustery beach.

Then we were done. It was the strangest feeling I have ever had. We picked up the Jerry can as we were leaving the beach, and Brook painfully heaved it a little ways until he started to complain about how much pain his back was in. I took the lid off the can and began to dump the water out. "Angel, how can you waste all that water?" Brook exclaimed, but it was time to dump out that water, it was time to empty out that Jerry can, and it was time to call it a day, all the way.

We had more fun with our family that day than I'd like to admit. We had a huge dinner that evening, and more people had arrived to celebrate with us. My little sister LeiLani and her boyfriend arrived, along with my two best friends. Some of our beach buddies came to dinner and we ate and drank and celebrated. The next day, I had planned a victory lap at a park in Wilmington, so I had to run all sorts of errands before I could rest my weary head that night. I looked over all of the people that I loved and appreciated in that room, eating and laughing, and I felt God again. Such a peace and wholeness rested in me as I slipped out from the merry making into that cold night.

My two best friends are twins named Shawn and Deidre. We have been beside each other through middle school awkwardness, high school drama, and young adult lessons. Every milestone that I have hit, they have been present at, and this was no exception. We went out to pick up balloons and cake, decorations and food for the wrap up party the next day. We caught up as we drove around Wilmington picking up party supplies for the victory lap and presents for KO's 2nd birthday. They filled me in on their lives and I had so much fun! I kept saying, "I can't believe its over," and they showered me with smiles and hugs. We returned to the beach house laden with goodies and we wrote celebratory messages all over everyone's car windows with one of those window pens. I went to bed just as my final sister arrived to make it to our victory lap the next morning. As I fell asleep I counted all the loved ones I had under one roof supporting me and my husband, thirteen in all. How blessed I was!

The next morning, KO woke up to his second year of life. I got up and I took him to see his birthday balloon! It was a giant Thomas the Train and he was ecstatic. We kept the celebration going from the night before, and we all just ate and laughed. Shawn, Deidre and my mother helped me prepare the park for the victory lap, and everyone arrived to join us for our celebration. We had pictures provided by Wendy for people to look at, the Jerry can, printouts of our blog entries and my favorite part: the maps. Wendy had procured state maps of all of the states we had walked through from her AAA office. We had outlined the route Brook had walked the night before and I was transported all the way back to Oregon, and through the ten states we traversed one last time. It truly was a gift to see the final map, with the whole trek highlighted on it. Family, friends, our entire church body, and even a few strangers showed up to walk around the park and cheer on God's incredible work. Our victory lap was filled with laughter, stories and joy.

"If you feel God calling you to take a leap of faith, you better jump full force." Photo Credit: Wendy Hinman

As we finished our lap and ate cake under the park shelter, Brook gave a short speech. He gave God the glory for the walk, thanked every single person present and far away for their donations, prayers, and help. Then he charged the crowd that was gathered there. "If you feel God calling you to take a leap of faith," he began, "then you better jump full force. Don't hesitate, don't calculate, and don't try and run away. If you're issued a challenge from God then you are a blessed person, and you will be far more blessed if you see His invitation for faith all the way through."

We left Wilmington, NC that afternoon exhausted from five and a half months of poor sleep, constant traveling and in Brook's case, a 3,300 mile walk through every terrain and weather pattern imaginable. We also left with the satisfaction that we had completed the task at hand. God had seen us through in order that entire communities in Africa might not ever have to struggle with a walk for water. Our Living Water had made water for life a possibility, and we were eternally grateful for His provision as we drove down I-40 back home.

The Aftermath and the After Party

"For by grace you have been saved through faith. And this is not your own doing; it is the gift of God." Ephesians 2:8 ESV

People have asked me if I have any regrets from the walk. Typically, I find that people want to know what we did wrong and what we would have done better had we known in the beginning what we knew at the end. One of my biggest regrets was that I didn't capture the bear in a photo in Crested Butte. We also both lament from time to time that neither of us thought to have Brook carry a sign on his back pack as he walked. I would have done a lot of the day to day survival things like food prep and storage differently, given the chance. We both wish there had been a way to take more time to explore the nation and see sights, but overall, as we retired from the biggest career we'd had, we felt that we'd done a decent job at meeting our goals and accomplishing our task.

It's been one week since we finished our walk. I have spent time in both my parent's and my in-law's homes and I feel more transient in my home town than I ever did on the road. I wonder where I will go when this grace period is over and what will become of my little family. We are trying to readjust to living in society, and Brook experienced the most trying time this past week. He is so pitiful. Trying to figure out what to do with the abundance of energy he has gotten used to expending each day can't be easy. On the road, he would walk 8-10 hours a day, some days constantly without any breaks. Now he's supposed to be resting and relaxing, but he is struggling just to get through a movie without having to get up and run a lap around the house. All that alone time took a toll on him.

Brook is not a social butterfly by nature but being alone for five and half months certainly made him immune to the rituals by which we live in society. Thanksgiving was a real hurdle for us. Typically, we try to dress up and look presentable for the Thanksgiving festivities, myself delightedly and Brook from the sheer desire to stop my nagging. This year was no different, but as we put on our pretty clothes we felt so awkward. It was like we weren't wearing our own skin; as though we were pretenders. Family and friends arrived at my folk's house for the big meal and I watched my husband try earnestly to navigate his way through conversations about jobs, college, movies he hadn't seen, and other everyday life that we'd missed out on the road. The worst of it was that Brook wasn't talking to me about his anxiety; he just kept clenching his jaw and letting his eyes rove around as though he couldn't focus on one person or one thing. We had a long way to go before we'd be able to function properly in this type of environment.

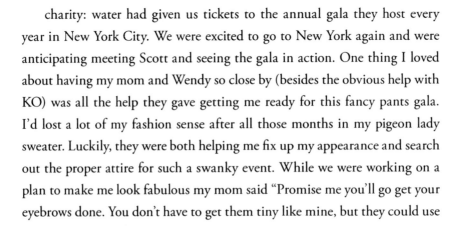

charity: water had given us tickets to the annual gala they host every year in New York City. We were excited to go to New York again and were anticipating meeting Scott and seeing the gala in action. One thing I loved about having my mom and Wendy so close by (besides the obvious help with KO) was all the help they gave getting me ready for this fancy pants gala. I'd lost a lot of my fashion sense after all those months in my pigeon lady sweater. Luckily, they were both helping me fix up my appearance and search out the proper attire for such a swanky event. While we were working on a plan to make me look fabulous my mom said "Promise me you'll go get your eyebrows done. You don't have to get them tiny like mine, but they could use some work."

If I hadn't already been keenly aware of my bush man eyebrows, her polite begging got the point across that I needed to de-hair myself for this important night. I made a mental note to get my eyebrows waxed and shaped. I missed being on the road when I realized what kind of pain and annoyances had to be done in the day to day world, such as eye-brow maintenance. I mean, who cares about anyone else's eye brows? I certainly don't notice people's brows when I meet them unless they have a uni thing going on, and even then it doesn't bother me. What a silly thing to have to keep up with. I just about put on my Pigeonette sweater and stomped off into the great wilderness again after I considered how silly things can be in the day to day world. Looking back and remembering how desperate I'd been to file my nails and dress up a few months previously, I realize how ironic this sounds.

Brook was at ease when it came to his big debut. As soon as we got the email from Scott Harrison, I knew the purple pants were coming with us, and so I did my best to work with his zaniness. It was not an easy task. In fact, getting that man to look presentable after he'd worn the exact same shirt and pair of shorts for five and a half months was a miracle in itself. When we returned from the walk and went to find the beloved purple pants, we discovered that they were lost in storage, and that we had to come up with a whole new look for him. Brook was devastated.

Brook had gained an average of one pound every single day since we'd been back from the walk. He'd been working out at the gym and running all the time, but our families were stuffing us and I think that between the lack of walking 8-9 hours a day burning calories and the 1 hour workout sessions, he'd likely see his body change for quite a while. He was not amused. Try shopping for men's formal wear during the holiday season with a non-decisive, moping, frantic adult male and a shrieking, potty training toddler and you'll experience two things: absolute torture and my unfortunate reality for about a week in December 2011. Somehow, after a few battles with each other, a razor, some hair clippers, and about 185 prayers from me to God imploring patience and divine intervention, we transformed him from a bearded, stinky, wild man walker into an almost suave, still bearded, philanthropist. The only thing we hadn't figured out was his shoes.

You've read about shoe shopping before we left for the trip, and about how miserable it was from the road, and not to get too dramatic here but those were times that we depended on shoes for his physical well being for life. Shopping for a dress shoe for him was the most ridiculous experience I have ever endured. It made all the other shoe shopping stories I've shared look like a fun afternoon jaunt. For the gala, he first wanted a trendy sneaker to go with his suit. So we looked for days at Converse high-tops, Pumas, Vans, and a million other colorful sneakers. After he'd tried on the thirtieth pair of purple accented shoes, he decided he wanted a boot so he could have some lift.

We started to look for a boot that fit his criteria which was: dressy, functional, could be transferred to a work environment, was black, had a lift, and wasn't six hundred dollars. After another million or so pairs we came up with zilch. Then we tried for just a simple dress shoe that'd give him the lift he wanted. We were actually in NYC the day of the gala searching for shoes in department stores for his picky, ridiculously expensive tastes when he found a four hundred dollar pair of Hugo Boss sneakers that he said felt like wearing baby skin. He commented that they'd been marked down to "only" two hundred and fifty dollars, when I gave him the evil eye and made it very clear that he was not getting a pair of shoes that cost that much until I got a pair of shoes that cost that much. Yet again, after hours of my life had been wasted trying to locate the 'perfect shoes' for an impossible to please man, he ended up wearing his old, comfy, worn in, walked a few hundred miles across the country in 'em sneakers. I wish I could say that the rest of the shopping experience for his clothes for the gala had been different from this, but I bought and returned 10 things and spent thirty hours(for once I calculated!) looking for his clothes with him.

On the other hand, after browsing online for a few weeks, I found what I was looking for. I walked into H&M, picked up a dress, and bought it in a matter of half an hour. My shoes took about ten minutes to swipe my card for, and they cost a grand total of five bucks and some change. I bought a necklace and some earrings and in one day I had my outfit ready. I felt nearly as successful as I packed our suitcases for the trip to New York knowing we'd not show up to the biggest party of our lives looking like we'd been living in a car for six months as I did finishing the walk.

We handed our precious son over to his grandparents, and on December 11th, we flew into La Guardia in New York City. Our Uncle Al and David live in Brooklyn, so we stayed with them. They took us out for dim sum in China Town as soon as we got there and it was fantastic. All the energy of the city was stampeding around us that Sunday as we went and saw Times Square and all the major shopping sights along Fifth Avenue. When Brook looked in the Armani window and said "I think that's exactly the kind of suit I'd like to wear to next year's gala," I died laughing as I explained what an Armani suit entailed so far as cost and tailoring. We couldn't even get to Rockefeller plaza because the mobs of people pushed us back. Between the crowds, busy subway rides, dim sum in Chinatown and high energy, it was a classic New York day.

The following morning we took the subway all the way out to The Cloisters, which is a museum that is designed to display different European monasteries from medieval times. Unfortunately, it was closed when we got there, but we leisurely strolled around Fort Tryon Park with Uncle Al and heard stories about his life growing up across the Hudson in Tenafly. After the Cloisters, we headed out to the financial district to see where all the protestors had been squatting our entire trip and were disappointed to find a small band of people who closely resembled bums.

The "Occupy Wall Street" protestors had been cleared out of Zucotti Park a few days before we ended our walk across America. They had been gone for a few weeks before we arrived in New York City and though we missed out on seeing any real action, we did get an eye full. What we witnessed were seven individuals, I counted, standing there with various old caps, coffee cans and buckets collecting 'donations' while holding signs that said things like "Donate to keep the cause going" and "Ask not what you can do for your country, but what your country can do for you," and of course, "We are the 99%." It was disappointing. We left the band of misfits and grabbed a gyro from a vendor on Wall Street and walked along the water while we watched the helicopters taking off to give people rides with views of the city. And then it was time to get ready for the gala.

We got back to Al and David's and showered, trimmed Brook's hair, beard, groomed and shellacked ourselves as glamorous as we could. As it is miserable to have to read what people wear and how they do their hair, makeup, etc., I will refrain from giving that lengthy description. Suffice it to say that after a good deal of time we were ready to go, and so we called the car service that was sponsoring the gala and headed into town.

As we got into the car, my stomach was in knots and I was acutely aware of the butterflies flying all around inside of it. My mind was racing and I worried about how I looked, if I'd be able to converse with people, if I'd be obviously awkward, and if I'd get to meet one of my favorite celebrity's, Tyler Perry, who was helping to host the auction at the event. The driver distracted me from my fears; he was a guy who had served in the army and been at Fort Bragg, which is in Fayetteville, NC, so we got to speak to him about familiar territory. When we arrived at the gala there was a line around the block waiting to get inside. We got in line and proceeded to freeze along with one hundred or so trendy New Yorkers. The woman in front of us started chatting with us about the charity, their work and how she was involved. The real estate company she worked for actually donated a percentage of all their transactions to charity: water, and in the few years they'd been in existence had funded enough to dig six wells.

All across America, Brook and I were in touch with businesses as we sought donations from the corporate sector. Many gave, if not to us, to noble individuals and causes. I love that about the free economy and America in particular. As a consumer, I am more likely to take my business to fellows who feel that it is their duty to care for others as one of their business principles. So I applauded this woman and her employer who waited in front of us in the freezing cold that evening.

Then came the inevitable question, "How are you guys involved with charity: water?" and we for the first of what felt like a million times, explained our walk. That perked up the ears of her employer, who had been waiting near her in the line. He came over and was so excited to talk to us! He had seen a twitter post about us that Scott Harrison had made when we finished our walk, and he had actually visited our website and loved reading about the journey. As we entered that gala, finally emerging from the winter cold to check in, I felt unnerved that someone who lived so far away from where I had been on the road, had heard about the walk and gotten so excited about it. I continued to feel overwhelmed and insufficient from then on that evening.

Brook, however, was the image of sophisticated New Yorker. I kept looking at him wondering how on Earth he, who had been muttering to himself for the past five months about the condition of people's low tire tread as he trudged from one coast to the other, could act as though he was a New York high roller. It would later prove my salvation that he was so calm and assured, but throughout the evening it truly comforted me, even if I thought he was the strangest person I've ever loved.

As we were saying goodbyes to these kind entrepreneurs and checking in our coats, the woman looked down and mentioned how much she loved my Manolo Blahniks(for those of you that do not know, those are hideously expensive designer shoes). I am sure my eyes popped out of my head for a second or two, as I had purchased the lovely sling backs I was wearing for five dollars at a discount store, but I casually thanked her and complimented the lovely craftsmanship of my shoe maker, whoever the heck they were.

We handed our coats to the coat check and emerged into the largest room I have ever been in. The ceiling was probably seventy five feet high, and it was cavernous feeling because the lights were turned low. The first thing you saw as you entered the room was a model of a well pump and there was clean, clear water coming from it. The music was pounding and as we were still on the early side, the room wasn't as packed as it eventually would become. We got drinks at one of the four open bars located in the room, and wandered around admiring the exhibit sections that detailed the work charity: water had done through the year.

There was a catwalk in the room, and its purpose was to encourage individuals to walk for water. You had to carry two full Jerry cans, weighing about forty pounds apiece around the catwalk. For every person who walked, there were donors that gave money to fund more projects. There was also a photo corner where you could stand in front of one of those obnoxious fans that blew your hair out like a model's and get your picture taken with your ridiculously good looking companions. Brook and I took part in the catwalk, but avoided the photo session and the fan.

There were humongous movie screens on the far wall as you entered the building and they were playing footage of well digs and images of mostly women and children enjoying the benefits of clean water. My favorite part of the whole cave, as I have come to call that dear place, was a wall with letters people had sent to thank and honor little Rachel Beckwith. Rachel was the nine year old I told you about earlier, whose story had punctured the heart of America.

As the cave filled up with flashy, incredibly attractive people, I was struck at the similarities the gala had to my senior prom. There was loud, bass thumping music that you could feel through the floor to your feet all the way up through your body to the top of your head. My ears were sore in half an hour. People were dressed up in their exquisite gowns and suits, coiffed and lacquered in pounds of makeup and hairspray, and everyone was going around buzzed on something or other and checking out everyone else. Obviously the people were older than the high school students at my prom, and as the evening benefited a ground breaking charity there were concerned and sincere individuals throughout the room. However, the overall feeling, for me at least, was not unrelated to that of a high school formal. At least there was no ice sculpture. I would have lost it had there been a seven foot tall frozen statue of a Jerry can somewhere in the room. Maybe there was and I missed it, the place was huge so it's possible.

Eventually the time came for Scott Harrison to make a speech, and get the live auction started. The room grew quiet as we all prepared to hear our fearless leader share his words with us. The cave was hushed; the lights that remained on were from the bar and the exhibits, which cast an eerie glow in the peripherals of the room, bringing the focus to the stage. The mega movie screens, which had been providing the majority of the light had gone black for a moment. My heart began beating infernally in my chest and even as I type this I can feel my butterflies returning because I just felt that something was about to happen. Something I'd never seen, or heard, or felt was about to transpire.

I am taller than Brook, and he wanted me to record Scott's speech, so I had his iThingy and I was trying to get it to record, but as I am technically impaired I kept asking "Is it on?" He exasperatedly would grab the confounded thing and adjust it for me. We were in the middle of this debacle when all of the sudden the screen lit up.

And there, on the largest screens I have ever seen, was a picture of our family. I almost missed it at first because I was so wrapped up in the iThingy, but Brook barked "ANGEL!" and I looked up, and there we were. I had the biggest, worst hair day in my life staring me in the face, in front of a few thousand fantastic looking New Yorkers. It was a picture from our final day of the walk, right as we were charging full steam into the ocean. I craved our son being able to remember this moment with us; I missed him so entirely right then because he had made it across the country at the young age of two! Scott charged up and opened his evening with, "This guy, right here behind me walked all the way here, across America to make it tonight. Brook Hinman, where are you at?" My knees were shaking, I nearly wet my pants and I started sobbing and cheering and laughing and hugging Brook. I was the loudest, most obnoxious wife you can imagine at that moment, because the pride and joy I felt for my husband's work so over powered me I was smitten.

Scott blessed us in that moment more than we could ever thank him for; it was an incredible honor to be, well honored, in front of so many noble people doing truly miraculous things for others. I was unprepared for the emotional toll that I experienced in that moment of recognition. I realized later that evening that though we might be capable of incredible feats, we humans don't need glory. All the attention that we got in that moment flooded me with what I can only express as insufficiency, and as every person standing near us walked over to shake our hands and congratulate us I cowered inside.

The night was dedicated to Rachel Beckwith's memory, and her mother came on stage to share about her daughter's legacy. I missed KO even more in that moment, I just wanted to hug and kiss him and whisper in his little ear how proud I will always be that he made it with me in the wilderness all those months. I couldn't have made it without him, I realized then, and I was so thankful for little Rachel, helping so many of us understand that we can't make it without each other, especially if we don't live with the hope of helping others out.

Jessica Biel came on stage after a bit; she was hosting the event for the evening. She was giggly, bubbly, and assured. I was yet again reminded of prom because her speech was delivered in a party spirit encouraging everyone to conserve water by imbibing as much as possible for the evening, not unlike a typical prom queen oratory! I realized as she gave her speech that I was in the same room as one of the most reputably beautiful women in the world. This made it difficult for me to stay focused on the work of charity: water. Soon after her speech there was a live auction.

Tyler Perry was the guest assistant to the auctioneer. Now don't get me wrong, I admire and applaud Tyler Perry. He is a bad mamma jamma, but he didn't wow me that night. I was hoping he'd get into it and heckle people more, make more jokes, entertain. But he just ended up buying 500,000 dollars worth of the auction and though it was awesome that he gave so much money to the clean water crisis and did such a great deed, I felt like a little balloon had popped in my heart. I do so hope to meet him one day and tease him for not living up to my standards.

Brook and I had pushed our way through the crowd and had made it to the stairs leading up to the stage, and were standing about ten feet from Tyler Perry when he was failing to wow me. Even though his most famous character Madea is larger than life on the television screen, I was surprised at how big a guy Mr. Perry was in person. He towered over the auctioneer and had Brook been standing beside him, it would have looked like a dwarf and a giant! Again, I felt overcome by knowing that the wealthiest man in Hollywood was standing ten feet away from me.

When the auction was over, Brook and I looked at each other and walked up on stage. The people who had bid in the auction were getting their picture taken with Jessica Biel and Scott Harrison and so we figured we might as well do it too. Brook actually brushed up against Jessica's arm as we were waiting to take our picture with her, but she escaped before we got a photo opportunity with her. We did get our picture with Scott, though. And he invited us to the after party as well as to his office he next day to talk.

We thanked him for the unforgettable time he'd given us that evening, and we left to mingle. I'd had a few drinks and I needed to use the bathroom, so I headed down what felt like a million stairs in my "Manolos" and finally arrived at the end of the line that was only about thirty five ladies deep. I was minding my own business and waiting patiently when I finally made it to the front of the line. As I emerged from the toilet there was a statuesque woman with incredible hair and gorgeous skin, just dripping in glamour standing at the sink. I have seen this woman in Vogue modeling designer duds I will only ever touch if I somehow find them in a rummage sale. She saw me and said "Oh my! Can I have my picture taken with you?" I nearly died right there on the floor. From what I could tell, a super model had just asked to have their picture taken with me. I smiled and chatted for a minute, took my picture with her, and headed out. I nearly imploded waiting to tell Brook as I searched him out in that blasted cavern. When I finally did find him he was chatting up Rachel Beckwith's mother!

I thanked her for what she had done as a mother for me, by raising such an epic child. What an example to live by! She was the most genuinely sweet woman I have ever come across, especially so recently after such a tragedy. I was yet again overpowered inside when she explained that she had read about our campaign on twitter and followed our website. For me, that was the coolest moment of the entire night. God had arranged for our paths to cross as I had been praying so earnestly for her, and she had actually heard of our walk. Never could I have planned such a night, and for that I am grateful that God gave Brook and me the gala to celebrate not only charity: water's incredible achievements, but also to celebrate His. God was the celebrity in the room that evening, He was in every picture of a smiling child pumping clean water, and though I felt inferior from the second I walked into that cave, He is never inferior or undeserving of praise.

We were abundantly blessed by the gala. I wish I could say that we were wise enough to end the evening right then, after such a surreal moment meeting Rachel's mother. But alas, we had been invited to an after party by Scott Harrison. We figured we couldn't turn down such a tantalizing offer. Brook and I retrieved our coats from the coat check and departed from the cave into the bustling New York City nightlife. On our way out, I grabbed a Jerry can. I had asked a few charity: water staff members if they'd mind me taking one. I so wanted a trophy to take home to KO. I figured it'd be the best present I could bring him back from our trip. It was a Monday night at about 12 o'clock, but there was still traffic bustling and people walking the streets. The after party was a few blocks away so we walked amidst all of this energy in high spirits as I joyfully swung the Jerry can around.

I'd had more than enough to drink, and luckily Brook had not kept up with me, so while we walked I exclaimed about how incredible it was that little old us were going to an after party, which is something we had only ever heard of in movies. Brook kind of laughed and looked a little concerned at my behavior, but I think he figured I was just being goofy like always. We got to the party and Sami, Rachel's mother, was right in front of us so we chatted some more. Then we shuffled into an elevator and made it up the umpteen floors to the party.

This shindig was in a super trendy hotel on what appeared to be at least twenty floors up, in a pent house type suite. There were two bars, and the elite donors and celebrity types were milling around. The women were dazzling with jewels and gowns. The men were all posed with one knee propped up with their foot resting on some piece of furniture, leaning over chatting into the women's ears, just like in magazine ads. The loud music continued blaring at this party. It was like we had just stepped into a condensed version of the gala, only this one had a few extra six foot and taller body guards wandering about with earpieces. I was intoxicated and I felt about as out of place in that room as I had felt at the Labor Day community yard sale way back in Kansas.

Brook was chatting with some people and I wandered off. I met a man and began talking with him about his work. He asked how I was involved with charity: water and when I explained what we had just done, he wanted to do shots of tequila with Brook and me to celebrate our completion of the walk and our, as he called it, "inspiring story." We threw back the drinks, and that shot of tequila penetrated my evening with a stunning blow.

242

Brook was stuck in a conversation with someone and I needed to sit down, so I found a seat where I could peer out the floor to ceiling window to the city. I remember looking out of the window down at the living creature that is New York. I saw cars whizzing by aggressively, billboards with people smiling at me, and then all the lights and music overcame me, and I shut my eyes. I don't remember anything else.

Now before I tell you any more, I'd like a moment to prepare you. Psalm 107:2 is a declaration to "Let the redeemed of the Lord say so, whom He has redeemed from trouble." As I set out to write this book, I wanted to tell the entire story of our journey truthfully and completely. I could easily have left this section out, but I feel that transparency is of the utmost importance. Some of my closest family members and friends suggested that I didn't share this with the rest of the world. But I need to share my failure with you, and whoever else reads this, because it was in my failure that God's blessing of clean water became the very clearest it had ever been to me, as was the miracle that it forgiveness. Hear my story, my testimony of God's love and abundance of living water, as I learned it that fateful day with patience and understanding, if you will.

I am a girl that was raised in the Bible belt in a dry county. Where I come from a lady doesn't behave the way I did that evening, drinking too much and causing public humiliation. I also had been raised to behave better, and I have never ever been a partier before; this was a first time experience for me. While I will never judge anyone for over drinking having been there and done that, I'll have you know that when I greeted the world in the early hours of the next morning, I was about to experience the crushing feelings of failure and utter self loathing.

I woke up about four and a half hours after closing my eyes in that den of my personal peril. Before I could bring myself to open my eyes, the pungent odor of throw up greeted my nose. I heard beeping, talking, the whir of wheels being moved across the ground and TV's. I peeped open my eyes to see the familiar trappings of a hospital; I had been taken to the emergency room. My chest indented as my heart crumpled when I realized where I was. The first thing I asked Brook was, "Did I let KO down?" My eyes frantically began searching the room for the Jerry can. It had been left, Brook explained, when he and one of the six foot something body guards had to carry me out to the ambulance. I began to cry. Not sob like I had earlier when they'd shown our picture on the screens, but silent, painful, ashamed tears.

The nurse came over and he asked me how I felt. I shot him daggers and looked down at my barf covered dress and he read my mind, "That was a pretty dumb question, wasn't it?" he asked. I drank some water, emptied my stomach a bit more, and then begged Brook to get me out of there. I didn't need to be at a hospital, I was just hung over. We waited the infernally long time it takes to get discharged and I had to walk barefoot to a taxi, as I had lost one of my precious "Manolos" in my unfortunate display of idiocy. My eyes clouded over with more tears at the irony of my walk of shame that morning. After a night spent celebrating a walk that brought health and life to others, I was humiliated that I had to walk barefoot and filthy from an emergency room. The taxi driver that gave us our ride was not pleased with his passenger load but kept his wits about him as I stunk out the back seat of his car and threw up in my barf bag as he drove along in the early morning traffic. Being the fool that threw up at 7 a.m. in the back seat of a taxi is a role that I will never get cast for again.

I am a forgiving person naturally, and I live a life for a God who forgives and forgets permanently. But that day, I hated myself. I had planned to go ice skating in Bryant Park, something I'd always dreamed of doing. I had a job interview that afternoon for a position I'd dreamed of, in a city I loved, and there was no way I was going to make it. I had just had the opportunity of a lifetime and I felt as though I blew it. What really caused the self loathing to sink in was the fact that I had let my son and my God down.

As I wretched over and over again in my poor uncle's bathroom, I wondered how I had gotten there. This is the best I can come up with. I don't ever drink liquor, so I had that against me. I was mixing liquor, wine, beer and champagne which is always a horrible idea. I hadn't eaten a blasted thing because I was too jittery and surrounded by rail thin women. The music was so darn loud I couldn't concentrate on my body and how I was feeling. I was exhausted; I'd just come out of a five and half month battle against the elements and was not used to this kind of energy output. I am not a partying type of gal. I am two beer dear that loves Jesus and belongs in bed with my two year old around 9:30 at night. After the flood of reason washed my brain with excuses, I realized that though there were many reasons why I had flunked, the source of my failure was my sinful self. Instead of turning to God in prayer that evening when I felt inferior and overwhelmed I turned to a bottle, which was just about the dumbest thing I could have done.

As I grappled with my disgusting failure, my phone wouldn't stop ringing, beeping and obnoxiously blaring every two seconds. "How was it?????" "SEND ME A PICTURE!" "I am dying to hear how it went...please call me!!" Everyone I loved was calling, texting and emailing me and I was miserable. I had just rolled into my uncle's house at 7:30 a.m. after the night of my life, and I couldn't get a moment of quiet. I gathered up my courage and called my mother.

She excitedly answered the phone and I remorsefully told her my tale. "Angel!" she inhaled deeply, like only my mother can when she is shocked, "I never expected this from you." Great, my mother was going to join in on the loathe Angel party. But she surprised me. "Baby," she sighed loudly, "just let this one go. I can tell you want to hold on to it, but the ones we want to hold onto are the ones we've got to let go the most or they'll keep holding us back. You got held back one night and one day, don't let it steal anymore of your time here on Earth." As I hung up the phone I remembered why I love my mother.

My dad wasn't quite so understanding when I called him next "You did what?! Well, that was pretty darn stupid wasn't it?" and then he started to laugh at me again. My father is of the philosophy of learning from the hard knocks of life, but I could tell that his laughter was tinged with disappointment. We ended our conversation after about a minute. He told me to drink black coffee and go for a walk, pray for some clarity and feel better. I texted one of my best friend's and I begged her to pray for me. She texted me back that she was praying but to come on home with my head held high, because she was still proud of me.

Believe it or not it was a call from my little sister Gabby that forced me up out of my pity party later that day. "You have got to be kidding me. You mixed wine with liquor?! Haven't you ever heard, "Wine with liquor, never sicker?" Girl, for someone so smart you are soooooo stupid sometimes."

Of course, how could I forget that age old rhyme of reason? Gabby has always had a bit of the "my big sister is perfect" complex, so to hear her call me stupid slapped me into reality. I realized there was nowhere I could go but up, and I had to make this whole disaster a life changing moment. I pulled myself out of bed and headed for the shower.

Every shower I took over the summer was a welcome one. While we were in the dirty playgrounds, cornfields, Wal-Marts and back yards of America without regular access to bathing we cherished moments of rushing water pouring over our heads. However, there has never been a shower in my life that was as cleansing as the one I took after I got off the phone with my little sister.

Stepping into the warm water released the tension in my head instantly. I let the water fall over me and stared down at the drain where the barely dirty drops disappeared before my eyes. Then I knelt. I folded my knees and bent so low my nose touched the drain. The water was my blanket, and it covered over me. I began to weep. I begged God to make me better. Not physically, because I knew I deserved every ounce of misery I was experiencing but spiritually. I begged him to heal me. In my naked posterity, I humbled myself, and told God how sorry I was for being such a blasted idiot. I told Him how foolish I'd been to not lean on Him in my weakness, and realized that I wouldn't be doing it ever again. I prayed that no one would be lost because of my mistake, but rather that not only would I learn from it, but that I could help others not to make a similar error. Most of all, I prayed that He would forgive me for not being a healthy example of who He is in me. I let my light go out that night, and as I was engulfed in the comfort of cleansing water I prayed he would not just restore my light but that he would install a better bulb that shone brighter. As my tears mixed with the shower's drops I felt God there, lifting my eyes to the glorious showerhead that I loved so much in that moment, the Living Water cleansing every aspect of my life.

He reminded me that though I had failed for a moment, what I was feeling, the sheer bliss of healing water was going to be felt all over another woman's body somewhere far away because I had suffered through the journey. He had not forgotten my suffering and He forgave me, as well as promised me that He had suffered on the cross in order that I might be forgiven so graciously. I was forgiven, and I was graced with a shower that exposed my God's superiority in my moment of complete inferiority. And He did it with a shower, where I could be reminded of the precious gift that clean water is. My God is great!

I emerged from the bathroom and evaluated who I was as a person. I was 22, a pigeon lady who just crossed the country in an SUV that I had wrecked in five separate states with my two year old son, while my loony husband walked 3,300 miles to raise money for a worthy cause. I worship a God who is love, who forgives ugly, puke covered deeds. He also is a God who carries us when we can't go on any further. I am loved, I am in love, and I have His love in me. I climbed back into bed and I opened my journal, the one I'd kept on the road, and I opened to a page I'd written a few months before, back in September.

9/13/2011

God is everything I need.

He is my ambition.

He is my energy.

He is my purpose.

He is my time!

He is my patience.

He is my love.

He is my peaceful place.

He is my rest.

He is my hero.

He is my provider.

He is my truth.

He is my sight.

He is my joy.

He is my acceptance.

He is my knowing.

He is my witness.

He is my righteous judge.

He is my endurance.

He is my life giver.

He is my second chance.

As I read my own words of encouragement, a few more tears marched down my cheeks, and I added one more sentence to my list.

He is my living water.

This time, the tears weren't shameful or depressed; they were triumphant warriors tromping away from a battle that they had victoriously won. I was forgiven. God revealed how blessed I am to have access to clean water and promised to restore me with his living water after my night of doom.

I was comfortable with who I was in that moment. I had some work to do with God on my weaknesses, and I still felt like I'd just gone a few rounds in the ring with Mike Tyson, but I was going to quit my belly aching (literally) and move on. I am going to tell my story, the whole thing, as honestly as possible in order to represent our walk in all its glory and lack of splendor. Brook and I only hope that as we are closing the book on our walk across America, there are people somewhere who don't have to walk so far for their water. When they do have to walk for their water, we pray that there will be clean, healthy water waiting for them at the end of their trek.

Brook went to the charity: water office that day while I was having my shower epiphany, and he returned laden with hats and t-shirts and a deep satisfaction that he'd gone. He nearly didn't go because he wanted to take care of me, but I kicked him out the door, and I am glad that I did.

"Scott said something about us going to Africa on a well digging trip, what do you think about that, my darling Pigeon Lady?"

"Well Billy, it looks like our walk is only beginning."

Epilogue: The Number Breakdown

rook requested that I include a section at the end of the book with his numbers, so here it is. Our second campaign closed in December with a final donation amount of 14,899 dollars towards a fancy "Brmm Brmm" that has already begun drilling wells in Ethiopia. Altogether, with the help of our generous donors, we raised $29,523 dollars for charity: water and the clean water crisis. Brook walked exactly 3,300 miles from Cape Meares, Oregon to Carolina Beach, NC which made him about as happy as anyone could be. He walked through ten states, four mountain ranges, extreme temperatures that ranged from 15 degrees to 115 degrees, and he ate an estimated 350 peanut butter foldovers. It took us 171 days to complete our sojourn. We stayed approximately twenty percent with host families, another forty percent in hotels or motels, and the final forty percent in our car or tent. Brook walked through five pairs of shoes, KO and I played at approximately 100 different playgrounds or parks and our family consumed about 97 cans of beans. Most importantly, an estimated 1,500 people will gain access to clean water from our endeavor. Our greatest prayer is that as they get those glasses of clean water to drink; they will also accept His living water that will sustain them, as it did us, when nothing else could. Praise God for His work, and for bringing my family out of the wilderness!

Acknowledgements

God carried us when we were weak, Jesus witnessed to us when we were lonely, and the Holy Spirit fed us when we needed spiritual sustenance. Without the Trinity we would not have made it, so to our Heavenly Father, we owe all our thanks. Brook and I would like to extend our deepest gratitude to the donors who gave to our Water Walk America campaigns, and who bestowed the precious gift of clean water to so many lives. Also, to the host families across America; we owe a huge thank you! Your homes were all wonderful, refreshing us in our time of need and true blessings from God. We pray for you all often and hope your hospitality is repaid a hundredfold.

To Scott Harrison, the charity: water team and staff, and all of the inexhaustible workers in the field that bring clean water to those in need we'd like to utter our praises. The work you do is incomprehensible, and sure to be rewarded by God. You all kept us informed, helped us understand a problem that needed our help, and included us in your work. For that we thank you. Keep up the mission!

To Rachel Beckwith, and her strong and inspiring mother Sami, who I can never thank enough, I send my highest thanks and greatest appreciation. Your little girl did a miraculous act that will bless mothers for generations to come.

To our family and friends who supported us through our journey with prayers, financial help, hotel rooms, encouraging messages and love: YOU

ROCK! And we hope you know how much we appreciate and love each and every one of you.

To my beloved Billy, who kept on walking, I am so grateful God has given me you! Your walk inspires me today; never forget those nights in Scout Junior or those days on the road! These memories will carry us far away when we need an escape. Also, thanks for helping me on our marathon editing and writing sessions. This book wouldn't "flow" without all your creative juices!

I'd like to make a special praise to my fierce son KO, who at two years of age has suffered for the well being of others more than most adults can claim. You are my trooper, little one, and I always thank Jesus for your company, especially out on the road!

Pastor Kevin: Thanks for encouraging me with my transparency and testimony. Reminding me that amidst our failures we become the strongest through Him who strengthens us was just the push I needed to make this work whole.

To every person who helped me complete my dream of finishing this story; those at Westbow Press, my church family and community for your anticipation of the book, and again to my friends and family, thank you.

To you the reader, thank you for purchasing this book. Your purchase of this book means that people all over the world and here at home in America are receiving practical assistance through clean water from the author royalties of this book.

And to Isaac, whose image is still in my mind, thank you! I pray that that your village will have clean water for the rest of your life and beyond. I thank all of the water walkers around this world; you kept us going when we could not have continued. You are the real heroes of this story and you are all in our prayers.

After completing the walk, Angel and Brook settled down with KO in their hometown of Winston-Salem, NC to try being responsible adults. As she chases after KO, tries to keep her Billy from turning into a calculator and balances a career at a local non-profit, Angel looks to Jesus' teachings for her constant support. Angel continues to write, seek God's smile, and is working hard not to wreck her awesome 'new' 1984 Volvo station wagon that she named Doris May.

CPSIA information can be obtained at www.ICGtesting.com
Printed in the USA
BVOW011514201212

308590BV00010B/151/P